AF589091

Praise for *Gospel of Lies*

In addition to telling her own heartfelt story of overcoming the dogmas and misinformation with which she was raised, [Promise] collects under a thematic heading a variety of arguments that one is likely to hear when voicing doubts or concerns. Promise offers careful and incisive responses to those arguments and shares additional context that can help folks struggling with doubt and pressure to think more clearly and make better informed decisions about their own lives. Gospel of Lies *will no doubt be an essential tool for evangelicals deconstructing amidst unsympathetic or hostile relationships.*

—DAN MCCLELLAN,
Bible scholar and NYT bestselling author of *The Bible Says So: What We Get Right (and Wrong) About Scripture's Most Controversial Issues*

Promise inspires me. Those who have never deconstructed a high-control religion may not realize just how much courage it takes to acknowledge nagging doubts, to challenge the sacred, and to defy scriptures which command the faithful, "Do not trust in your own understanding." The road out of fundamentalism is often jarring long before it becomes liberating, and I'm convinced that Promise's candid personal story will help to make the deconstruction journey easier and better for a great many people.

—SETH ANDREWS,
exvangelical / podcaster / secular activist

Gospel of Lies *is the book I wish I had when I started deconstructing, even though I grew up in a garden-variety Catholic home. Experiencing a fraction of Promise's upbringing shed a lot of light on why she is so passionate about speaking out against religious dogma. This book also demonstrates the real, dangerous ideologies that fester deep inside the typical American evangelical home. I took notes and highlighted pages to ensure I didn't miss anything and would be able to take her wisdom into real-life conversations with our callers on The Line. Reading this felt like being supported by your brilliant big sister - it's powerful, informative, and inspiring.*

—ALYSSA LJUB,
Co-Host on *The Line*

Promise has this unique ability to say things clearly and concisely whilst being humble and provocative at the same time. As a queer survivor of evangelicalism, it was validating to read her stories and how she eloquently confronts the harm of evangelical beliefs. The grip of indoctrination from a young age is coercive and formidable. Something as personal as faith should be permitted, not enforced. For all of the people I worked with in ministry who were closeted atheists, this book is an answer to their godless prayers. From an array of personal experiences to practical frameworks and insight, Gospel of Lies *is bolstering and bridge-building for anyone impacted by the conversation around God.*

—MIKE MAESHIRO,
Founder of Numa and host of the *Confessions of a Reformer* podcast

In Gospel of Lies, *Promise traces her journey from unquestioning devotion to unapologetic atheism with her unique blend of compassion and honesty. She exposes the cracks in doctrine that sermons never acknowledge and gives voice to the doubts believers are trained to suppress. Because she knows the language, the fear, and the cost of leaving, her story will resonate deeply with those still trapped inside faith—and those who have already escaped. As Promise writes, she may have lost her faith, but she gained so much more in return. Once you read this book, so will you.*

—HEMANT MEHTA,
Editor of *FriendlyAtheist.com*

Gospel of Lies *is a courageous and methodical confrontation of the arguments, impacts, and traumatic manifestations of modern evangelical Christianity. Promise Backlund exposes the circular logic of a rigged system and replaces it with a process of reclamation grounded in reality. This generous and powerful book is for anyone confused by Christian Nationalism and the cognitive dissonance we witness as a fruit of evangelical faith.*

—TIA LEVINGS,
Author of NYT Bestseller *A Well-Trained Wife: My Escape from Christian Patriarchy*, and *I Belong to Me: A Survivor's Guide to Recovery and Hope after Religious Trauma*

GOSPEL *of* LIES

SURVIVING AND RESISTING EVANGELICAL EXTREMISM

Promise Backlund

To those who bravely ask the questions they are most afraid of.
May you find excitement in the uncertainty,
and comfort in not being alone in it.

Table of Contents

Foreword

You're very fortunate to be reading this book.

I don't mean you're fortunate because it's a great book by a great person (though I believe that's true); I mean you're fortunate—because you exist.

If you're reading this, you exist, which puts you at an advantage over those who weren't so lucky, which includes many if not all proposed gods.

If you're reading this, you were taught to read, which means you are fortunate in many other ways. You're fortunate that someone cared for you and nurtured you. You're fortunate that someone taught you to read and that you were able to learn.

You're also very valuable.

You're valuable to those who care about you, and I hope that you're valuable to yourself. While part of your value is connected to your relationships with others, your value to yourself is what allows those relationships to exist and grow.

But are you also brave?

We are fearful, curious, cooperative creatures faced with the daunting task of understanding the world. It requires some bravery to take on the challenge of honestly exploring reality—to seek the truth and to be willing to accept it where found.

It takes bravery to acknowledge you've been wrong, to modify your opinions when they aren't worthy. It takes bravery to say, "I don't know" and to continue to explore your path and to learn and grow.

It takes bravery to stand up against the authorities who pretend to have delivered the truth.

Understandably, some folks take shortcuts and invent stories to ease discomfort. Those stories are then shared, as if true, pretending to offer answers and hope. Those lies that gain popularity because they're useful are codified and thrust unto people before they've learned how to doubt or that doubt is an option.

If you pretend to have the truth, you stop searching for it.

We have a moral obligation to seek the truth and to share the truth. We have a duty to ourselves and to each other to defeat confusion and the conflict it creates. We have an obligation to take the knowledge we've gained from others and to expand it and to share it, to clear the path for others, instead of cluttering the path as we meander.

Promise's path may be very similar to yours, or very different, but *Gospel of Lies: Surviving and Resisting Evangelical Extremism* is a heartfelt attempt to let others see that path and to inspire them to seek the truth and to allow us all to benefit from what she's learned.

You have the advantage of living now, with countless people's experiences and discoveries to guide you on your journey. You live at a time with the greatest access to knowledge and understanding in the history of humanity. What will you do with it?

You're fortunate, you're valuable and I hope you're brave.

Promise is and she's willing to help you.

Are you brave enough to seek the truth?

Are you brave enough to share it?

—Matt Dillahunty

Introduction

"The heart is deceitful above all things,
and desperately wicked: who can know it?"
—JEREMIAH 17:9

I WAS RAISED TO BELIEVE that I was bad, but it was good that I was bad because that meant I could let "God" help me be good every day. It wasn't my personhood or individuality that made me special or of value; rather, it was my lack of value that now somehow made me...valuable? I was raised this way because my parents and their parents happened to be raised this way and truly believed in this God. I was destined to believe as well. And I did believe, not just because of the underlying fear I carried but also the underlying hope. Hope that if there was a thunderstorm, someone powerful was watching over me. Hope that when I was nervous during my piano recital, someone would magically help me remember the notes. Hope that my friend with cerebral palsy could someday be healed. Hope that when we had money problems, God would provide more work for my dad. Hope that when scary things were happening on the news, it was all just part of some grand, perfect plan. A plan in which the creator and author of the universe cared about me and the things I cared about. I was addicted to, and dependent upon, the hope that something bigger, better and more powerful than me was out there doing good. Because the alternative was too painful to contemplate. When those moments of doubt intruded, when my curiosity peaked enough to encourage a glance behind the curtain, I had to look away. There *had* to be a god; the god of my father, and his father, and his father. My entire life felt dependent on this fact, yet even at a young age, the questions would creep in and the answers (or lack thereof) were only satisfactory enough to hold me over until adulthood. My fear of hell, loss and other things that go bump in the night was enough to fuel my childlike faith and motivate me to quiet my doubts. It was less of a choice and more of a programming, but off the dogmatic deep end I went.

Jesus was my everything. As a child, he was the imaginary friend who protected me when I was scared of the dark. He was the patient and kind inner voice that consoled me when I'd frustrated my parents. He was the sweet, smiling face from the Jesus movies my grandmother would always have on at her house, proclaiming that the kingdom of heaven belonged to us children. What could be more special than that? As a teenager, Jesus was the big brother looking over my shoulder, the North Star that I based all my long-term dreams around. I didn't need to worry about the future or planning out some grand career. I would follow my "calling" and be sure that whatever I did or achieved pointed back to Jesus.

It was easy to stay committed in this steadfast, one-sided love affair. Our family conversations at home always circled back to Jesus and God. If we pointed out a beautiful sunset, the credit and conversation were immediately shifted to our "amazing creator." A trip to the zoo or aquarium was just a reminder of how creative God was. A trip to a science museum was an opportunity to point out the "worldly" agenda to indoctrinate us in the evils of evolution and the Big Bang Theory. Bedtime reading was almost always an illustrated Bible story. Easter was "Resurrection Day" and Christmas was "Happy Birthday Jesus Day." I wasn't allowed to believe in Santa Claus because my parents believed that when I found out the truth about him, I'd think God was just a story as well. The irony. My mom homeschooled me for my entire K–12 education, always using Christian curricula. Christopher Columbus was a saintly hero, the earth was only 6,000 years old, dinosaurs were a conspiracy theory and my math books were full of Bible verses. My friends were all Christians, and most of them were homeschooled as well. I had everything to gain by embracing Jesus and Christianity as ultimate truth, and even more to lose if I were to make the grave mistake of entertaining any doubts. And yet, looking back, I know they were there. Buried deep beneath the fear and hope were questions waiting to be boldly asked.

2016 was the beginning of the end for me, and by 2017, I would finally admit to myself that I no longer believed in the god I had clung to so ardently. A combination of newfound bravery, fury and my desire to grow all snowballed together, allowing me to finally face these unanswered questions. The bravery had come from finally experiencing some difficulties in life, no longer being sheltered within my exclusively Christian bubble. The fury was fueled by realizing that the very Christian leaders I had admired and compared my "moral code" to were all but worshiping a businessman turned politician who was the antithesis of the Jesus I had been taught about. The desire to grow stemmed from there. Perhaps it also had something to do with reaching my mid-20s and further developing the skills necessary to confront what I had avoided for so long.

Maybe fellow Christians and leaders had lost track of the true gospel, but I wasn't going to. I was going to grow my faith even more and become closer to Jesus than ever before. I was going to know the Bible inside and out and I was going to have all the answers to present to my new non-believing friends. I would spend hours at a time in my "prayer closet," taping my favorite scriptures to the walls, reading verses out loud, worshiping and attempting to commune with my chosen god. I read all of the apologetics books, and, of course, the Bible. I went to ministry school and followed my "calling" as a worship leader.

Eventually, I was ready to let those buried questions face the light, because while I was very aware that I should "lean not on [my] own understanding" (Proverbs 3:5), I had also reached the conclusion that the truth should not be afraid of questions. Surely what I believed was true, and getting to the bottom of those questions would only fortify my beliefs. But the more I asked, the more I read and the more time I devoted to prayer, the less convinced I became. I had entered a field of intellectual land mines, each stone I turned shaking a new foundation. The shakier things got, the more I had to realign my center. The goal was no longer to solidify what I believed but instead to prioritize truth, whether or not I liked or understood what that truth was. I soldiered on, grieving the assurance and certainty I had falsely depended on.

This book will highlight many of the questions and assumptions I had and the conclusions (or lack thereof) that I have reached since. Most relevant now, though, is the final question I landed on: Do I have a good reason to believe any god exists at all, much less the one I had been indoctrinated to believe in? The question was terrifying, soul-crushing and blasphemous. The answer was a thousand weights removed from my shoulders and the beginning of real freedom. I had peeked behind the curtain and found no great and powerful wizard, only smoke and mirrors. I had shaken my fist at the sky, and no lightning struck me down. I ate the fruit from the tree, and I didn't die.

Having reached this new place of freedom from religion, I had hoped to move on privately with my life; not make waves or even ripples. As a pastor's kid raised to "influence" others, I thought I would finally get a reprieve from the limelight. I kept my atheism to myself and sugar-coated it for others as "belief in the universe," whatever that was supposed to mean. And then COVID-19 happened. And then the January 6 attack on the United States Capitol happened. Again, all of the voices I had grown up respecting were proclaiming conspiracy theories and dangerous rhetoric that I knew would propel Christian nationalists forward. My unique personal insights and experiences made my silence feel like complicity. What started as an attempt at anonymous online dissent turned to hundreds of thousands of social media followers, hosting debate call-in shows, public speaking and more. During this time, I had the honor of hearing the stories of thousands of fellow indoctrination survivors. I have also faced intense amounts of vitriol and hate from those who feel personally offended by my criticisms of Christian nationalism and evangelical rhetoric. But there have also been hundreds of successful conversations and debates, addressing the lies and harm that some have defended. These conversations are what inspired me to share with you the most common arguments, questions and traumas I've faced.

If you are lucky enough to be unfamiliar with the level of indoctrination or blind belief that I and many others experienced, thank you for being curious enough to want to understand and help others who have. I truly believe two of the biggest threats to the free world are religious extremism and religious nationalism. As Christian nationalism grows in power, it should be a concern to all who value human rights. I hope this book provides you with a glimpse into what those of us who have dared to leave the fold are up against so that we can work together to dismantle delusions and restore truth. If you are reading this and relating to any bit of it, my hope is that you not only feel seen and validated but also gain more confidence and the language to voice your own unique story.

Evangelicalism taught us that we are our own worst enemy, that our hearts are "desperately wicked." Here's the truth: You are fully capable of making good decisions for yourself. You are free to set whatever boundaries serve your mental health best. You are much more than whatever challenges you are currently working to overcome. You are also so much more than whatever you are naturally gifted at. Neither your best nor worst quality has anything to do with your value. You have probably already overcome more than you could have ever imagined, and you will probably experience even more wonderful things than you have so far imagined. You are not "saved" or "unsaved," "sinful" or "redeemed." Reality is not some binary, good versus evil battlefield. There are gray areas and nuance and a full spectrum of experiences and possibilities. But if it were black-and-white, if I were forced to either embrace my desperate wickedness or reject truth, then I would proudly take the title of desperately wicked. I hope you'll join me in courageously living in the reality of the known and unknown, instead of the comfort of lies.

CHAPTER 1

Facing the Invisible Monsters

"The only thing we have to fear is fear itself."
—FRANKLIN D. ROOSEVELT

WE MUST START at the worst part—the scary part. The part that prevents even the most intelligent from doing what must be done when presented with extraordinary claims about gods, the universe and ourselves: questioning whether it's true or not. Without a doubt, one of the most crippling symptoms of evangelicalism is fear. What a brilliant weapon this fear can be—a physiological and psychological emotion so powerful it tells you to "save yourself now, think later." But sometimes, that feeling occurs so frequently or so intensely that your brain decides it will stay on that path long-term. Even long after exiting religion, so many find themselves stuck in fight-or-flight mode simply from the evangelical messages they were fed concerning hell, demons and spiritual warfare. Fear is a useful tool when encountering true danger, but how do we determine if a threat is real? When both a scary fact and a believed lie can bring about the same emotional and physical responses, how can one regulate themselves long enough to determine which one is the truth? This is why we must start at the worst part.

My childhood was full of anxiety, nightmares and the constant fear of hell, demons and even angels. After all, the only thing more powerful and terrifying than seeing a demon was seeing an angel, or, worse, God himself. Countless nights, I lay in my bed shaking, begging God to come into my heart just in case I had done something bad enough to make him go away. I would say "Jesus!" out loud, repetitively, because I had been taught that this would keep the demons at bay; they feared his name alone (Luke 10:17). Even when I would try to imagine heaven and its beautiful streets of gold, I would fall into a state of anxiety over the concept of "forever." How could there be something that lasted that long? Wouldn't it get painfully boring to just stay in one place, eternally worshiping one god for hours on hours? I could barely make it through a church service as a child, much less imagine heaven as anything other than daunting. And so, at a very young age, I developed a massive fear of death and an almost equal fear of living. My obsession with fear was crippling, and whether it made me the perfect candidate for evangelical beliefs or my beliefs made me the perfect candidate for anxiety, I'll never know. What I do know is that it made me unwavering in my faith. My fears about life were dismissed as a weak mind allowing "spirits" to influence me. My fears about the supernatural were praised and regarded as maturity and discernment. My faith validated my fears, rather than helping me overcome them. The church and Christianity see this foundation of fear as a tool of control—all the motivation I needed to dive headfirst into whatever hopeful news Christianity had to offer me. The scam was working. I had been infected with a disease by the same source that was offering me a cure, and I couldn't refuse. In the words of the late and intellectually great Christopher Hitchens, I was "created to be sick and commanded to be well." You don't have to be a child to be manipulated by this sort of religious weapon. Fear of dying, fear of the unknown, fear of the future; these are all things humans grapple with, opening up plenty of vulnerable places for evangelical dogma to sink its teeth into.

Post-religion, I don't find myself with fewer fears. But I'm no longer ruled by them. My fears serve me, and I no longer serve them or the trigger responsible for them. While evangelicalism taught me to war against parts of myself by commanding that "anti-Christ" thoughts be silenced or by rebuking natural human emotions beyond my control, I have now learned to love and accept all of these parts. They now get a voice. My fear makes its arguments, but so does my curiosity, my passion, my responsibility and my joy. Having courage doesn't have to look like overcoming all my perceived failures or battling spiritual forces. It means taking inventory of all the tools and information available, letting my fear know it must exist in the world of reality and be held accountable for its claims. I have now learned to befriend my fear, knowing it's the part of me that is taking things seriously and bringing potentially important things to my attention that more careless emotions may overlook. Now I face my fears, turning on the light to reveal the source of whatever strange shadows are attempting to haunt me. Now I can find joy in doing things that scare me. It's proof that I'm alive and present.

DAMNED TO HELL, OR CREATED FOR IT?

"If there is no hell, a good many preachers are obtaining money under false pretenses." —BILLY SUNDAY

The first religious fear I ever overcame was my fear of hell. Had I never confronted my belief in hell, I'm not sure that I would have had the courage to question anything else about my faith. What makes this lie especially sinister is how the fear of hell can live on long after you have rationalized how silly a concept it is. I have talked to many who have stopped believing in the inherency of the Bible, stopped believing in blood atonement, maybe even stopped believing in any gods at all, and yet that fear of eternal torment stays with them. How many more never dare to question their beliefs due to this threat of eternal damnation? Indoctrination through fear is especially effective when it targets the most vulnerable: children.

By 3 years old, I could already tell you Jesus Christ loves us so much that he died on the cross to save us from our sins (Romans 5:8) so that we could live with him forever in heaven, worshiping God and dancing on streets made of gold (Revelation 21:21). I could tell you about the mansions God was preparing for us in heaven (John 14:2). And I could even tell you about how there would never again be fear or suffering (this "no fear" aspect was particularly enticing to my anxious young self, scared of her own shadow). I could also tell you the other part of the story—the part that kept me awake at night, shaking with anxiety: If we didn't accept Jesus as our savior, we would go to hell and suffer for all of eternity. Depending on which illustrated version of the Bible I had looked at that week, or which grandparent or parent I had talked with about the subject, hell took many different forms in my imagination. Sometimes I envisioned it as an actual pit of fire guarded by

Satan and his demons, something akin to the scene in *The Lion King* where Scar enlists his hyena minions to do his dirty work. Other times, I focused on the eternal separation part, horrified at the thought that I could never again be with the people I loved, imagining myself as one of the poor unfortunate souls Ursula had captured in *The Little Mermaid.* Whatever aesthetic it took on, fear of hell was a daily part of life. This fear was instilled in me at a young age by the adults I trusted most, long before I learned how to think critically. I was easily convinced by the good versus evil narratives found in most of the content I was allowed to consume. It is truly a brilliant way to minimize the risk of someone ever straying from the fold. Every thought or action went through the filter of "Whatever you do, don't put yourself at risk of going to hell." So many nights I sat in my bed begging Jesus to forgive me, reminding him that I accepted him as my savior, just in case my harsh words toward my sister or attitude toward my mom had put me at odds with him. Of course, some Christians now love to point out what terrible theology that was, but what did that matter? I was 3, 4, 5 years old and couldn't tie my own shoes, much less understand concepts like blood atonement, eternity or salvation. This was my life as a child, training my brain to never question or doubt at the risk of my soul. I didn't know how to ask for evidence. Kids were supposed to be able to depend on what their parents told them. I was believing the unseen, practicing blind trust, becoming faithful.

Hell is an afterlife claim, of which we have no evidence, and yet 61 percent of U.S. adults believe in its existence.[1] What "hell" is varies depending on whom you ask. Some believe it is simply eternal separation from the Christian god, but the majority believe it involves some sort of psychological torment, and possibly physical suffering as well. And while even more Americans believe in heaven (73 percent),[2] much of the shared message of the Christian gospel relies on eternal punishment, not reward, for motivation. Driving across the Bible Belt of America, you are almost certain to come across billboards stating "HELL IS REAL" or "Where are you going? HEAVEN or HELL?" usually with depictions of flames (and sometimes even a little cartoon demon). I have yet to see a billboard with images of heaven citing eternal paradise as

1 "Spirituality Among Americans," *Pew Research Center* (Pew Research Center, December 7, 2023), https://www.pewresearch.org/religion/2023/12/07/spiritual-beliefs/.
2 "Few Americans Blame God or Say Faith Has Been Shaken Amid Pandemic, Other Tragedies," *Pew Research Center* (Pew Research Center, November 23, 2021), https://www.pewresearch.org/religion/2021/11/23/views-on-the-afterlife/#:~:text=In%20the%20case%20of%20hell,or%20probably%20can%20meet%20Satan.

a good reason to believe. Fear is a much more powerful tool, and threats of torment create a sense of urgency that a person *must* believe now or burn.

It's difficult for me to find anything more sinister than baselessly convincing people of the terrifying threat of suffering infinite consequences for finite actions. Weaponizing this against the most vulnerable group of people—children—is an evil I can only forgive when it comes from parents who truly are terrified of the same consequence and believe they are protecting their kids. On the other hand, this train of thought always leaves me wondering what sort of person would choose to bring a child into the world knowing there is a chance the human they create will go on to an afterlife of *infinite* suffering. Anyone who makes the choice to become a parent hopefully knows their child will face challenges, hardships and other difficult circumstances over the course of their lives. None of it lasts forever, though. Infinite suffering is something we have no knowledge of. And life also comes with all sorts of positive and neutral experiences between the periods of struggle. Eternal torment, however, is inhuman by definition, as humans are finite. What sort of loving parent would risk a consequence so unnatural and cruel for someone they love, with stakes so high that they extend beyond the natural world? Similarly, and yet so much worse, what supposedly all-knowing, all-powerful, all-loving god would create beings bound for eternal torment? If this god is all-knowing, as is often claimed, it would know exactly which of its creations would end up in hell long before they were brought into existence.

Let's run these concepts through a simple logic exercise. Hypothesizing that all these evangelical claims about hell are real, consider someone who is now in eternal hell. Let's call him Evan. Evan was an atheist and, even on his deathbed, he remained unconvinced that Jesus was any sort of savior. For his lack of belief, he was consigned to hell. Now, let's rewind to Evan's childhood. He was raised as a Christian, fully exposed to the Bible and its teachings. That being the case, there is no excuse for his position. He knows the gospel and still chooses not to believe. Isn't he ultimately "sending himself to hell," as many apologists claim? Let's keep going. Rewind to before Evan was born: God is in heaven, knitting Evan together in his mother's womb (Psalm 139:13), knowing exactly what choices Evan will end up making and choosing to create him anyway, knowing precisely the endless suffering his creation will face after death. God has created a being knowing he's bound for hell. Usually, I hear a retort at this point claiming that foreknowledge does not take away choice, that awareness of an outcome doesn't remove free will. And that would be true if we were simply discussing a being that knows all. But we are discussing the claimed creator of all: an all-knowing and all-powerful god. If I know the winning team for a football game, that's simply foreknowledge and doesn't mean much. But if I am also the creator of every rule, of every player and their athletic abilities, of the weather and the physics of how the ball and players are impacted by it, the way the grass grows under their cleats...you get the point. I am now not only the creator of all of these things, but also of the outcome of the game. The game is rigged.

This thought process is largely what started my evangelical undoing in my early 20s. I remember having a conversation with a pastor who had some theologically progressive views, and he hypothesized that hell was something temporary, something that could be defeated. Matthew 16:18 was brought up, referencing the gates of hell that would not prevail. It felt like a blasphemous yet thrilling conversation. Why would the god I believed in be okay with the permanence and horror of eternal suffering? This toe-dip into critical thinking opened up a whole new world for me. I was dogmatically bound to a god who claimed omniscience, omnipotence and love, and I found those characteristics to be utterly incompatible with the idea that anyone this god created would go to hell. Thus, I couldn't sustain that belief while maintaining intellectual honesty. Confident that any loving and all-knowing god would know my heart and not judge me for questioning this aspect of my faith, I finally felt comfortable exploring the theology of hell. What I found was less than helpful. A few ambiguous verses and the use of fear as motivation seemed to make up the shaky foundation of something that had held me captive for most of my life. Every Christian pastor I spoke with had a slightly different take on it, and theologians couldn't even come close to agreeing on what or even *if* hell was. My first real rodeo with a primary tenet of my faith quickly changed from a bucking bronco to a broken mechanical bull ride. All of the anxiety and terror I associated with hell, simply because I was too afraid to question my faith and explore other possible truths, just slipped away.

COMMON ARGUMENTS YOU'LL HEAR

"Telling someone about hell is the loving thing to do! It's not a threat, it's a warning!"

Warnings are as valuable as the truth behind them. Pretending there are no negative consequences to a false warning is irresponsible and thoughtless. If there is a monster in my closet, of course I want to know. If there is not a monster in my closet and I am unable to check for myself and I live my entire life with the negative psychological impact of fear, then this baseless threat is an act of abuse. There absolutely are negative effects from the belief in hell. Fear of hell, sin and punishment from a god are all common symptoms of scrupulosity—a subtype of OCD that can cause significant disruption to everyday life and your emotional state. Many of my fellow ex-evangelicals who have shared their stories with me describe PTSD-like symptoms when referencing their fear of hell. Some have been professionally diagnosed with mental health conditions, including PTSD and OCD, directly tied to their religious trauma. Again, if this "monster" and its actions were real, this mental health issue would be an unfortunate side effect of life. But it's no more real than a make-believe boogeyman. Convincing anyone otherwise has horrific mental health implications and should be considered as helpful as the boy who cried wolf.

"God doesn't send you to hell. You choose it!"

I don't *choose* hell, and I don't *choose* heaven. I don't believe the choice exists at all. Post-belief, this argument sounds as silly to me as someone saying, "Zeus doesn't send you to Hades; you choose it!" You can't tell me I landed on Monopoly's "Go to Jail" space when I'm not even playing the game. But that's me. The argument many evangelicals make is that God would never do anything so awful as send someone to hell; he just has to let the laws he created play out as promised and ensure his believers have "free will." If your path leads to a bad place, tough luck. If this sounds like something an abusive partner or parent would say ("I only hurt you because I love you"), that's because it is. A creator that knows your outcome before you were even created obviously decided that outcome. There is only the illusion of free will. Were the Christian god a real god, and were you to go to hell, not only would he be sending you there, but he would have created you for it and it for you. Not simply damned to hell, but built for it.

"If there's no hell, that means horrible people don't get punished!"

Now we're getting somewhere: the actual need for this belief that so many cling to. We want to hope that there will be some sort of justice, or some revenge, on the worst of society. If there's no hell, then the Problem of Evil* becomes an even bigger issue. Someone can go their whole life doing horrible things, harming untold numbers of people, never getting caught and then simply die without ever having to face a consequence for their actions? It's a hard pill to swallow, but our desire for an alternative does not make it so. I would love to believe I will see my loved ones in a peaceful afterlife and that the wicked will be punished, but all the wanting in the world does not conjure up an actual afterlife. The sooner we can face this loss of certainty and grieve the peace and justice we hoped for, the sooner we can appreciate what we have here and now and take responsibility for what is in our control.

"God is just. That's why there's a hell!"

Punishment fitting the crime is something I associate with justice. Infinite consequences for choices made in the finite does not sound like a just punishment. Not only is this a completely disproportionate and literally immeasurable consequence, it offers absolutely nothing for the victims of the crime. A serial rapist dying peacefully at 90 years of age and then finally being held accountable for his atrocious acts does nothing for anyone harmed by him. It did not prevent him from assaulting his victims again and again and again. It did not heal the trauma of the victims. Even more ridiculous: If you follow the evangelical beliefs, this man could repent on his deathbed and find himself eternally *rewarded.* To refer to this system as a form of justice is laughable. The pushback on all of this is often that God *is* just because he is an infinite being and therefore all sins against him deserve infinite consequence. Even us lowly humans are more merciful in this regard. Children are almost never tried as adults in a court of law, as we are aware that their cognitive development and moral maturity are not the same as an adult's. This god, though, is apparently so petty and easily offended that he demands an unnatural consequence for the natural creature in the natural order he himself created.

"But what about all the near-death experiences people have reported?"

People who cite near-death experiences as evidence of an afterlife somehow ignore the "near" part. These experiences are evidence of brain activity, in many ways the opposite of death. Neuroscience tells us that there can be

*A philosophical argument that tries to reconcile both a world with suffering *and* the existence of an all-powerful, all-knowing, all-good god.

many contributing factors to NDEs, including temporal lobe stimulation, decreased oxygen and the effect of drugs and medications. Unsurprisingly, these reported experiences seem to follow the culture that person has already been exposed to or are often a reflection of a faith already held or considered in the past. Some NDEs consist of absolutely zero gods or afterlives, just a sort of nothingness. Also unsurprisingly, those NDEs are not the ones people like to cite. One of the most important traits that is consistent with every story from a person who was near death is that it's a subjective experience and we are relying on a fallible human to report on it. Even if we give them the benefit of the doubt and assume they are being honest in their reported experiences, we still must defer to the very unreliable human memory. When I hear a near-death experience story, I am no more compelled to believe it than I am a story from someone who took DMT (a psychedelic drug) or had a vivid dream. Even the most extreme, inexplicable NDEs have offered no evidence of an afterlife—only a perplexing "hmm."

Hell falls apart rather quickly when you realize it cannot exist, at least as claimed, in the realm of a loving and just god. It also completely contradicts the claim of free will—unless you consider free will to include those choices made under the duress of a metaphorical gun to your head or choices made after being programmed to make them. The claims fall completely flat when evidence is demanded of them, especially of the scientific sort. We have no knowledge of any afterlife, fiery or otherwise. Scripture itself is ambiguous at best on the claim, and Christians can't agree amongst themselves on what exactly Jesus is talking about when he references Sheol, Gehenna or things like "weeping and gnashing of teeth." The claims lose even more steam when you recognize the ways they have been weaponized to control and manipulate the masses. If you still find yourself wondering about hell claims, you could (and I encourage you to do so if it is of interest) spend time reading all the theological positions on hell and the different flavors it has taken on over the years. Much of the stereotypical fire and brimstone preaching we still hear from some evangelical preachers was popularized in America in the 1700s during the First Great Awakening by Jonathan Edwards and his peers. Later on, 20th-century preachers such as Billy Sunday and Billy Graham also put charismatic emphasis on the threat of hell, with Graham being a proponent of the idea that "God will never send anybody to hell. If man goes to hell, he goes by his own free choice." Researching all of this with intellectual honesty will destabilize anyone's theological position of hell, and for some, it's the most helpful route. I find it to be unnecessary, though, as I can summarize my disbelief in hell quite simply (and you will find this response repeated throughout this book): *There is simply no reason to believe hell exists.* Neither the popularity of the claim nor the consequences, were they true, amount to evidence of it being fact. Make up any other after-life claim, popularize it, make the stakes of disbelief high enough and you have just as much reason to believe it exists as you do hell.

THE DEVIL, HIMSELF

"But who prays for Satan? Who, in eighteen centuries, has had the common humanity to pray for the one sinner that needed it most, our one fellow and brother who most needed a friend yet had not a single one, the one sinner among us all who had the highest and clearest right to every Christian's daily and nightly prayers, for the plain and unassailable reason that his was the first and greatest need, he being among sinners the supremest?" —MARK TWAIN

One of my earliest memories is of visiting my grandparents and sitting under a piano bench attempting to engage in the spiritual warfare I had heard so much about. I vividly remember my grandfather asking me what I was up to. His 6'2" frame shadowed my view as I looked up from my sheltered position. "I'm trying to talk to Satan," I earnestly answered. At just 5 years old, my life was already consumed with evangelicalism and all the angels, demons and stories that came with it. Even my private moments and thoughts couldn't escape it. "Hmm, I'm not sure you should be doing that. What are you trying to talk to him for?" Grandpa Jack's voice was kind, curious and a bit shaky from the Parkinson's that was slowly but surely overtaking his body despite the amount of prayers and faith we were dwelling in for his healing. Immediately, I felt I must be doing something wrong. If anyone knew about this stuff, it was my grandpa, after all. He had been a pastor and missionary for over 50 years, and to this day, he is still the image of faith to me. He devoted his entire life to the god he fervently believed in. I remember anxiously explaining that I was going to try to get Satan to ask Jesus for forgiveness. The Bible says Jesus will forgive anyone if they just believe in him and ask for his help. Which, to me, meant that if I could get Lucifer to apologize for what he did, Jesus would forgive him and there wouldn't be any more hell or demons. I wish I could remember what my grandfather's response was, but I can't for the life of me. I'm sure he had a laugh, and luckily, I have no recollection of him shaming me, but I also don't recall a solid answer that would undo the seed of doubt that ended up staying with me for years and years, just waiting to bloom.

Throughout my childhood, I maintained a fascination with the evangelical character arc of Lucifer, most certainly because I viewed him as a cautionary tale. Despite my prized Marvel graphic novel edition of C.S. Lewis's *The Screwtape Letters* that depicted him as a horned, muscular figure of death, I imagined him more as the beautiful, angry fallen angel that Alexandre Cabanel depicted in his famous painting *The Fallen Angel*, hiding his face, with angst and tears in his eyes. Pride was to blame for his fall. Questioning God and comparing yourself to him were the worst possible things you could do. I never quite understood this. If God was so perfect and amazing, and we were supposed to strive to be like him, why was it so horrific that one of his own creations attempted to compare stats? But like most evangelical rhetoric, I knew it was taboo to question the subject. Nothing could be more dangerous than advocating for the devil himself. And yet I still found myself hoping and praying that God and Lucifer would make amends, not just for the sake of the world, but because of the deep empathy I felt toward their fractured relationship. Even more confusing was that my childlike perspective was praised by Jesus in the Bible (Matthew 18:1-4) and yet clearly concerned the adults around me. Satan was bad. Evil. And there was nothing more to it. Imagine my surprise when I learned as an adult that this narrative of Lucifer being an angel taken over by pride, thrown out of heaven and turned into "Satan" or "the devil" was even less biblically based than the idea of hell. St. Augustine popularized this idea of a fallen angel by piecing together a few ambiguous Bible verses with John Milton's fictional work *Paradise Lost*, shaping the dramatic and emotional story many Christians now associate with Satan or Lucifer. Learning this was one of the first times I was able to be honest with myself about the amount of theological acrobatics being used to make up and maintain so much of what I had been taught as inherent Christian truth.

What's especially fascinating about the Satan/Lucifer narrative is how much evangelical rhetoric depends on it. For starters, there is no nuance or gray area. You are either on God's side or you're against him. What better way to influence massive numbers of people than to make everything high stakes? An enemy is needed in order to justify the black-and-white thinking that gives comfort to so many. Outsourcing one's judgment to someone else simplifies things, certainly. It also absolves one from any accountability for those judgments. Even more helpful, if anyone who doesn't serve God is automatically serving Satan, you can easily dismiss and make an enemy of them. No reason to approach people we don't understand with curiosity and compassion if they are working for the devil himself and could lead us to sin. The local yoga instructor? Practicing new-age Satan worship. The atheist organization? A gathering of Satanists working to remove God from society. The gay couple down the street? Actively embracing sin and following the devil's plan for their life. There's no bridge-building with the enemy, and when you make the enemy everyone except those who share your beliefs, you've effectively shielded yourself from ever learning anything new.

Another important and potentially more sinister role this Satan character plays is that of a mental terrorist. I remember being taught that every thought I had should serve Christ (2 Corinthians 10:5), and what wasn't serving Christ was subject to the lies of the devil. Satan is, after all, called the father of lies, and any thoughts of fear or anxiety were considered to be from him. You can imagine the turmoil this put me in, especially in my early 20s when dealing with a panic attack disorder. There was an entire battle playing out in my mind, constantly attempting to control and "take captive" my thoughts, which I believed Satan was influencing. When religion can convince you that your own thoughts are either holy or evil, in a continuous battle for your identity, that's power. External control isn't even necessary when your own thoughts must be regularly filtered, corrected and policed.

Ultimately, I find Satan's most important role to be as one of God's scapegoats. In line with the evangelical black-and-white thinking, one of the earliest things I was indoctrinated with is that everything good and perfect comes from God (James 1:17) and anything negative or bad comes from the devil. You pray for safe travels before a road trip and everything goes well? Thank the Lord! You pray for safe travels before a road trip and wind up in a terrible car crash? That was an attack by the enemy, and that pesky free will (more on that later) prevented God from intervening. You pray for help with an important exam and pass with flying colors? God did it! (Never mind that you stayed up all night studying.) You pray for help with an important exam and fail? What distractions from the devil have you fallen for lately? The beauty of a rainbow, the wonder of mountains, the power and joy of waves on a beach? All credited to God, who loves us so much he designed this world for us. A destructive flood that wipes out innocent lives, a city-destroying earthquake, a famine that causes children to starve to death? Well, that's just the enemy going about his business with a little help from his friends Sin and Free Will. It's the perfect system in which God is never to blame and is always to be thanked. Creator of all and responsible for none. It is Satan, God's creation, who seems to hold the most power and influence.

COMMON ARGUMENTS YOU'LL HEAR

"Satan has dominion over Earth."

This belief is typically harvested from John 12:31 and is where much of the scapegoating comes from. However, it instantly presents a problem with the claim that God is all-powerful. Similar to the hell claim, if God is all-powerful and yet Satan is ruling over Earth, that is by God's own design. To say that God is sovereign yet Satan rules Earth is to say that God ordained it that way since the beginning of time. This makes Lucifer a hand-designed colleague, if anything, and certainly not an unwanted enemy.

"Satan wants to destroy you!"

If Satan's goal is to lead people away from God, this is a terrible strategy. If I want my friend to come hang out at my house instead of some other person's house, my strategy would be to make them happy, comfortable and offer them all of the things they want. The rebuttal here is generally, "Yes! He does do that; he makes you so happy and comfortable that you abandon God!" Well, which is it? Is he behind the children's bone cancer? Or is he serving tea and cakes on the patio? And furthermore, why is he so much more emotionally invested in us than our all-loving creator? It paints a picture of an absent god, answering prayers at the rate of chance, versus a very active devil that is working overtime to both comfort and harm us as often as possible.

"God allows Satan to tempt us, but ultimately, it is our choice to fall for temptations."

God sure does grant a lot of privileges to his adversary. How interesting that he decided to create a universe that allows for one external being to influence both our thoughts and daily lives. I hope you're seeing a pattern here of what appears to be some sort of alliance between God and his worst enemy. God allowing mere humans to be faced with temptations from a powerful supernatural being is akin to putting a child in a room with a magician and then punishing them when they fall for the magic tricks. The odds are stacked against us when this free will is issued with a voice whispering the wrong answers in our ear. This claim also fails to acknowledge that many things impact a person's choices even when not being "tempted." Poverty, childhood trauma, health issues, addiction, education and more are all things outside of an individual's control that play a big part in what choices they have the chance to make.

"The greatest trick the devil ever pulled was convincing the world he didn't exist!"

Some variation of this silly and popular phrase has been around since the 19th century, although the exact rendering above was spoken in *The Usual Suspects* (1995). It sounds quite dramatic at first. How spooky that we could be deceived by the most evil force of all time and not even know it! But this could be said about anything. The greatest trick little green aliens ever pulled was convincing the world they didn't exist! The greatest trick magical unicorns ever pulled was convincing the world they didn't exist! It's a circular argument that offers up zero evidence and somehow tries to convince us that the lack of evidence is, itself, the evidence for a positive claim. It's all smoke and mirrors, designed to use fear to keep you from questioning the false dichotomy that either you believe in the devil or he's deceiving you into thinking he doesn't exist. The people asserting this are usually the same people who claim Satan's greatest sins are pride and the desire to be worshiped as God. So which is it? Does he want our adoration and acknowledgment? Or is he content to deceive us that he doesn't exist?

Despite the lack of biblical foundation for most of Satan's story, you can see how fundamental this character is to maintain one of evangelicalism's most powerful tools: us vs. them. There has to be a "them." By introducing this evil villain who taints the hearts and minds of men and has power over the world we live in, the well has been effectively poisoned. We can now demonize fellow human beings and claim that the devil is working through them. It sows seeds of distrust, and instead of allowing us to observe things through the lens of reality and nuance, we can simply say that Hollywood, the government or any other subculture or flavor of humanity that makes us uncomfortable has been taken over by Satan. At best, this allows for people to turn a blind eye to real issues that need to be addressed; at worst, it can justify horrific bigotry and violence. Desegregation can be framed as Satan using the government to destroy God's order, with MLK Jr. and others acting as his agents of rebellion. Self-proclaimed prophets can claim that "the gays" are triggering hurricanes as judgment for destroying godly marriage. Pop star Taylor Swift is a servant of the devil used to influence teen girls with feminism. The Capitol must be stormed because of the evil cabal that has taken over. While Satan is simply a boogeyman, the implications of believing that he's more, or even pretending to, are dangerous and detrimental to the progress of society.

Fear of invisible monsters is a powerful tool, but courage and a nice dose of skepticism quickly reveal that it is nothing more than a sleazy con man.

CHAPTER 2

Eat the Apple

"The only good is knowledge, and the only evil is ignorance."
—ATTRIBUTED TO SOCRATES

HISTORICALLY, AND FOR GOOD REASON, we have labeled those who ban books and discourage the pursuit of knowledge as "the bad guys." The Soviet Union, Hitler's regime, the Qin dynasty and modern-day North Korea and Russia all fit the bill. But what do we call it when a group seeks to demonize knowledge and pushes for one specific book to be centered in place of it? This is known as religious extremism, and I experienced it firsthand through evangelicalism. It's well known that over the years, American evangelicals have been huge fans of "cancel culture" and attempting to ban certain books or even music. The '80s featured the infamous satanic panic full of demands to burn and destroy heavy metal and rock albums that were accused of promoting Satanism and demonic activity. In the '90s, evangelicals protested and called for libraries to ban books like *Harry Potter*, claiming it was influencing children to participate in dark magic. Evangelicals have also been the first to jump on boycotts against companies that have been inclusive toward queer people, or even just toward people of other faiths. The American Family Association and Focus on the Family are two of the Christian fundamentalist organizations leading many of these attempts to demonize media that doesn't fit their conservative agenda. For truly "devout" families like ours, this limiting and banning of certain media consumption was normal. Only Christian music was allowed, movies were limited and most books my peers were reading like *Harry Potter* or *The Baby-Sitters Club* were strictly forbidden. Anything with magic was not permitted because it undermined God's power. Anything with dating, kissing or other forms of immodesty was also not allowed because it encouraged lust and inappropriate behavior. Various forms of other "questionable" media were also banned from our house because of references to evolution or other scientific claims that went against our understanding of Genesis. The general rule of thumb was that if the book, song or movie didn't center around Christianity, or at least Christian values, it was probably not going to be allowed. Even my parents' decision to homeschool their children was to "protect" us from the scary liberal agenda of public schools and to make sure that they had full control over every bit of content we consumed. Of course, there is a normal amount of oversight by parents when it comes to their children's media consumption in order to keep kids safe from things that are not age-appropriate, but this was different. This was fear-based censoring designed to control what I believed about the world around me and to guarantee that I was sticking to Christian doctrine. In other words, it was indoctrination. Looking back now, it seems most of my time as a Christian was spent being protected from, or protecting myself from, the thing that ultimately led to my disbelief: knowledge. The demonization of broad knowledge was covered up with the encouragement to pursue specific knowledge—curated, carefully packaged and presented to me in a way that kept me on the straight and narrow evangelical path.

That path very much included daily Bible reading, starting from childhood. My Christian homeschool curriculum had me writing out verses to practice penmanship. It often used Bible stories as examples for math problems. When I wasn't reading the Bible itself, I was reading historical fiction (or even nonfiction) that revolved around characters referencing the scriptures. At bedtime, we read my illustrated children's Bible stories. When my parents would drop me off at my paternal grandparents' home, I always hoped it would be a TV day when I could watch *The Gospel According to Matthew*, but more often it was a Bible-reading day when my grandmother would use her felt board (a fabric-covered board upon which felt figures could be displayed in order to tell a story) to illustrate whatever chapter she decided we would study. Sunday mornings, of course, were spent at Sunday school learning about—you guessed it—the Bible. Even home discipline revolved around the Bible. Talking back, forgetting to make my bed or causing trouble with a sister usually led to being assigned a passage of scripture of my father's choosing to copy over and over—sometimes for what felt like an eternity and definitely until my hand ached. For "fun," once a week I got to go with a friend to Awana, an international Christian program for children, where we were rewarded with prizes and recognition for Bible verse memorization. I knew the Bible and I knew it well. Or so I thought. What I really knew was the meaning I was taught to derive from it, a very specific narrative that had been chosen for me. Contradictions were skipped over, ignored or repackaged. The historicity of it was exaggerated, simplified or even straight-up lied about. The questions or confusion I expressed were constantly met with "Well, you're taking it out of context," or "We'll find out one day when we get to heaven." It seemed there was an unspoken rule that required us to accept the Bible and its claims—or modern assertions of those claims—or face the consequences. Cherry-picking the more palatable parts and reinterpreting the difficult-to-swallow ones was allowed and even encouraged, as long as the Bible itself wasn't doubted. Often, I felt I was talking to a wall when asking questions in Sunday school or even at home and that I was walking on theological eggshells if I didn't rein in my questions. One core memory of experiencing this doubt as a child occurred when I first heard the story of "The Emperor's New Clothes." In it, a prideful emperor is visited by con men who have learned of his love of beautiful, unique garments. They convince him that they can make a magical outfit for him. The catch is that the garments are invisible to foolish or unworthy people—or so they tell him. The emperor falls for their scam and parades himself around town completely naked, too embarrassed to admit he cannot see his "clothes." He is met with cheers of approval and praise from all of his townspeople, as no one wished to be seen as foolish. Suddenly, a child in the crowd cries out, "But he doesn't have any clothes on!" And just like that, they are all exposed as frauds. I found myself relating to the child upon hearing this story, and yet was scared to admit that I, too, did not see the "clothes," or the God, that everyone around me was constantly praising. I felt ashamed and at a crossroads. Do I express my doubt or accept the burden of belief? I chose the latter. Something must be wrong with me, not everyone else.

Satan must be blinding me and trying to tempt me to stray. I didn't dare be like the child in the fairytale; I had to commit to my faith or risk unraveling the entire foundation of my world. So I continued to believe, suppressing my doubts, taking every opportunity I could to credit anything unknown or ambiguous to God. It wasn't "good luck," it was God's favor. It wasn't my conscience, it was God's voice in my ear. It wasn't just nature, it was God creating sunsets for our enjoyment. I trained my brain to see the emperor's clothes. I followed with naive faith, placing my trust in religious leaders and family members. The Bible was true because it must be true.

COMMON ARGUMENTS YOU'LL HEAR

"The Bible is God's word: It says so!"

This is a massive claim and yet falls completely flat, as it relies on itself to prove itself. Outright circular reasoning. The Bible claiming something about itself does not make it true. If a person were to write a book and somewhere in it claim they are "speaking for God," would we accept that? Hopefully not. Even more scathing, "the Bible" as we know it does not claim to be God's word. The few, vague verses that are used to defend this idea (like 2 Timothy 3:16–17, which claims "all Scripture is God-breathed") were written before the New Testament was even compiled and refer solely to the Old Testament, not even specifying which books it includes. Even today, different branches of Christianity have different canons: the 66 books evangelicals are most familiar with and more for Catholics and Orthodox Christians. So which Bible is God's word? The one with 66 books? The one with 81? When you remove the option of circular logic and instead apply historical facts to the compilation of the Bible, many evangelical claims immediately fail.

"No other book has been as influential or important!"

No doubt, the Bible has been influential and has held varying degrees of subjective importance to many. But how did that happen? It turns out that being on the wrong end of a sword, imperial power or both certainly helps motivate someone to convert. When you have the political pressure of the Roman Empire or the threat of European colonizers hanging over your head, the Bible isn't such a tough pill to swallow. Threatening Jews and pagans with exile or even execution is a convenient way to fast-track a religion's popularity. We must also acknowledge the immeasurable influence of other notable books. The Quran, *The Analects of Confucius*, the

Rigveda, the Book of the Dead, Newton's *Principia*, Darwin's *The Origin of Species*, Marx's *Communist Manifesto* and Hitler's *Mein Kampf* have all had a massive impact on the history of humans and caused, for better or horrifically worse, significant changes. When measuring something as subjective as influence or importance, the answer to which book has had the most impact often depends on which area of the world you find yourself. Yes, we should be aware of religion's impact and influence, but it is not evidence for the claims that it makes. If, over the next thousand years, a new religious text contradicting the Bible became more influential and popular, would Christians concede that their faith was incorrect? I think not. Being at the top of the bestseller list is not evidence of something being true. It is a look into what humans choose to popularize and how forced conversions, politics, storytelling, tradition and fear can all collide and influence the masses.

"Biblical prophecies are being fulfilled!"

War, famine and natural disasters have been taking place long before and after the creation of the Bible. Stating that "wars and rumors of war," earthquakes and nations going against other nations (Matthew 24:6–7) will occur at some unspecified time is like a weatherman predicting that "this year we'll have rain, some cloudy days and some thunderstorms" in a climate that generally allows for it. And that's the problem with the claimed "fulfilled" prophecies. It's doing a disservice to the word "prophecy" to say that these are anything other than vague predictions almost guaranteed to occur. *Cosmo* magazine horoscopes and Nostradamus use the same cryptic, sometimes poetic method that is easily used in retrospect to claim an accurate prediction but in reality could be applied to many different events or circumstances. For centuries, this is exactly how people have made the claim that biblical prophecies are being fulfilled, all while citing wildly different things as evidence of that supposed fulfillment. This is not prophecy fulfillment; it's retrofitting history to support an agenda. We see the same thing when we look at the "prophecies" in the Old Testament that are claimed to have been fulfilled in the New Testament. Vague assertions can easily be reinterpreted to fit subsequent events. Even more so, there was nothing keeping the authors of the Gospels from embellishing or even outright fabricating some of the events in their stories to appear as fulfilled prophecies. There was also nothing stopping Jesus from acting out these prophecies in hopes that it would validate his message. What's even more absurd is when an event in an earlier story is claimed to be the fulfillment of a prophecy that wasn't even written about until after the event in question.

Another problem with biblical prophecy is that there is zero verification that any of the events in question actually occurred. It's the equivalent of me writing a book claiming something will happen, then another person authoring a follow-up book years later claiming the thing did happen and pronouncing it a fulfilled prophecy. This retrofitting occurs throughout the Bible including the Book of Daniel, an apologist favorite for referencing "fulfilled" prophecy. We could spend this entire book discussing each claimed prophecy and why it is invalid, but I instead encourage you to do so on your own and recognize the vagueness, prescriptiveness or outright failures found therein.

Conveniently, when bringing up biblical prophecies, apologists do not mention the failed ones. Matthew 24:34 makes it very clear that all of Jesus's assertions about the sun darkening, the moon not giving light and the stars falling from the sky along with the apocalyptic wars already mentioned will occur within the time of the generation he is speaking to—including his return to Earth. Obviously, these prophesies did not come to pass. Paul goes on to make the same failed prediction in 1 Thessalonians 4:15–17 when he claims that he and others living during that time will experience the second coming of Christ. Ezekiel 26:7–14 claims Tyre will be destroyed and never rebuilt, yet you could book a flight there today and stay at a hotel in the city. Prophecies are not being fulfilled—only vague predictions that anyone could make. And there is nothing impressive about Daniel claiming to predict the rise and fall of multiple kingdoms, long after those kingdoms have risen and fallen. This isn't prophecy; it's merely post-dating a story.

"The Bible is consistent."

Consistent with what? Certainly not itself. What were Jesus's last words? In the book of Acts, did Paul's companions hear the voice but see no one, or see the light and hear no voice? Was Moses face-to-face with God, or, as the authors of the New Testament write, is that not possible? Was it God or Satan who inspired David to take a census? And was Jesus born during the reign of Herod or the census of Quirinius? All of these and more receive inconsistent answers in the Bible. That which is consistent, or at least isn't contradicted, is thanks to the exact canon chosen by early Christians and the strategic decision to omit certain texts that were originally included.

Consistency is also not to be expected when a book is actually a collection of many books written by multiple authors over the course of hundreds of years. Most importantly, consistency alone does not indicate validity. There are many prolific creators of fiction, covering novels, short stories, comics and even poems. Regardless of how consistent or detailed their works are, whether we're talking about Tolkien's hobbits, Marvel's heroes or Disney's Woody and Buzz, the works themselves remain fictional.

"That's where faith comes in."

If words could win awards for carrying the most weight of claims, "faith" would be a shoo-in. And yet what a lazy word it is. For starters, like many religious terms, good luck getting a consistent definition from its users. Most often, it boils down to belief in something without evidence. Hebrews 11:1 claims, "Now faith is confidence in what we hope for and assurance about what we do not see." Well, what's the use in that? If we apply faith as our gap-filler when there is no bridge of evidence to a belief, that makes absolutely any and all beliefs untouchable. Why not spend all my money on lottery tickets and just have faith that I will win the lottery tomorrow? Why not forgo those mortgage payments and have faith that the bank will just let me keep the house anyway? Why not jump off a roof and have faith that I'll grow wings and fly? Faith is an excuse for not being able to bear the burden of proof. It is a fortifier of ignorance that results in baseless arrogance. Faith is useless when applied to any aspect of reality and is no different than someone saying, "Just believe it for no good reason." If faith isn't a good enough reason to believe that I'll fly after jumping off a roof, it's also not a good reason to believe in other things that defy what we know about reality, such as the existence of gods or afterlives. My final question to Christians who declare "faith" as a sufficient reason to believe is this: If you wouldn't believe in someone else's god based on faith, why should I believe in yours?

A BETTER BIBLE

If the Bible were to be read for what it is—a collection of writing from many authors over the course of hundreds of years that requires social, historical and cultural context to even begin to make sense of—we might disarm it of some of its potential dangers. But evangelical rhetoric more commonly does the opposite—presenting the Bible as a single unified message from God, fully relevant to modern life and interpreted in a way that supports a specific narrative, rather than aiming to understand the text itself or question whether an objective interpretation is even possible. It is used not as a tool to try to understand the past and what ancient people believed but as a weapon to attempt to control what people believe today and will believe tomorrow. The Bible is often referenced as the go-to source for God's wisdom, but even without getting into the horrific atrocities humans have committed using it for justification (as we will discuss in later chapters), I often wonder how many of the Christians who purport to believe in the Bible have truly read it, even through an evangelical lens, and considered what they're reading. Even some of the less controversial, decent parts of the book are open to interpretation and could very easily be made better. For example, the beloved "Do unto others as you would have them do unto you" (Luke 6:31) sounds nice at first, but let's apply this to reality. I love big, extravagant birthday plans with lots of people and things to look forward to. My husband prefers more low-key, spontaneous celebrations that he doesn't have to anticipate. If I were to "do unto" him by celebrating his birthday with the kind I would want, he would not feel very loved at all. And vice versa. This "golden rule" looks a bit tarnished compared to "Do unto others as they would have you do unto them." Jesus's famous words of "Love your neighbor as yourself" (Mark 12:31) are also given a major upgrade when changed to "Love your neighbor as you would a fellow human deserving of love," because plenty of people do not, in fact, love themselves. Or what about Ephesians 6:5, which commands slaves to obey their masters? Wouldn't a better use of scripture have been to say, "Hey, everyone! Don't ever own fellow humans as slaves. That's wrong"? Honoring your mother and father (Ephesians 6:2) sounds sweet, but with tens of thousands of child abuse cases reported each year in the U.S., it sure would be helpful if "unless they are abusing you, in which case you owe them nothing and should be protected from them" had been added to the verse.

Again, if the Bible were simply viewed as a window back in time, we'd write off these imperfections and lack of ethics as a product of the past. But evangelicals don't see it that way. To them, the Bible is an extension of God himself and must be respected as such. In fact, seven out of 10 white evangelicals believe U.S. laws should be more influenced by the Bible than by the will of the people.[1] To wish for something so unclear, inconsistent and archaic to have precedence over democracy is as dangerous as it sounds. Which parts of the Bible do they want to be influential? The part where God endorses genocide (1 Samuel 15:3)? The part that says women should not be permitted to lead (1 Timothy 2:11–12)? Or the part that says anyone who is not a believer is an enemy (Matthew 12:30)?

"You're cherry-picking!" is often the response to pointing out some of the more loathsome verses of the Bible. Well, of course, the Bible must be cherry-picked to find any specific stance or message. That's exactly what evangelicals do and why it's so dangerous. Permitting the Bible to inform laws or promote certain lifestyles requires treating it like some Ouija board where the reader can jump from verse to verse, claiming a supernaturally inspired message that was, in reality, hand-picked to align with their own personal agenda. Again, not a tool, but a weapon. But of course, this is the way of humans. We are all biased, we often have an agenda and we are not the most reliable narrators. Which is why it is so fascinating that throughout the history of god-claims, none of these supposed gods have figured out a better way to communicate with us other than through humans, who write, rewrite and reinterpret what they believe these gods have said. And none of these religious texts have ever left us with any way to prove the writings were inspired by an actual deity and are not just the musings of the people writing them. All-powerful gods reduced to stone tablets, papyrus scrolls, councils and politically influenced consensus.

My realization of how chaotic, ethically confused, contradictory and fundamentally human the Bible is began with my desire to grow deeper in my beliefs and to know the Bible so well that I could convince anyone of its truth and worthiness. I was in my mid-20s and headed for ministry school. Outside of my sheltered upbringing, I was finally starting to meet people who believed different things than me. Thanks to the internet, I was even exposed to some atheist arguments, usually in the form of abrasive memes saying something like, "Sky Daddy loves you unconditionally, under a few conditions." I was beginning to understand that despite what I was taught, not everyone thought or believed like me. And many of them had some pretty

1 "Half of Americans say Bible should influence U.S. laws," Pew Research Center (Pew Research Center, April 13, 2020), https://www.pewresearch.org/short-reads/2020/04/13/half-of-americans-say-bible-should-influence-u-s-laws-including-28-who-favor-it-over-the-will-of-the-people/.

compelling arguments for their views. I wanted the strength of my arguments to match the passion I felt for my beliefs. Like any people-pleasing, overachieving eldest daughter of a pastor, I decided to start my homework before ministry school even began. Reading through the Bible was no big deal; I had done it several times before and was already reading the Bible daily. Now I would just read it through from the beginning, a few chapters from the Old Testament and a few from the New Testament every day. But this time, I would read them as objectively as possible, letting personal curiosity be my teacher, looking at the work through the lens of some of my new non-Christian friends to try to anticipate questions or pushback they may have. That broke open a whole new world for me. Suddenly, the Bible I had grown up with wasn't the Bible I knew—completely ridiculous-sounding at times, full of inconsistencies, leading me down various rabbit holes for hours while trying to understand what I was possibly supposed to get out of it without arrogantly assuming I knew the mind of God. The dissonance between what I had been taught about the Bible and what I was seeing with my own eyes was growing with every moment I spent reading. It was no longer a god-breathed firm foundation for my faith. It was a patchwork quilt stitched together by ancient humans with varying agendas and motivations.

BIBLE STORIES YOU MIGHT HAVE MISSED

One of the many surprises my reading journey took me on was realizing how many Bible stories are flat-out ridiculous, graphic or just plain weird. Reading them makes it clear why Christians cherry-pick which parts of the Bible to focus on. Some of them just don't make for a nice Sunday morning sermon.

King Saul and the Necromancer: 1 Samuel 28

Saul suddenly finds himself terrified after seeing his opposition, the Philistine army, assembling for battle. He realizes he needs some sort of advice but he inconveniently expelled all mediums and practitioners of magic and God seems to be ignoring his pleas. He manages to find a witch and disguises himself so she'll be more inclined to help him out. Sure enough, she conjures up the ghost of Samuel, who gives him quite a talking to, criticizing him for disobeying God and telling him the Philistines will defeat him. This upsets Saul, causing him to fall to the ground, and it didn't help that he hadn't eaten anything in a day. The witch feels bad for Saul and makes him some food, but fails to provide any additional help. Saul eventually dies, and the Bible points to his use of a medium as one of the reasons why. Apparently, God holds a grudge if you seek outside help while he's playing hard to get.

Paul Talks a Boy to Death: Acts 20:9

It turns out that sitting in a window while Paul preaches is not the best idea. A young man, perched on a window ledge, fell fast asleep as Paul spoke late into the night. He fell three stories and died. Paul wasn't worried, however. After putting his arms around the boy and proclaiming "He's alive!" Paul gets a snack and keeps preaching until the next morning, when the boy somehow awakens and goes home, alive after all. Was the boy healed of all injuries? We don't know. Was the boy truly, verifiably dead when he fell, rather than just knocked unconscious? We don't know. Was this story used when I was a child to tell me I should be able to sit through any length of church service? Yes.

Jesus Gets Hangry and Casts a Spell on a Tree: Mark 11:12–14

In perhaps one of his most human moments, Jesus gets hungry while traveling and spots a fig tree. When he realizes it isn't producing fruit, what does he do with his all-powerful god abilities? He curses the tree with a declaration that no one would ever eat of it again. Never mind that it wasn't even the correct season for fig trees to produce fruit. Why Jesus didn't decide instead to simply use his godhood to have the tree grow figs anyway, or pull another "five loaves and two fish" moment (during which he miraculously fed 5,000), I'm not sure.

Ezekiel Has a Shitty Cookout: Ezekiel 4:12–15

God tells Ezekiel to cook his meal over a fire fueled by human feces, because he wants this to be a symbolic act of how the people of Israel will be driven out of their land and forced to eat "defiled" food from gentiles. Understandably, Ezekiel really doesn't love the idea and objects. Great news for him, God concedes and says not to worry...he can use cow dung instead. What a relief. Very similar to when God asked Abraham to sacrifice his son and then said "just kidding." Lower stakes, but I guess he still loves a good fake-out.

42 Prophet-Bashers Versus Two Bears: 2 Kings 2:23–24

Elisha, another prophet of the Lord, is traveling when a large group of boys from a nearby town begin to mock him. Why are they mocking him? For being bald. Apparently, Elisha doesn't joke around about his hairline because he immediately calls down a curse from God resulting in two bears coming out of the woods and mauling 42 of the boys. Interesting that this story was never brought up in Sunday school. I guess it's not a good look for the god of the universe to participate in such ego-driven, prideful reactions.

Touched by a Foreskin: Exodus 4:24–26

This is just one of many stories involving something that the Bible seems to find important: foreskins. (Remember in 1 Samuel 18 when David gifts 200 of them to Saul?) Immediately after asking Moses to go speak for him in Egypt, God abruptly gets the hankering to kill him instead. We're never told why. Lucky for Moses, his wife suddenly decides to cut off their son's foreskin and touches it to Moses's feet, obviously causing God to spare Moses's life. Obviously...

Prostitute or Daughter-in-Law?: Genesis 38

Judah's oldest son, Er, marries a woman named Tamar, but then God kills him because he was "wicked." As was tradition, Tamar is married off to the next son, Onan. He is also killed by God for being, you guessed it, wicked. Judah's next son in line is too young to marry Tamar. She waits around until he is old enough, only to be ignored. She comes up with a plan to disguise herself and convince Judah to unknowingly hire her as a prostitute. He does, she gets pregnant and her scam is praised by her father-in-law/baby daddy.

Equine Emissions: Ezekiel 23

Instead of just being direct and clear with his feelings about the two kingdoms of Israel, God decides to tell Ezekiel a story of two sisters. In short, the sisters "prostitute" themselves, but the Lord decides to go into long, graphic detail while telling his story. He mentions specific sex acts and body parts, and then there's this lovely verse: "There she lusted after her lovers, whose genitals were like those of donkeys and whose emission was like that of horses." In the end, God makes sure to include graphic scenes of them being humiliated and punished for their lewdness. Amazing to think of all the books I was not allowed to have as a child, yet the one containing this story was handed over to me as soon as I could read. I guess graphic violence and sexual content is totally fine as long as God is the one telling the story.

EVE WAS FRAMED

Despite my dogmatic devotion to the Bible, none of the stories were ever that interesting to me. Most were long, complicated and either very weird or not very entertaining, especially when read straight from the source instead of some illustrated retelling. But the story of the Garden of Eden always haunted me and left me with the most questions. On the surface, it is a simple story with an important outcome that supposedly convicted me due to Eve's original sin. But I also found it quite scandalous. The first humans were naked, walked and talked with God and snakes and then ate fruit and BAM, everything was ruined. My initial, childlike understanding was the common telling of the tale. A perfect god creates a garden for his creations where everything is blissful and lovely. They have everything they could ever need. Except for Adam, who had one need. And her name was Eve. With that need met, what more could he want? Apparently, a fruit snack. Cue Eve wandering in the garden, cue the devil as a serpent (an equivalence that the Bible doesn't even make), cue the forbidden questioning. This is one story from the Bible I find myself replaying and relating to. I'm empowered by the story of Eve:

One day, like she did every day, Eve walked through the garden. It was the only home she had ever known. Her very existence was sparked by the loneliness of a man, or so it was claimed, and yet her own loneliness was beneath notice. She didn't mind; the garden was her companion. Bare-skinned, with the warm sun and a perfect climate causing her to know only comfort, she breathed in perfect air scented with flowers and frankincense. Every animal her friend, every tree bearing an offering for her. Except for one. The Tree of the Knowledge of Good and Evil. She walked by it often, feeling some odd sensation she had no name for, though she imagined it was something close to "longing." Something that made her feel as if she were created to be near it. It's not as though it looked special or more appealing than any other tree; all the fruit in the garden was perfectly appealing. She only knew what it was because Adam told her that God had forbidden them from eating the fruit of that specific tree. Perhaps that was part of the attraction, but there was something bigger at play. Something written in the stars. The Tree of Life was there too, but it did not draw her to it. Eve was already living, after all. But today, that inexplicable tug brought her closer to the Tree of Knowledge than ever before. Close enough to hear a faint voice. "Did God really say...?" it whispered, but she could not make out the rest. Eve cautiously crept close enough to make out a small serpent with its legs wrapped around one of the most fruit-laden branches. "Did God really say you cannot eat from any of the trees?" the serpent repeated now that Eve could hear it better. "We can eat from the trees, any of the trees. Just not this one," Eve replied, her heart pounding as the conversation drew her in. Animals, Adam and God had all said many things to her before. None had asked her anything. "We cannot even touch it, or we will die," she continued, as the serpent slithered softly down the limb toward where Eve sat to rest. "It isn't true. You won't die," it said. The serpent's voice sounded so familiar Eve could barely distinguish it from her own thoughts. The serpent continued, "God knows the truth, that eating it would open your eyes to see like Him. You would know good from evil." This time, the serpent spoke loud enough that Eve looked around expecting God himself to interject. In fact, where was he now? All her existence she need only think about him and there he was, quick to walk alongside her. Yet now she felt entirely alone with her new serpent companion. She stood and turned to face the tree and found herself looking into the serpent's amber eyes. For a moment, they changed to look exactly like her own, and then reverted back again. Somehow, she knew that the snake was not lying. Now that she was closer than ever to the fruit of the tree, she could see it for what it was. It was welcoming. It was good. It was knowledge. Her hand began to move and before her mind could react, it was reaching for the fruit. How easily it was plucked and pulled down to her lips. How perfect and delightful the flavor as she bit down. Her mind was catching up now, and it felt like a fog lifted. She didn't just feel things anymore; she knew them. Even more so, she realized how much she did not know. And for the first time in her life, she felt that she had something to offer someone. She had access to something useful that the others in the garden did not, and she wanted to share it.

"Adam!" she called out, much louder than necessary. He was standing right there, hidden behind branches, watching everything play out. Too curious to stay away, but too bound by God's warning to join the conversation. "Oh, Adam, you must eat the apple too!" Her confidence, her joy, her new composure. It was all very convincing and he found himself joining her. They

sat under the tree together, reveling in their newfound awareness. Everything had changed. Colors were brighter, scents were stronger, the sky was bigger. But their awareness didn't just apply to the external. "My skin..." Adam said, pointing to the hairs beginning to raise across his arm. Eve examined hers as well, a chill rushing over them both. "It's...cold," Eve whispered. Clouds slowly swirled in front of the sun, the breeze turning into frigid air. Adam agreed. "We need to be covered," he said, getting up and clutching at whatever large leaves he could find. They both covered themselves, anticipating that this feeling of exposure could be worsened if observed by God. Suddenly, the wind shifted again. They could hear God approaching, and their new awareness went through their bodies like a shock. Hiding felt instinctual, and yet even as they hid in a nearby bush, Eve thought to herself, "Now that I have knowledge, maybe God will ask me things and let us join him in creating." The hope of being accepted, the fear of not, all bubbled up, bursting at the sound of an angry God. He had never been angry before. She should be surprised by this emotion. Instead, her newfound knowledge gave her understanding. Of course he was angry. He had lost control. He was afraid of another being his equal. And she knew, from then on, she would be to blame.

Eve's "choice" was referenced as the answer to so many of my questions about life, whether as serious theological positions offering explanations for things like suffering in the world or as half-jokes blaming her for period cramps and childbirth pain. As a Christian, I accepted this rhetoric, and, instead of giving credence to my questions and doubts, I trusted that God must know best.

But now, with freedom of thought, the absurdity of the story is so clear it's impossible to avoid. For starters, did the all-knowing God not see this coming? Did he not know before he created Adam and Eve exactly what choices they would make? Humans are so complex; similar in many ways, yet also wildly different from each other. Some are more curious, some more cautious. Some more volatile, some more restrained. Some introverted, some extroverted. Did God himself not design Eve's temperament? Did he not decide what colors would excite or deter her more? What ideas she would most likely entertain or reject? When he created the garden, did he not know that the tree would most certainly be eaten from? Did he not decide exactly how accessible to make it or how appealing to make its fruit? Did he not create the serpent, give it the gift of speech, make it clever enough to ask questions? If all of this was not actually his doing, then whose was it? And if he didn't know how his specific design choices would impact outcomes, then is he truly all-knowing? Perhaps if he had created Eve to be more restrained by rules, like some people naturally are, she would have refused the fruit. Maybe if he put the tree somewhere harder to reach, she would not have seen it in the first place. But no, he created the exact circumstances that he knew would result in this rebellion. He, quite literally, according to the Bible, handcrafted Adam and Eve to introduce disobedience and thus suffering and sin into the world. Evangelicals often refer to God as a father and compare his relationship to humans to parenting. But what sort of parent puts a loaded gun on a table and leaves their toddler alone in the room with it? Much less an all-knowing, all-powerful parent that created the gun, the child and the room and then put them all together knowing every detail of the outcome in advance. Not a good parent. Eve was never even told what the extent of the consequences of her actions would be. No one said, "Hey, if you do this, billions of people will suffer. People will die from agonizing diseases, children will be horrifically abused and this will be your legacy." Would this information have curbed her appetite? Maybe. But God apparently was more concerned with blind obedience than informed free will.

The counterargument to many of these questions is generally to claim that humans would have chosen to disobey God, chosen to sin, no matter what, as it is part of their nature, and that the option to do otherwise was necessary to allow for the opportunity to exert free will. This brings about so many more questions. Is there no free will in heaven? The place that is claimed to be perfect, where we only make perfect decisions in the eyes of God? Why is it so different on Earth? Why not just skip the "Earth" part and create everyone in heaven, completely forgoing all the suffering and evil?

Does God himself not have free will? He seems to be doing just fine making choices that do not damn him to hell. Why is it only humans who seem to be fraught with this condition? Does free will require an option with negative consequences? Do I have free will when told I can choose between pasta and pizza? Or do I only have free will when presented with pasta or poison?

And even ignoring all these questions, if this was the absolute best that an all-knowing, all-powerful god could do, why did he create anything at all? If your options are A) construct a universe where some creations will receive eternal reward, but where every other creation will suffer abuse, fear, torment or worse for all of eternity or B) don't create anything and no one will know what they missed out on for better or worse, why would you pick option A? These are the questions that ultimately led me to realize the only truth I could garner from the story of Eve: If this god-character is as all-knowing and all-powerful as claimed, then everything in the story was doomed—no—*designed* to happen. Eve was not responsible for introducing sin into the world; she was framed for it by her own creator.

COMMON ARGUMENTS YOU'LL HEAR

"God doesn't want robots, so he gave us free will."

Let's address the biggest problem first: Free will isn't even in the Bible (not that its absence has diminished the popularity of free will as an evangelical belief). There are no verses that mention it explicitly, only implications that humans are held accountable for what they do, and there are lots of verses that contradict the idea of free will. Proverbs 16:9, "The heart of man plans his way, but the Lord establishes his steps," seems to paint a reality in which God ultimately has a plan that is designed to be carried out. In Exodus 4:21, God says he will "harden" Pharaoh's heart, therefore determining that the ruler will free the Israelites. God goes on to manipulate, and go against, the free will of others in Deuteronomy 2:30 and Joshua 11:20. And according to John 17:12, Judas was destined to betray Jesus so that scripture could be fulfilled. Where is the free will in that? If the idea is that God wants us to choose to love him, is that not possible without the introduction of evil and suffering? My best friend does not need to threaten me with negative consequences to get me to freely choose to love her. And how silly as well, to imagine a god who is so wrapped up in ego that he needs his own creations to do so in such a specific way.

Another major problem with this idea of free will is that most, if not all, choices people make are influenced by their childhood, culture, biological makeup, education, traumas and other things that are completely outside of their control. Not to mention, none of us had the free will to decide if we would be born to begin with. Neuroscientists have learned that our actions often precede our consciousness, massively undermining the idea that we have the sort of free will many Christians (and others) believe we have.[2] Using the defense of "free will" to excuse suffering and evil is easily contradicted by both science and the Bible. Most notably by the evangelical

---

2 Ezequiel Morsella and T. Andrew Poehlman. "The Inevitable Contrast: Conscious vs. Unconscious Processes in Action Control." *Frontiers in Psychology* 4 (September 9, 2013). https://www.frontiersin.org/journals/psychology/articles/10.3389/fpsyg.2013.00590/full.

god-claim: If the god who created you is both all-knowing and all-powerful, you do not have free will. He knew exactly what would happen based on what and who he decided to create.

"It wasn't God's fault; Satan deceived Eve!"

Guess what? Genesis does not refer to the serpent as Satan. That idea didn't come about until centuries later and was based purely on a reinterpretation of the text, not anything in the original story. As discussed in the previous chapter, so many of our ideas about the character "Satan" were theological developments influenced largely by sources outside of the Bible. The story of Adam and Eve has nothing to do with Satan. Just a snake that God created with the ability to talk. Also fun to note is that the Bible never claims it was an apple that Eve ate, just a fruit. Western European art is largely to credit for that visual depiction.

"We don't have to interpret Genesis literally for it to have meaning!"

Some evangelicals have realized that science disproves a literal interpretation of the Genesis story. While I appreciate that they do not deny science, it leads me to a question: Why then would you still believe in original sin, the entire reason for Jesus's story arc? If everything else in Genesis is just story and myth, why let "sin" be the thing you continue to take literally? As we will get to in the next chapter, it's because without this key moment of original sin, the rest of the gospel falls apart. If we aren't being held accountable for the choices made by two humans thousands of years ago, there's no need for Jesus's sacrifice and no hellfire scare tactics to motivate converts.

IGNORANCE IS...DANGEROUS

The first woman supposedly came from the rib of a man. I am still embarrassed to share that up until my de-conversion I believed men had one less rib than women. Which is only slightly less embarrassing than my refusal to believe in the existence of dinosaurs. Eventually, I came to admit that they probably existed, but only 6,000 years ago, alongside the humans of that era. I guess that isn't too crazy when you take into account that I also believed Earth was only 6,000 years old. You can imagine the mental gymnastics it takes to conclude this is a rational line of thinking, but as a young child who was only ever Christian homeschooled, it wasn't too difficult. Still, these ideas became increasingly problematic the more knowledge I gained over the years. I have a core memory of walking into an enormous room featuring the bones of both a Giganotosaurus and an Argentinosaurus in the Fernbank Museum of Natural History in Atlanta, Georgia, where I grew up. Naturally, I was in awe—and even a bit scared—but my mother quickly reassured me dinosaurs no longer roamed the earth because God had created humans to rule over them, which they did until the dinosaurs died out. So there was nothing to be afraid of. As a lover of reading, I obsessed over each exhibit label, only to be told that there was no such thing as billions or even millions of years ago. What could that mean? Was the museum lying to us? Maybe. More likely, I was told, the scientists were very bad people who hated God and wanted us to doubt his creation. My first conspiracy theory: Science was evil and wrong unless it supported and confirmed what our evangelical dogmas required. Science was merely a distraction put in front of us by the enemy. While this sort of undermining of reality may sound extreme, surveys have shown that 40 percent of American Christians believe that God created humans as we presently know them to be, which directly contradicts the science.[3] It's quite chilling that so many people take comfort in this anti-science mindset, rejecting everything we have learned so far about the universe and its evolution. These anti-science beliefs result not just in laughable, conspiracy-minded adults, but the dangerous, real-life consequences that result from their denial of reality. Anti-vaxxers, climate-change denialists and even flat-earthers are not hard to find within Christianity.

Evangelicals have done an excellent job of making knowledge their forbidden fruit. The rhetoric surrounding education was so scary to me as a child that even going to a Christian university caused me to worry about being radicalized. Colleges were said to be Marxist factories that would brainwash vulnerable young people and cause them to lose their faith. The fear of public universities indoctrinating students with horrible ideas like evolution, feminism or liberalism was a great selling point for private Christian schools. They didn't need to offer notable alumni, expert professors or really anything other than "We'll protect your children from the dangers of secular education." Homeschooling is popular in some subsects of evangelicalism, and 53 percent of parents who homeschool refer to the "desire to provide religious

---

3 Megan Brenan. "40% of Americans Believe in Creationism." Gallup, July 26, 2019. https://news.gallup.com/poll/261680/americans-believe-creationism.aspx.

instruction" as their reasoning.[4] Somehow, they fear indoctrination from outside sources but conveniently turn a blind eye to the actual indoctrination they are committing at home. If you teach truth, if what you believe follows logic, then exposure to more information should be welcomed, not feared.

COMMON ARGUMENTS YOU'LL HEAR

Something that's important to note: I am not a scientist, which is why I will not be going into depth on arguments related to evolution, abiogenesis and other such topics. These apologetic claims against science, however, are generally based on blatant misunderstandings of what science is and its claims. And yet, even if one were to accept their denials of science, it still offers no support for their supernatural, religious claims. My homeschool education taught me to reject Darwin's theory, the Big Bang Theory and similar scientific beliefs, so there was a period of time when I first stopped believing in the existence of any gods that I also didn't necessarily believe the answers science offered. I was uneducated and I knew it, so I took the time to learn—starting with basic high school biology textbooks, Richard Dawkins's *The Greatest Show on Earth* and other resources that eventually caught me up on what we currently know about our universe and revealed that the pseudoscience I had been taught was an outright lie. One of my favorite things about humans is our deep desire to know—we crave and seek out information so that we can survive, and our curiosity drives us to keep learning and exploring. But as soon as we compromise our desire for true knowledge in exchange for baseless, fill-in-the-blank answers to serve an agenda based on dogma rather than fact, we lose our edge and integrity.

"Evolution is just a theory."

Do you know what else is "just" a theory? Atomic theory, the theory of gravity, germ theory and plate tectonics. In science, theory isn't a casual speculation or guess like it is in everyday conversation—it's a well-tested, evidence-based explanation of how something works. But even if something like the theory of evolution were disproven, all we would be left with is a gap in our knowledge about the natural world. There still wouldn't be any reason to fill that gap with unproven supernatural claims.

---

4 "A look at homeschooling in the U.S.," Pew Research Center (Pew Research Center, February 20, 2025), https://www.pewresearch.org/short-reads/2025/02/20/a-look-at-homeschooling-in-the-us/.

"Something can't come from nothing! Creation must have a creator!"
Nothing? What even is that? As soon as you define it, it becomes...something. And with quantum physics, nothing is something. So we are already off to a rough start. The biggest hole in this argument is that it asserts everything must have a cause, and then goes on to say that the cause of the universe is something that does not have a cause: God. At that point, why can't we just assert that the universe has always existed in one form or another and needs no cause? I don't believe something came from "nothing." Neither I nor scientists claim to know for certain what, if anything, caused the creation of the universe, but we are learning more all the time, and maybe someday we will know if our universe even has a beginning, but in the meantime it is dishonest to insert "God" when the answer is "We don't know yet."

"We didn't come from monkeys!"
Correct. We did not. And hearing this phrase should be an automatic cue that your interlocutor not only has a complete misunderstanding of the basics of evolution but is also following a tired apologetics script. We didn't come from monkeys—what we have actually learned is that we share a common ancestor with them. We *are* apes, and this is where evangelicals usually base their massive misunderstanding of evolutionary claims. What I find most humorous is that as a Christian, I had no problem accepting that God made Adam from literal dust and Eve from a rib, yet I could not accept the theory of evolution. Christian propaganda had to work hard to build a straw man for evolution that was more ridiculous than their own creation story.

"Look at the trees!"
When asked what my least favorite argument from theists is, this appeal to perceived beauty or design is by far the one I am most tired of. Often when I question what evidence a theist has that there is a creator, the response is something close to, "Well, just look at the trees!" or "Haven't you ever seen a sunset?" The entire premise of this argument is based on the subjective idea that nature is beautiful and that somehow beauty is equal to intelligent design. While most of us would agree that many parts of nature are beautiful, we would also agree that there are many ugly, brutal things about nature. "Look at the poison ivy!" or "Look at the mosquitoes!" or "Look at that oncoming tornado!" don't quite have the same ring and yet are just as natural as trees and sunsets. Our subjective appreciation of how something

physically appears or feels is not an indication of anything other than an ability to observe and enjoy.

"Science confirms the Bible."

Well, which is it? Is science anti-Biblical or does it validate the Bible? Science is often demonized, denied and proclaimed a conspiracy by Christians but then conveniently used as an attempt to prove the Bible. As we have established, "the Bible" is not one entire book. It's many books with many different claims. So while there are some true things in the Bible (including historical cities that we have archaeological evidence of), it is also full of claims that are easily disproved by science. For example, there is no evidence of any global flood. None whatsoever. The earth is also not the center of our universe, despite the Bible's claim. The earth doesn't have "four corners" (Revelation 7:1), nor is it set on some immovable foundation. And placing certain sticks in front of mating animals will not actually cause them to produce offspring that look a certain way, contrary to what the Bible may stipulate (Genesis 30:37-43). If science had indeed confirmed the Bible, it would have at least verified its most central claim— the existence of God. But it has not done that.

Knowledge should only ever be the enemy of lies and the friend of skepticism. The truth of Eve's story is that she did what she was designed to do and was punished for it. She was told she would die (the scripture says "in that day," not a spiritual death like evangelicals claim), yet she did not. Instead, she ate the metaphorical apple as so many brave women throughout history have done. From Marie Curie to Hypatia of Alexandria to Malala Yousafzai, the pursuit of knowledge has been an act of courage. The character of Eve risked her life to gain knowledge, either fulfilling her destiny or defying the plans of an all-knowing god. Evangelicals painted over the story of Eve as a fearless, earnest woman to portray her as a maliciously rebellious wrongdoer. But I think this character arc should instead serve as a lesson in how powerful knowledge is, so much so that gaining it can even frighten the gods. Any belief worth holding is worth questioning. The truth is never afraid of questions. And a god that fears the enlightenment of his creations is a weak god.

CHAPTER 3

The Cure for Which There Is No Disease

"In him we have redemption through his blood, the forgiveness of our trespasses."
—EPHESIANS 1:7

THE GREATEST LOSS I EXPERIENCED on my journey out of religion was the loss of Jesus. He was my strongest emotional connection to my faith and a beloved figure throughout my life. When not having to focus my attention on the more gruesome parts of his story, I was obsessed with him and found comfort in thinking of him. To say I remember my first introduction would be a lie, as this character felt as much a part of my life as my parents were. My mother was writing letters to me about Jesus before I was even born, and all my earliest memories of her involve her talking about Jesus or heaven. My early memories of my father are of being quizzed on Bible facts and praying together at bedtime. We have home videos from before I can even remember, when I could barely even talk, being told to say "Happy Birthday Jesus!" I was asked if I knew what Christmas truly represented before I could continue to open my presents. Any time someone complimented my physical appearance, I parroted back, "Thank you, Jesus made me this way!" just like I had been taught. Jesus was the point of everything, or at least that's what our household aimed for, as it was clear my parents were actively hoping and trying to raise children that loved Jesus.

I remember learning that Jesus, as an extension of his father, God, was perfect. He was loving, kind, patient, joyful—everything you could want a human to be. I imagined him always with a warm smile; I'm sure it had something to do with the VHS tapes my grandmother constantly played for me featuring Bruce Marchiano as Jesus with a perpetual grin on his face. Jesus represented the opposite of anything negative that life put in my path. He was not annoyed by my childlike behavior, which I was ashamed of and told to put aside to set a good example for my younger sisters. He even said that the kingdom of heaven belonged to children (Mark 10:13–16). During my awkward preteen years, I comforted myself by believing that Jesus was my true friend even when I felt rejected by others, because he knew my heart and could see that I was really trying.

Later in life, when I faced heartbreak and betrayal, I would remind myself that Jesus had been betrayed far worse than me and must be feeling empathy toward me. How amazing, I thought, that the god of the universe could also relate to my pain. This made Jesus feel like so much more than some distant, unknowable deity that saved me from my wretched sins, although he was very much my savior. He was the ultimate friend—his redemptive nature making me feel unconditionally loved for all my complexities, flaws and goodness. My journal entries were made out to him. After all, as an all-knowing god, he knew what they said before I even wrote them.

My mind was always asking "What would Jesus do?" thanks in part to a popular trend of wearing WWJD bracelets as a constant reminder. My daily prayers featured phrases such as "Make me more like you, Jesus." In worship services at church, I would sing the repetitive songs declaring "Worthy is the lamb that was slain," weeping as I focused on the idea that someone loved me so much they sacrificed their life for me. When you are a lonely teenage girl, dreaming up an entire person who loves you is not difficult to do and truly provides a sense of hope. I fully believed this was what everyone described as a "personal relationship with God." I had convinced myself that Jesus was not just a character in a book but alive and well, and active in my life. In reality, I had credited my own inner voice, the most compassionate parts of it, to the character of Jesus. Instead of recognizing that I could be my own support system, I outsourced it to God. This was entirely the result of having been conditioned since birth to believe something was true and then being encouraged to look for evidence to support it. And so, at every opportunity, I credited things to Jesus. When I shared my belongings with a friend, I was showing Jesus's kindness. When I thought of something nice to say to someone, that must have been Jesus prompting me. If I did a good job singing in the church nativity play, Jesus was responsible. Confirmation bias was a constant.

The external pressure to devote my every waking moment to God was also very real. I was caught between the validation I received from others, such as friends' parents telling me how much they admired my relationship with God, and the disappointment I felt from my pastor parents when I wasn't taking enough notes during a sermon or willing to discuss with them what I was learning through my relationship with Jesus. I didn't mind discussing Bible passages in youth group, leading ministry teams at a young age and offering to pray with my friends at church. But to me, this fabricated relationship with Jesus was very personal. The prying and prodding from my parents made it feel as if they were demanding evidence that I was maturing the way they wanted, instead of respecting my personal journey. Looking back, they absolutely had reason to be fearful. I was independently developing my ideas about what and who Jesus was instead of trying to please others with the outward appearance of my spiritual life. I wanted it to be genuine. I wanted my belief to be mine, not that of my parents. In my own way, I was fighting their indoctrination, only to replace it with an invention of my own. I may have been following the god of my father, but I was loving my very personal rendition of Jesus.

With Jesus at its focus, Resurrection Sunday was always a big day in our Christian home. We weren't allowed to call it "Easter," as that word was based on the name of some pagan goddess and it was implied that merely using the word might result in us accidentally worshiping her. Of course, we spent the day at church, often ending with a big family lunch. Some weekends, we even attended or held a Passover seder the Saturday evening before (even though we were not Jewish) in solidarity with what the Bible taught was Jesus's "Last Supper." Cosplaying as Jesus's own people was, and remains, very popular in the more charismatic branches of evangelicalism. But whether we pregamed with religious appropriation or not, Resurrection Sunday was a serious day. So serious that my family decided

Easter bunnies and baskets and egg hunts would be reserved for a separate day dubbed "Spring Bunny Day" so as not to steal Jesus's thunder.

Up until my mid-20s, I spent Resurrection Sunday ruminating over gruesome depictions of a man being beaten and violently nailed to a cross. And I was personally responsible for it. I had been told many times as a child that "Even if you were the only person on Earth, you would still be full of sin and Jesus would still die just for you." This wasn't just a story; this was personal. The recognition of Jesus's bloody sacrifice was central to our Christian faith, and from a very young age I was taught that my sinful nature required a truly disturbing consequence—the death of my god. Passion plays, gold crucifixes hanging around our necks, movies and Bible illustrations were all designed to drive home how violent yet vital this death was and to provide contrast to the "good part"—the gospel, the proclaimed truth that Jesus was not dead. In fact, I realize now that this "sacrifice" only caused him to miss out on one earthly weekend before coming back to share his trauma with his disciples in the form of hole-y hands and ghostly magic. What a relief his resurrection was supposed to be for us. God didn't actually create a version of himself that was also his son just for him to die a grotesque death and for that to be the end of the story. No, it was much more complex! He created a version of himself that was also his son so he could die a grotesque death, fulfill a blood sacrifice owed to himself and then come back to life again just to disappear into the sky. His death was not true death, we acknowledged. As far as our guilt and allegiance were concerned, however, it was true *sacrifice*. And in terms of power, Jesus had reached his peak by defeating death. God had humbled himself to live as a weak, mortal human, and we were expected to believe this was his ultimate act of power.

It's no wonder I was so terrified of death and dying at such a young age. The threat of death and what came after was something I was subjected to over and over again, not as a natural part of the cycle of life but as a terrifying monster that Jesus, too, was faced with. I was 13 years old when Mel Gibson's *The Passion of the Christ* premiered. It was the first R-rated movie I was not only allowed to see, but required to. *Harry Potter* was banned for its magic, *The Notebook* for its premarital physical relationship and *The Punisher* for its violence—but here I was required to watch a graphic depiction of something I believed to be extremely real and personal. Not only was the movie traumatically violent and graphic, but I will never forget the sounds of the grown adults around me. Some crying, even loudly weeping at times. They acted as though they were literally watching the crucifixion play out in real time. I found myself crying as well, but more because of how uncomfortable I was with all the blood onscreen and grieving adults surrounding me. A few years later, I remember discovering *Saving Private Ryan*, Spielberg's epic WWII film. It was also incredibly graphic, full of war scenes and death. I remember feeling ashamed that this movie drew so much emotion from me in ways that scenes from *The Passion* did not. One particular scene of a man sacrificing his life for other men touched me so deeply, I pondered why this sacrifice seemed more "real" to me than Jesus's. I realized it was not just because my own grandfather had fought in that war and was living proof that it truly happened but because these men did not get to come back after three days in the grave. Their deaths, their sacrifice for men and country, were permanent. They were not sons of gods with the comfort of resurrection or redemption. They sacrificed not because they were created to do so but because it was the right thing to do at that moment. They did not need to believe the very souls of every single human in history were dependent on them taking action; they were willing to sacrifice for just a few. They were living and dying by their convictions. And yet, at the end of the day, these men were simply sinners, still in need of Jesus's ultimate sacrifice. And yet this "sacrifice" amounted to a death far less permanent than their own.

The Christian glorification of death, blood and violence always turns my stomach. Such an odd, nonsensical story that my faith revolved around. The most freeing thing I ever did was let go of it and no longer allow myself to feel emotionally manipulated into the worship of loss and suffering and judgment. My own resurrection came after I stopped believing in Jesus. As a Christian, I had metaphorically died. Even though I had killed my own hopes and dreams and pleasures to replace them with God's so that I might die to sin and live to righteousness (1 Peter 2:24), the righteousness never came and I remained simply human. Irony of ironies, I came back to life the day I left Jesus in the grave. I found hope and true freedom, and all the parts of me I had lost along the way were just waiting to be resurrected. The good news is not that someone saved me by paying a blood sacrifice to themselves or by cleansing me from the wickedness they themselves instilled within me. The good news is that I was never in need of saving in the first place.

COMMON ARGUMENTS YOU'LL HEAR

"The resurrection is proven."

To say a claim is proven is to state that the truth of the claim is irrefutable. However, when it comes to something supernatural, like being raised from the dead, a claim is all it is. There is absolutely no known evidence of the resurrection of any individual after being dead for three days, or even two days, or even one. The claim of Jesus's resurrection was not recorded until decades after it was said to have occurred, meaning we have absolutely no records from the time of the event, which immediately weakens any case believers might try to make. And there are no claims of Jesus's resurrection outside of the Bible. Supposedly, a man came back from the dead after three days, many people witnessed it and yet no one wrote about it until years after the fact and those authors were strongly biased. No Roman or Jewish historians, or anyone outside of Christian circles for that matter, backed the claim. And the accounts that we do have in the Bible contradict each other. Anyone claiming that the resurrection is "proven" is appealing entirely to circular reasoning, but the Bible cannot prove the claims of the Bible.

"The disciples wouldn't die for a lie!"

The victims of Jonestown and Heaven's Gate, members of apocalyptic cults who died in mass suicides, would like a word. People die for their beliefs all the time, and it does not make those beliefs any more or less true. Islamic terrorists have flown planes into buildings for their beliefs, beliefs that Christians would most certainly consider to be false. We also don't have any evidence that these disciples were actually martyred; we only have stories recorded long after the claimed events, most with contradicting details. While Christians most certainly have been persecuted and killed for their faith throughout the years, so have disciples from other faiths. Christians have been heavily responsible for persecuting believers of other religions as well and engaging in violent tribalism. Martyrdom is not limited to Christianity, and historically, Christianity has even been responsible for violent persecution against those of other faiths.

"The eyewitness testimonies are reason to believe!"

This apologetics claim was one of those that temporarily stopped much of my lingering curiosity and confusion. I took it on faith when pastors would tell me there were over 500 witnesses to Jesus's resurrection. How could

500 people make up such a story? Imagine my surprise when I learned that this claim is entirely based on 1 Corinthians 15:3–8 in which, decades after the supposed event, Paul claims Jesus appeared to Cephas, the 12 disciples and then a crowd of 500 people. We do not have any testimony from that group of 500 to support the story. Only Paul's claim that it happened. Not only is this not evidence, but it adds even more unproven claims to the story of Jesus.

"There's an empty tomb!"

Apologists often reference an empty tomb as evidence, but unsubstantiated reports of an empty tomb, even the physical existence of an empty tomb itself, are evidence of only one thing: an empty tomb. Other than that, we simply have legends and possible evidence of grave robbers. I remember going to Israel as a teenager and coming back claiming that I had been to Jesus's tomb. The truth was, however, that I had been to two of his claimed tombs: one more commonly accepted by Orthodox and Catholics, the other by evangelicals, and neither based on anything other than myth and tradition. Stating that something is fact certainly adds a flair of confidence to a claim, but it does not make it so.

"Jesus was a real person—so obviously, the Bible is true."

While this can be a controversial topic, sources outside of Christianity, such as the writings of Roman and Jewish historians, do indicate there was a Jewish preacher executed by the Romans who was later worshiped as Jesus. What we do not have is unbiased historical evidence of anything supernatural. There are no eyewitness accounts of any of the resurrections, earthquakes or healings that are associated with Bible stories about Jesus. Claiming that a person existed thousands of years ago and having a fair bit of evidence to back it up is one thing; claiming that a person existed thousands of years ago and still exists today—as a god, no less—without providing any evidence is misguided at best, lunacy or deception at worst.

A BLOOD-OBSESSED GOD

How bizarre to think back on how frequently blood was referenced during my time as a Christian. We sang song after song about Jesus's blood washing us clean. I wore a necklace with different colored beads, each attributed to a “phase” in salvation, the red one representing Jesus’s blood in the center. Communion was something we frequently practiced, taking time to sit and reflect on pieces of bread and cups of grape juice as though they were the literal flesh and blood of Jesus. Even Christian radio’s attempts at pop music contained casual references to blood. Why is that? Evangelicals hold the belief that humans are ultimately deserving of eternal punishment due to God’s demand for justice. By dying and shedding blood, Jesus is said to have fulfilled that demand.

This is known as the theory of penal substitutionary atonement. When we break it down step by step, it is revealed to be quite archaic and nonsensical. First, as we discussed in the previous chapter, we have an all-knowing creator that designs his creations to fail—commonly referred to as “original sin” or a “sin nature.” This creator then designs a system with an impossible standard, where simply being human relegates you to the status of a sinner in need of redemption (Romans 3:23). These are God’s rules; he knowingly demands more than is possible from his creations and then holds them as debtors for their failure to meet those demands.

God’s need for blood sacrifice to offset one’s sins is nothing new. As early as Leviticus 17:11, he makes it clear that blood—lots and lots of blood—is the required offering: “For the life of the flesh is in the blood, and I have given it for you on the altar to make atonement for your souls, for it is the blood that makes atonement by the life.”

His system demands perfection, and as that cannot be reached, he requires animal sacrifice to appease his needs. This all-knowing, all-loving, all-powerful god that is beyond space and time could simply decide to forgive, but instead he wants something very much resembling a pagan tradition practiced across many different religions and superstitious beliefs. He wants animals—killed and burned—as worship, as atonement and on holidays for good measure. He even says the very smell of it is “pleasing” to him (Leviticus 1:9).

For some reason, this practice suits this timeless god for hundreds of years. And then, one day, he decides it’s time to switch things up. The verse John 3:16, which is beloved by evangelicals and one of the first I ever memorized as a child, sounds quite generous and loving without context: “For God so loved the world, that he gave his only Son, that whoever believes in him should not perish but have eternal life. This is how much God loved the world: He gave his Son, his one and only Son.”

After years of requiring animal sacrifice, God decides he will send his son (who evangelicals also believe is God himself; more on that later) to take the place of these animal sacrifices and calls the solution to the problem he created "love." Who decided that a sinful world should exist? God. Who decided that the world would owe God a debt for this sin? God. Who decided that literal blood from animals would be a sufficient debt payment? God. Who decided that the blood of his only son would become the sole solution to the sin of the world? God. Who decided that his creations would sin in the first place? God did. He knew all of this would happen and still decided to move forward with his plan regardless of how many of his creations suffered because of it.

Christianity paints Jesus's sacrifice as a beautiful, necessary gift. It asserts that humans should be grateful and humbled by the act. But it actually reveals the same pattern abusers follow. A narrative is created that there is some problem with the victim—a problem that doesn't actually exist. Abusers commonly convince their victims with lines like, "You're nothing without me" or "No one would love you except for me." The victim is continually made to take the blame for everything, even if it was the abuser's fault, and then they are made to feel as though they should be grateful the abuser would even be with them at all. It's a vicious, shameful cycle designed to subjugate the victim. But evangelicalism is dependent on you accepting this exact premise: that you are sinful and only God can save you.

Sin is pointed to as the root issue, but the problem is that sin is completely fabricated. According to 1 John 3:4, sin is lawlessness; the act of going against God's laws. Which is interesting because evangelicals also believe sin is something you are born with, something unavoidable (Romans 3:23). Sin is both an act you can commit and a condition you have no control over. It doesn't even require physical action. Simply having an "impure" thought in your head, even if it was never acted upon, is enough to warrant eternal punishment (Matthew 5:28). All of which is problematic when we acknowledge that we cannot control our thoughts; we can only influence them and manage how we act or don't act upon them. The concept of sin is clearly not there to promote better behavior; it is there to shame and control. It is a condemnation meant to convince you that you are in need of a cure.

COMMON ARGUMENTS YOU'LL HEAR

"Everyone has sinned! Sin is just 'missing the mark.'"

Missing what mark? Set by whom? This statement assumes that there is some divine goal that can be "missed." Is that standard set by the Bible? Surely not, as the Bible doesn't have a consistent message on lifestyle or morality. Christians cannot even agree amongst themselves what qualifies as sin: Is alcohol okay? Dancing? Birth control? The denominations vary with their stances. So who gets to determine what the mark is? And if everyone has sinned, the more accurate accusation would be that we are all human. It is a brilliant tactic though, because if you can convince someone that just existing is evidence that they are diseased, you position yourself to sell them a cure without having to prove one is even necessary. It's like a door-to-door ghostbuster convincing you that all houses have ghosts, and because you are a homeowner, you are in need of his (invisible, naturally) services.

"Christianity isn't a religion; it's a relationship with Jesus."

Sure, if we want to completely do away with established definitions for various words, we can go with that claim. But what is the use of language if we are just going to misrepresent what words actually mean? Religion is typically defined as belief in or worship of gods, deities or other supernatural beings. Using that definition, what could possibly be more religious than the belief that you can have a relationship with a deity such as Jesus? The reason this phrase is so commonly spouted by evangelicals on their T-shirts, mugs, book titles and personal testimonies is to try to rebrand what they themselves admit is unattractive: religion—a system of belief typically made up of rules and regulations which controls the behavior of its followers.

A "personal relationship" with Jesus was a counterculture idea in the 1960s and '70s during the "Jesus movement." With the popularity of Eastern religions and New Age spirituality spreading in the U.S., Christianity needed to adapt and offer something equivalent to the freedom and love advertised by the hippie movement. It was quite a provocative thing to claim you could commune with a god. But the times called for a more emotionally compelling version of Christianity, and this peace-loving Jesus character rebranding was just the thing to do it. That trend of focusing on one's personal relationship with god and attempting to dismiss the institution of religion behind it continues today.

"If I'm wrong, nothing happens. If you're wrong, you go to hell."

This is known as Pascal's wager. Blaise Pascal argued that if one did not believe in the Christian god and he ended up being real, they risked the eternal consequence of going to hell. But if you did believe in the Christian god and he was not real, you simply wasted a bit of time. There are many problems here, the most egregious being that belief is not a choice. One cannot switch on and off a belief as simply as placing a gambling bet. If there were such a thing as a perfect lie detector test and you connected me to it while placing a gun to my head with the threat of "Believe you are a duck or else," it would not end well for me. I could quack like a duck, pretend to believe I was one and do everything I could to lie and save my life, but deep down, I'd remain unconvinced. Someone is either convinced of something or they're not, and you would think an all-knowing god would know whether that person's belief was sincere or not. Which brings us to the next issue with this wager: If God values sincerity, even if belief was a choice, why would he be okay with someone who chose him simply to avoid consequences? Isn't the whole idea that the evangelical god wants people who are genuine believers? This gamble also makes another significant error in that it assumes there are only two options: A) the Christian god or B) nothing of consequence. It fails to recognize that there could be a different god—one that's angered by the worship of the Christian god. Or perhaps there are multiple gods and you risk angering many by worshiping one. There could even be a god that is specifically bothered by belief based on a gamble instead of personal conviction and now you're on his bad side by accepting it. Ultimately, this argument also fails to acknowledge the value of what you *do* risk by devoting a lifetime to belief in Christianity. Time is an extremely valuable thing to waste, especially if this lifetime is all there is. Outsourcing your lifestyle, community and loyalty to this specific gamble is a massive risk. Better to be honest and go with truth than treat god-beliefs like a coin toss.

"God gives us a choice to accept his salvation."

This might be relevant if belief were a choice. But the problem is, I believe I can "choose salvation" as much as I can choose to go to Barbieland—which is to say I don't believe it's a choice to begin with. To reject Christianity is not simply to reject salvation but anything grounded in make-believe. It is also laughable to suggest that the evangelical God presents salvation as a choice. It's as much an option as being asked to do something with a gun held to your head. Refuse and the gun goes off. Sure, you can decline, but the consequence is death and eternal punishment. Acceptance of salvation is not a friendly invitation; it's a mandate.

"Christianity flourished because it's true."

Similar to the claim that the Bible must be true because it's popular, desirability is not evidence of something being true. Islam, Hinduism, Buddhism and other religious beliefs that contradict Christianity have also spread widely across cultures and civilizations. Popularity does not make something true. And, just like the claim about the Bible, it fails to take into account how much of Christianity's influence was imposed through theocracy and colonialism. When your social standing or very life is at risk, compliance with a new belief can be the only option. Another extremely effective aspect of Christianity is the threat it overtly advertises: believe or face eternal punishment. Fear can popularize a belief quite quickly, whether true or not. And it doesn't hurt that it also offers a reward if followed—that someday you'll no longer suffer and will live in eternal paradise. To the vulnerable who face a lifetime of poverty, disease or abuse, this bit of hope for a potential future is enough to convince them to believe even if they have no good reason to do so.

AN INCONVENIENT JESUS

Western Christian media has propagated a very simple, palatable Jesus character. He is seen as humble, warm, personable, morally perfect, compassionate and conventionally attractive. Sunday school lessons cherry-pick the sweet, uncontroversial stories about his life, usually painting him as a peacemaker. Worship songs and hymns lyrically describe him as "friend," "brother," "loving" and very much a being you can have a relationship with. If God is the bad cop of the Old Testament, Jesus is very much advertised as the good cop of the New Testament. Many of God's negatives (like designing his own creations with a "sin nature") are quite literally redeemed by Jesus. Along with the mental image of Jesus as a soft, relatable human, he is almost always visually depicted in his two most vulnerable moments: a baby in a manger or a dying man on a cross. These cultural images helped reinvent the God of the Old Testament as stable, wise and even relatable. Instead of honestly addressing the cultural context of the Old Testament, evangelicalism doubled down on its simplistic, literal and twisted interpretation. Given this, Christians needed a savior to smooth out the vengeful, egocentric, controlling god they extrapolated from the Old Testament. A lamb for their lion, if you will. The marketing worked, and as a child, many of my qualms about God were washed away with a simple "Yes, but Jesus!" response. God was often encouraging, even commanding, performing acts of violence in the form of war (or even by direct command), but sweet Jesus was there to tell us to love our enemies and turn the other cheek. God was too holy to look at without instantly dying, but Jesus walked and talked with his disciples. Where God required perfection and animal sacrifice when one failed to achieve perfection, Jesus said, "Just follow me and I'll take care of the rest." More than redeeming sinners, Jesus redeemed the sins of the evangelical god. A pretty effective PR move. However, the biblical character of Jesus is far more complex and far less divine than the sugarcoated version we are most often fed.

The problem begins when we acknowledge that what little we do know about him only spans a few years of his life. The Bible claims his ministry didn't begin until he was 30 years old. Imagine the number of hungry, disabled or otherwise needy people Jesus came across during that time without offering a single miracle. We are supposed to view Jesus as humble and relatable because he spent the majority of his life simply working as a carpenter and, apparently, just minding his own business. But this does not paint the picture of a supernaturally powerful god; it paints the picture of a normal man, a preacher who eventually gains some notoriety and has his unknown past written as if it were more deliberate than it actually was.

I remember thinking it was so cool, so edgy that the first recorded miracle performed by Jesus occurred when a wedding ran out of wine. He knew what an embarrassment this was for the hosts and displayed his first public act of supernatural power by turning water into fine wine. How cool was Jesus to care about such trivial things? He even cared about cultural norms! Having the power of God within him, however, he could have been performing all sorts of miracles any time he wanted. But no, he waited 30 years for this moment. He could have provided food for homeless people, healed a dying child or freed a household full of enslaved people. Instead, his first miracle was to help cater a party. That's fun and all, but there are even more inconvenient truths about Jesus. He tells his disciples to steal a donkey for him (Matthew 21:2–3), he claims that to properly follow him you must hate your family and yourself (Luke 14:26) and, as we discussed earlier, he curses trees for not producing fruit during their off-season as God intended.

Here's what I have witnessed evangelicals avoiding the most: Jesus makes it very clear that he has "not come to abolish them but to fulfill them" when referencing the law of the Old Testament (Matthew 5:17). He goes on to say that not even the "least" of the 600+ commandments in past scripture should be ignored and that to encourage otherwise is wrong (Matthew 5:19). This proves to be very problematic for any evangelicals who want to wear mixed fabrics, eat shrimp or gather wood on the Sabbath.

The most common argument put forth to negate Jesus's claim that the old commandments should still be followed is that his existence "fulfilled" the law like it was some sort of chore on God's to-do list. But Jesus very clearly says he did not come to abolish the law and that all of it should still be followed. Another technique for avoiding the old rules that are now inconvenient is to say, "We don't follow law, we follow Jesus. That's why he came; to show us the way!" as if that somehow isn't directly going against Jesus's command to follow the law. In fact, Jesus seems to love the old scripture and commands, so much so that he references them over and over. Not only does he say that he came to fulfill those laws, but he doubles down on them, telling his followers to hold themselves to even higher standards. Of course, murder is wrong, but now he says even feelings of anger or calling someone a "fool" puts you in danger of hellfire (Matthew 5:22). Adultery is punishable, but according to Jesus, if you even look at a woman lustfully, you should gouge your own eye out (Matthew 5:27–29). To Jesus, getting remarried is no better than committing adultery (Matthew 5:32).

Jesus makes his stance on these commands and others very clear. And yet I grew up around many divorced, remarried Christians and none of them were missing an eye. It's understandable that people would want to ignore these Old Testament laws today, but evangelicals, who pride themselves on their unwavering devotion to God, dismiss them just as easily as a nonbeliever does. The theological workarounds enable them to cherry-pick which commands are best suited for whatever their current agenda is. When Christians wanted to own other humans as slaves, Jesus's praise of the "meek" in Matthew 5:5 was used to encourage their submission, and his proclamation about freeing prisoners in Luke 4:18 was quite literally removed from some Bibles given out to enslaved people.

When conservative Christians protest immigration or welfare support, they ignore Matthew 25:40, equating the treatment of "the least of these" to caring for Jesus himself. And many evangelical leaders have opted for private jets, multimillion-dollar homes and cosmetic surgery over following Luke 12:33, in which Jesus says to sell all you have and give to the poor. When not being whitewashed and packaged to more easily convert the masses, Jesus becomes an inconvenient messenger for many evangelicals. If Jesus cannot be reduced to a simple, sacrificial savior designed to control one's allegiance to the Christian god, then he is simply a thorn in their theological side, exposing just how unimportant and disposable the opinions and pronouncements of their own religious figures are to them.

If you are born with a disease that could only be cured by believing in the sacrifice of a deity turned human, then believing in Jesus sounds like an incredible deal. But it is the ultimate scam. The truth is, you were not born inherently evil, wicked, bad, sinful or deceitful just because you were born a human. Religion teaches the former in order to shame you into submission, to coerce you into believing you are infected with a disease that does not exist. And it must convince you completely in order to scare you into devoting yourself to a cure that you don't need. But freedom is not found in animal sacrifices or the blood of a god's son claiming to provide salvation; it is found in the realization that you do not need saving. Losing my belief in Jesus was heartbreaking at first, but realizing that it was me all along who had demonstrated compassion, kindness and strength was life-changing. I had overcome tremendous challenges without requiring the blood of a savior. All the good things that I had credited to the supernatural were quite natural and part of who I was. I may have lost Jesus, but I found myself.

CHAPTER 4

When the Natural Seems Supernatural

"To surrender to ignorance and call it God has always been premature, and it remains premature today." —ISAAC ASIMOV

THE OVERHEAD HALOGEN LIGHTS were dimmed, and a slight chill hung in the air from the AC running on full blast. The stage in front of us was lit with moody, colorful lighting. The subtle scent of something warm and spicy wafted about, most likely frankincense and myrrh from someone's anointing oil (a blend of oils that is sometimes dabbed on the forehead or hands of an individual during prayer and worship). My 16-year-old best friend, Jessica, and my 15-year-old self were surrounded by hundreds of our peers, with some random older folks mixed in here and there. We stood in anticipation as musicians took their positions with instruments and microphones, and a lull fell over the crowd in response. The keyboardist began to play a suspended synth chord, filling the room with even more tension. A charismatic greeting from the lead singer, a twentysomething with a trendy hairstyle and baggy jeans, prompted anyone not yet standing to get out of their seats. The rest of the band joined in, the familiar melody signaling the start to a popular worship song, the lyrics to which we all knew. We would have known the words even without having heard the song, as they came from Bible verses we had memorized and repeated throughout our lives as Christians. Clapping in rhythm, we all began to sing together, declaring tenets deeply important to our shared religious doctrine. I felt chills come over my skin, and a smile that I could not contain broke across my face. My usually anxious mind could barely keep up with its own thoughts, overwhelmed by the loud music and the sound of my own voice singing repetitive lyrics to a driving beat. I felt a weight lift off of me. Hands began to lift all over the room, and I decided to raise mine as well, as though I were trying to touch the ceiling. It was supposed to be a sign of worship and adoration toward God, a symbol of surrender. I felt a rush of inexplicable energy come over me, though if I had taken a moment to really think about the sensation, some of it was probably due to feelings of anxiety that my less-worshipful peers were judging me. And yet, there was also the rush of feeling that I was participating in something bigger than myself, that God himself was pleased with my actions. Maybe I looked silly, but, like David in the Bible, I was willing to be "undignified" (2 Samuel 6:22) with my worship. With every movement made and lyric sung, I began to feel more and more euphoric. My heart rate increased, my hands began to tingle (most likely from holding them up for so long) and a warm sensation washed over me. I felt what I could only describe as indescribable joy. This must be supernatural. This *must* be God's presence.

Fast forward a couple of years. I stood in a different crowded room with that same best friend. Dark drapes covered the walls and a smoky haze lingered around the stage full of instruments. Anticipation hung thick in the crowd as we all talked amongst ourselves, trying to pass the time before the moment we were all hoping for. Suddenly, the dim lighting winked out to reveal string lights covering the stage equipment and keyboard. The crowd went silent and still, almost holding our collective breath. A charismatic leader stepped from backstage to thunderous clapping and yelling before taking a seat at the keyboard. His hands confidently played the first melodic notes, rich with nostalgia, and we all went silent again. He began to sing a song that we all knew and felt, and so we sang along. The lyrics were about the very city we were in—a city most of us were born in, raised in and deeply connected to. I felt chills come over me, and sweat caused by the warmth of the tightly packed crowd went cold on my skin. My heart pounded as though it would leave my chest. My hands tingled, perhaps from wringing them for the entire half hour leading up to this moment. I found myself swaying to the song, singing words I had only ever sung by myself in my room, now surrounded by hundreds of others singing those same words. Tears came to my eyes. We were all together at this moment, feeling something in unity. Having my best friend beside me, whom I knew well enough to know she was feeling the same, only increased the emotional power of the experience. Our collective voices made the room feel like it was vibrating. I was emotionally overwhelmed, feeling an indescribable joy. This must be supernatural. This *must* be God's presence.

Suddenly, someone lightly bumped into me and the smell of their spilled beer took me out of the moment. Wait, this couldn't be God. This was just a rock concert. The feelings, sensations and emotions were completely familiar though. I had experienced all of this (less the spilled beer and wafts of cigarette smoke) throughout my life at worship services. This was the same feeling I'd experienced just a couple of years prior at the aforementioned evangelical service. That particular event, the Ramp summer conference in Hamilton, Alabama, was just one of countless times before and after when I would have similar experiences. But that was a charismatic, evangelical event focused on children and teens "encountering God's presence." This, instead, was my very first non-Christian concert featuring my favorite artist. There wasn't supposed to be anything comparable between the two. With the lead singer's bare arms covered in tattoos, his occasional swigs of wine from a bottle and his fearless use of "goddamn" in his lyrics, there was no confusing this with a Sunday morning worship service. And yet, here I was, confused. I spent the rest of the concert in absolute shock. The emotional overwhelm never lessened; it only grew, peaking during a stunning cover of "Tiny Dancer" that resulted in one of the loudest, most joyful sing-a-longs I had ever been part of—even in church. The chills, the tingles, the warmth, the unity, the euphoria. It was all there. But was God? Was this his doing? I was terrified that maybe the answer was no. Maybe it was just humans and our brains, doing what we do. I settled upon a very silly workaround to ease my fears: God is omnipresent, so I guess he's at rock concerts too.

How naive and sweet. I was so bound by my dogma that I deemed my very human, natural emotions to be divinely inspired. My belief that God was as involved with a rock concert as he was with a worship service turned out to be closer to the truth than I realized. It turns out God was equally uninvolved. But my confusion was by evangelical design, as there is little difference between their worship services and a live concert. Music is already manipulative by nature; that's why we listen to it. We want to be made to feel something, to experience a release or even to distract ourselves from something we don't want to feel. Modern worship songs are designed to capitalize on this, often following a precise songwriting formula and arrangement strategy: The beginning focuses on creating a mood, paving the way for tension and release. Ambient synths, melodic hooks and repetition are all common. The lyrics tend to be very personal and storylike at first, setting the scene for a chorus that highlights all that is good about God. They also tend to be theologically ambiguous, and some could even be mistaken for traditional love songs. This helps the song appeal to a broad audience and increases its chance of achieving popularity. Key changes, crescendos, drum builds and dynamic bridges are all tools used to give the song a climax that inspires emotional release. Sometimes, there is even improvised singing or playing at key times during a song to promote the idea that this is all just organic, authentic worship for God. The vocals are often breathy and emotional, yet clear enough so the words can be understood and repeated. The song's vocal range is usually quite dynamic, ranging from soft, quiet singing to loud, belting choruses, often with octave jumps to heighten the climax.

Most of these formulas and sounds were taken directly from, or inspired by, major pop artists (which is why every other Hillsong or Bethel song sounds like a U2 rip-off). There is nothing new or revelatory about worship music; it simply follows the same musical rules that your favorite rock star does to create a song that makes you feel something deeply. No supernatural intervention needed.

This emotional manipulation is only amplified by every other aspect of a worship set. The lighting is often ambient and dimmed, sometimes fully programmed to display various colors and brightness levels at specific moments during the worship service, significantly impacting emotional impressions.[1] The worship leader is usually a charismatic figure with a warm and welcoming demeanor, acting as a spiritual coach or cheerleader throughout the set. They often encourage participants to stand, clap, sing, raise their hands, bow their heads or display some other behavior to fit the mood of the

1 Xing Xie et al., "Effects of Colored Lights on an Individual's Affective Impressions in the Observation Process," *Frontiers in Psychology* 13 (December 1, 2022): 938636, https://doi.org/10.3389/fpsyg.2022.938636.

moment. All of this and more manipulates your senses and expectations and profoundly impacts your perception of these "worship encounters." In the long term, these emotional moments can convince you that of course there's a god, I feel his presence at every worship service. This feeling of spiritual awe that's often aroused at religious gatherings is linked to increased generosity and cooperation, even in people less prone to agreeableness.[2]

In the short term, the result is a feeling of being uplifted, enthusiastic and confident in your beliefs. You are perfectly primed for the offering bucket that's about to be passed around. You're also ready to "receive a word from God," as the pastor often says in these churches. If the worship service caused you to feel closer to God, that must mean the message is from him as well. You can already see how a single experience can snowball, shaping your psychological responses to other situations and influencing your long-term perception of events.

EXPERIENCES AREN'T EVIDENCE

When talking to Christians about my disbelief in their god, I'm frequently told that it's because I haven't "experienced him for myself." That if I encounter God in some sort of profoundly spiritual moment, I'll believe like they do. But this assertion ignores the 20-plus years I spent as a Christian, having frequent spiritual experiences that I wholeheartedly believed to be God. As a worship leader and ministry team leader during mission trips, one of my responsibilities was to foster environments for others to experience the Holy Spirit as well. Not only do I have countless stories of my own encounters, but I was also witness to many others who claimed to have these deeply personal, spiritual moments. So when Christians refer to these "God-encounters," I believe them. I believe that they felt the sensations, the emotions and the indescribable feelings that they report. Just like the ones I felt. I understand just how convincing and meaningful those experiences can be.

Where I think people go wrong—where I know I went wrong—is not necessarily in their recollections of an experience, but in what they credit as the cause of an experience. Had I truly approached those spiritual events with skepticism and the goal of seeking truth, I would have reached more rational conclusions sooner. Instead, I was bound by loyalty and primed to believe

2 Claire Prade and Vassilis Saroglou, "Awe's Effects on Generosity and Helping," *The Journal of Positive Psychology* 11, no. 5 (January 2016): 1–9, doi:10.1080/17439760.2015.1127992.

supernatural explanations, based on my belief in God. If I hadn't been fueled by dogma, I would have realized that music, temperature, lighting, repetition (as in prayers or songs), crowds of people, expectations and emotional states can easily conjure up these same experiences. And even the most mystical-seeming situations were, at best, unexplainable. The honest conclusion would be to say, "I don't know what that was." But to further understand why personal experiences are not evidence of the supernatural, let's get into what we do know about the components that make up these experiences:

MUSIC Music's ability to impact our emotions, physical state and behavior has been widely studied and universally recognized. We've learned that sad music can make us feel more sad and upbeat music can lift our spirits. Our neurotransmitters, which directly affect our mood, also get a boost. Dopamine, specifically, is responsible for both the feeling of pleasure and the physical "chills" we get when listening to our favorite songs or ones that elicit a strong emotion.[3] Dopamine also rewards us with a sense of pleasure during certain activities and situations, like achieving a goal or exercising. This combined with music's ability to lower our heart rate and blood pressure and decrease cortisol (the stress hormone) makes it quite powerful. It even acts as a pain reliever for many people, which we'll discuss more when we address the topic of faith healers.[4] With music having so much influence over both body and mind, it must be taken into account when processing personal experiences that involve it.

CROWDS Being in large groups of people can impact individuals in a powerful way. It can amplify emotions, both negative and positive. It can boost our confidence in whatever activity the group is taking part in. Studies have shown that being in a crowd "decreased loneliness, increased positive feelings, a sense of meaning in one's life, self-awareness, and spiritual transcendence."[5] Humans are social creatures, so it makes sense that we can achieve a sense of fulfillment by being around each other. It's not just a fun time; it's part of what has helped us survive. French sociologist Émile

---

3 Laura Ferreri et al., "Dopamine Modulates the Reward Experiences Elicited by Music," *Proceedings of the National Academy of Sciences of the United States of America* 116, no. 9 (February 26, 2019): 3793–3798, https://doi.org/10.1073/pnas.1811878116.
4 J. H. Lee, "The Effects of Music on Pain: A Meta-Analysis." *Journal of Music Therapy* 53, no. 4 (Winter 2016): 430–477. doi:10.1093/jmt/thw012.
5 Shira Gabriel et al., "The Psychological Importance of Collective Assembly: Development and Validation of the Tendency for Effervescent Assembly Measure (TEAM)," *Psychological Assessment* 29, no. 11 (2017): 1349–1362, https://doi.org/10.1037/pas0000434.

Durkheim referred to the sense of connection and emotional state experienced during group gatherings as "collective effervescence." Further studies about this phenomenon have supported the idea that participants aren't just feeling some momentary positivity, but that it can even influence "their emotions, their power to act, their social positioning, as well as their beliefs and values."[6] Simply congregating with others is a powerful experience for us, one that many different religions, cultures and traditions have unnecessarily attributed to a god instead of recognizing it as a natural effect of humans gathering.

ENVIRONMENT Another thing that can heavily influence our brains is the nature of the place we find ourselves in. Studies show that even seemingly small things like wall color, room size, room layout, view and other architectural features impact things like mood and even heart rate. Just like music, our physical surroundings are inherently manipulative and must be taken into account.[7]

REPETITION Religious environments and rituals are host to plenty of repetitive lyrics, scriptures, sermons and movements. Some traditions involve repetitive prayer, mantras and even breathing exercises. The more we are exposed to something, the more inclined we are to believe it.[8] So it's no wonder that when we sing an emotional lyric over and over or repeatedly offer up a specific prayer, we begin to believe the message, even if we didn't before.

MEMORY There is quite a discrepancy between our confidence in the reliability of our memory and how reliable it actually is. Because we crave certainty and predictability, we are highly prone to recalling and reframing events in a way that aligns with our preferred worldview. We even "remember" things that never happened to begin with. Many studies confirm this bias that causes memories to align with our expectations of them, rather than reality.[9]

---

6 José J. Pizarro et al., "Emotional Processes, Collective Behavior, and Social Movements: A Meta-Analytic Review of Collective Effervescence Outcomes during Collective Gatherings and Demonstrations," *Frontiers in Psychology* 13 (2022).

7 K Strachan-Regan and O Baumann, "The impact of room shape on affective states, heartrate, and creative output," *Heliyon* 10 (March 2024), https://pmc.ncbi.nlm.nih.gov/articles/PMC10965811/.

8 Aumyo Hassan and Sarah J. Barber, "The effects of repetition frequency on the illusory truth effect," *Cognitive Research: Principles and Implications* 6, no. 38 (May 2021). https://cognitiveresearchjournal.springeropen.com/articles/10.1186/s41235-021-00301-5.

9 P.P. Raykov et al., "False Memories for Ending of Events," *Journal of Experimental Psychology: General* 152, no. 12 (2023): 3459–3475.

The risk of false or inaccurate memories is part of being human, and studies have proven just how easily some people "remember entire events that never actually happened to them."[10] When it comes to life-altering, faith-based assertions, such as the idea of encountering a god, our memory should be taken with a large grain of salt.

PATTERN RECOGNITION This is a valuable cognitive skill that humans rely on to read words, process traffic signs, recognize faces of people they know, learn a song, perform math and even make basic decisions. However, this can cause us to assign meaning to things without cause, especially when combined with confirmation bias. For efficiency's sake, this pattern recognition sometimes bypasses critical thinking and relies more on assumption, estimation and stereotyping. One study took a look at those more naturally inclined to pattern recognition and determined that "individuals who more readily learn, at an implicit level, patterns that are actually present in the environment may be biased toward belief in ordering Gods."[11] They also found that belief in a god increased one's pattern recognition abilities over time, which I find to be incredibly insightful when it comes to childhood indoctrination. A lower pattern recognition ability was found to make someone less prone to believe in gods. This is quite a blow to the idea of free will that evangelicals insist we have when it comes to choosing to embrace or reject a belief in God. If something largely beyond my control, such as my cognitive ability, is what determines the likelihood of my belief in a god, how is that fair?

Let's be clear about something: None of these things are fundamentally bad. Our susceptibility to these and other influences just makes us human. Manipulation is not inherently evil or wrong. Like so many things in life, the context of the intent and the outcome is what matters most. To manipulate something or someone simply means to control or influence it. We pay a lot of money to go to concerts with the expectation that we will be influenced by the event emotionally and even intellectually. Many people spend time designing their bedrooms or home décor in a way they hope influences their

10 Elizabeth F. Loftus and Jacqueline E. Pickrell, "The Formation of False Memories." *Psychiatric Annals*, 1995, https://journals.healio.com/doi/10.3928/0048-5713-19951201-07.
11 Adam B. Weinberger et al., "Implicit pattern learning predicts individual differences in belief in God in the United States and Afghanistan," *Nature Communications* 11, Article number: 4503 (2020).

mood when immersed in those environments. Being manipulated by people, places and our own subconscious is an unavoidable part of the human experience. This is why it's so important to practice skepticism and stay aware of when and how we are being manipulated. The danger comes when we lose control of our ability to determine the source behind the manipulation, when situations are wielded against us to encourage our participation in things we should avoid or follow agendas that are against our own best interests. It's one thing to be moved by music, crowds or other personal experiences. It's an entirely different thing to baselessly claim those feelings were caused by a god. Of course, modern worship performances aren't the only thing that people find themselves crediting as God-encounters.

OTHER TYPES OF EXPERIENCES

DREAMS Dreams have been perceived as meaningful to humans throughout history. In Christianity, Judaism, Islam, Hinduism and many other ancient religious traditions, dreams are a way for gods to communicate with humans. While the ability of dreams to create entire worlds in our heads may seem supernatural, it is so natural that evidence even suggests animals dream.[12] As dreaming occurs in the brain, it is not an easy thing to observe or study, other than determining that it is natural brain activity. What we have learned about dreams is largely dependent on humans' ability to recall and report them. The problem is that we can't verify or test those reports, so there is nothing stopping individuals from making up stories about dreams that never happened, claiming they came from a supernatural source. Even when reporting our dreams in earnest, it is impossible to recall them without being influenced by our emotional and psychological circumstances.

SLEEP PARALYSIS One of the darker sides of personal experience can be blamed on this scary condition. If you've ever experienced sleep paralysis, you understand why those prone to belief in the supernatural would easily credit this to demonic activity. Often occurring right as someone is falling asleep or waking up, sleep paralysis effectively freezes an otherwise conscious person. They can neither move nor speak. It's not uncommon for sleep paralysis to also include sensations of choking, chest pressure or other anxiety-inducing

---

12 "Animals have complex dreams, MIT researcher proves," MIT News, January 24, 2001, https://news.mit.edu/2001/dreaming.

phenomena. Sometimes you experience hallucinations or visions, maybe of the room you're in, and sometimes of dark, shadowy figures. While this may all sound quite spooky, it's actually a natural occurrence that around 30 percent of people will experience in their lifetime.[13] When your body goes into certain sleep cycles, it also goes into a state of paralysis to keep you from physically acting out whatever dreams you might be having. Sometimes these phases can have a sort of glitch and some level of consciousness is regained while your body is still in freeze mode.[14] It makes sense to feel disturbed by this sensation, but there's no need to credit demonic activity when your brain does a fine job of its own creating these eerie situations.

VISIONS These are images or scenes viewed through the mind's eye while awake and are often described as something dreamlike and unprompted. Some religious traditions, such as evangelical Christianity, attribute these experiences to communication from God. Others, like Buddhism, view them as a look into your subconscious and a tool for personal growth. Like dreams, visions are impossible to truly investigate as they rely on human memory and honest reporting. Anyone can claim they had a vision from God, as it is generally unfalsifiable.

NUMBERS Our human habit of pattern recognition combined with our desire to translate these patterns into meaning or story makes numbers the perfect target for claiming something spiritual lies behind them. Whether it's a license plate, sports jersey, apartment number, parking space, clock, birthday or countless other common things, we are constantly seeing numbers all around us. This creates multiple opportunities a day for our brains to unnecessarily assign meaning to them. In charismatic circles, seeing repeating numbers (e.g., 222, 444, 777) or repeating times (e.g., 11:11, 3:33) leads many to claim God is speaking to them, either just to say "Hi" or to point to specific Bible verses. Another example is when "prophets" claim certain numbers showing up in pop culture are messages from God. Hearing prophetic declarations about "2020 being the year of 20/20 vision!" or "March 4 is the day he is calling us to march forth into his calling!" were very famil-

---

13 Cleveland Clinic, "Sleep Paralysis: What It Is, Causes, Symptoms & Treatment," Cleveland Clinic, last modified July 9, 2024, https://my.clevelandclinic.org/health/diseases/21974-sleep-paralysis.

14 Vijay Bhalerao et al., "Recent Insights Into Sleep Paralysis: Mechanisms and Management," *Cureus*, July 26, 2024.

iar to me growing up. To this day, I can still play the game of projecting what prophetic claim the televangelists will make next based off of upcoming dates. Of course, there are also evangelicals who call this sort of thing "demonic numerology," continuing the black-and-white thinking that something is either a message from God or Satan. Not even arbitrary numbers are exempt.

FORMATIONS IN NATURE Sunsets and sunrises, clouds shaped like wings, grilled cheese sandwiches with the image of Mary: All of these and more have been cited as signs from God. Nature and confirmation bias have been combined in many indigenous and shamanistic traditions, not just Christianity. It is yet another outlet for our innate pattern recognition to seek out familiar and meaningful shapes and characteristics.

COMMON ARGUMENTS YOU'LL HEAR

"My church has real worship."

Anytime I expose the inner workings of a modern-day charismatic evangelical worship service, there is always someone quick to say, "Yeah, that's a perversion of worship! My church doesn't do that!" Two immediate issues I have with that are 1) this baselessly asserts that there's one specific way to worship and that their church has figured it out, when worship is a vague, subjective term with no objective foundation and 2) this response usually comes from attendees of church denominations that generally do not believe in more charismatic doctrines such as speaking in tongues or personal encounters with the Holy Spirit. Even so, whether you're in a Catholic church decorated with stained glass windows, echoing with vibrations from an organ playing sacred hymns or you're waving your hands in the air in the front row at a megachurch, you are being influenced and your dogma is being fortified by whatever flavor of church service you've chosen to participate in. You decided it was meaningful to you, so it is.

"Worship makes me feel better."

There are many reasons for this—the music, the company of like-minded people, physical movement or even worshiping alone and experiencing a reprieve from the more stressful parts of your life. None of these requires the involvement of a god to make you feel good. Meditation can achieve these same feelings, as can social interactions, concerts, hiking, sporting events and other activities that engage the body and brain in a way that causes dopamine release. "Feeling" something positive is not evidence of the supernatural; it's evidence that your brain is responding naturally to certain stimuli.

"Worship isn't for us: It's for God."

I remember this argument being made many times in response to someone admitting that they weren't "into" worship. But what kind of god demands worship from their creations? What sort of self-sufficient, perfect being requires or even allows humans to worship them with songs and musical performances? Pleasure at receiving unquestioned attention and adoration, earned simply by existing, seems consistent with a human who has a really big ego problem, not that of a god.

"God doesn't need us to worship him; we do it because we need it."

Presuming that God does not need or desire to be worshiped creates a bit of a logic problem when you consider that he created beings that feel compelled to worship him. Why design us to participate in a specific ritual or thought process that is otherwise meaningless? Worship doesn't feed the poor, clothe the needy or provide homes for the unhoused. While there are arguments to be made for the positive personal effects of worship, these are all centered around desired outcomes from listening to music, congregating with others, having routines and entering meditative-like states. None of it is exclusive to evangelical worship or religious ritual. More importantly, all those things can be experienced without the self-abasement and submissive mindset that worship requires. Those things we can argue are positive byproducts of worship and practicing one's faith can also be experienced outside of religion, without the undesirable and often harmful problems religion causes.

"I know God is real because I experienced him myself."

Many people claim to have experienced many different, opposing gods. So how would we know which experiences to believe? Which gods have actually revealed themselves to people, and which people are just lying or misguided? The problem is that these personal experiences are untestable, unverifiable and only convincing for the person who experienced them. When people credit these encounters to a god, they usually do not take into account the natural explanations surrounding the events. If Christ himself walked into my room right now and I were to retain my skepticism and critical thinking skills, I would be questioning my own memory, senses and state of mind. I would have countless reasons, backed by science, to assume there was a natural explanation. I would have no reason to assume there is an actual deity appearing in my room, one born over 2,000 years ago to a virgin. Personal experience is incredibly unreliable due to our limited and easily manipulated human faculties, and yet we are forced to rely on it every day. But our feelings surrounding an experience do not make it true, and often, the more emotional a response we have toward it, the more likely that we have a personal bias that must be questioned.

"I was speaking in tongues, so that must have been the Holy Spirit speaking through me."

The "gift of tongues," as some call it, has a more technical term: "glossolalia." It's a method of speech practiced amongst more charismatic Christians, and it generally consists of linguistically meaningless vocalizations credited as a supernatural language that only God can understand. It generally follows a pattern and cadence that resembles an actual spoken language. While many Christians reject speaking in tongues as an unbiblical practice, charismatic Christians who accept it in their doctrine consider it a sign of spiritual maturity. This belief comes from Acts 2:1–4, which says that believers "were filled with the Holy Spirit and began to speak in other tongues." Some believers go so far as to say you're not a real Christian until you have been "filled with the Holy Spirit," with the ability to speak in tongues being a significant indicator of that. But, like so many other things that feel unique when it comes to personal experience, glossolalia is not exclusive to Christians. It has been observed as part of shamanism, witchcraft and paganism. Even some Native American tribes practice glossolalia.

Scientists have studied this phenomenon, and some speculate that it's not an uncontrolled experience but rather a learned behavior that the practitioner participates in. One study "suggests that glossolalia emerged, and remained stable across centuries and continents, because of an optimal balance between, on the one hand, its dramatic effects on the practitioner and her audience, and on the other hand, its relative ease of acquisition and execution."[15] In other words, speaking in tongues as a tradition caught on

15 Yoshija Walter et al., "Brain structural evidence for a frontal pole specialization in glossolalia," *IBRO Reports* 9 (2020): 32-36, https://doi.org/10.1016/j.ibror.2020.06.002.

because it not only provides emotional impact for the person practicing it and their audience, but it also doesn't require skill or training. Another study found that "no extraordinary features appear to be involved."[16] Nothing that we know about glossolalia points toward a supernatural source; in fact, whatever information we do have about it suggests a natural, far more reasonable explanation.

"God answered my prayers."

Which god? And how could one possibly determine if a god were responsible for an outcome without first having evidence that a god exists? It is fascinating to me that Christianity considers humility a virtue, and yet the faith of so many of its practitioners hinges on their commitment to selfish thinking. To believe God has answered your prayers is to accept that he has ignored those of others. Prayers from children being abused. Prayers from families hiding in bomb shelters. Prayers from victims of domestic violence. But your prayer, the one that helped you find your keys in time to make it to work, the one that helped you recover from a cold faster, the one that helped you pass an important test, that is the prayer God answered. How arrogant and dismissive. How interesting that you are the one who benefited from God's "mysterious ways." This (hopefully) unconscious selfishness is the result of confirmation bias. Rather than challenge what we already believe and risk disrupting it, it's much easier to conclude that our experiences confirm our dogma. Rather than adjust our beliefs in accordance with reality, we adjust our reality to align with our beliefs.

"God always answers prayers, even if the answer is no answer."

This is just another irrational attempt to stick with a bias. If the belief is that God always answers prayers, one must have an explanation for those times when no answer is provided. Similar arguments are "God answered my prayer, just differently than I thought he would," or "God knows best, so whatever happened was his answer." If Jesus says it's possible to move mountains (Mark 11:23) and I pray for a mountain to move but instead find a road through it, Jesus did not answer that prayer, no matter how hard I try to change the narrative. "God helped me move through the mountain"

---

16 Yoshija Walter, "Neural Structural Changes Associated with Ritual Glossolalia (a Preliminary Study): Morphometrics on the Expertise of Praying in Tongues," SSRN, posted May 5, 2021, https://papers.ssrn.com/sol3/papers.cfm?abstract_id=3837534.

is a poor attempt to reframe an outcome to make it congruent with a personal belief. Saying that "No answer is an answer" is yet another unfalsifiable claim that even contradicts many scriptures. This theory suggests an answer that is indistinguishable from what happens if no god exists.

"I had a personal encounter with God that changed my life."

Ah yes, the powerful testimony of a transformed life. "I was a drug addict and then I prayed and got sober," "I was in prison, read the Bible, and now I'm a totally different person," "I had anxiety and depression, but I started going to church and now they are completely gone." These stories can seem convincing on the surface. How do you argue against someone immediately cured of addiction, depression or some other undesired trait? Life transformations are a very real thing that can happen, and often do. Therapy can be the catapult for some, while for others, the catapult might be a rock-bottom moment or perhaps a sense of responsibility such as a new child or relationship. Near-death experiences, ayahuasca or other plant-based medicines and even inspiring personal growth books can trigger positive changes. A god is not needed to transform your life, yet people often credit one for just that. Credit should go to the people taking it upon themselves to make the change—or to make the most of a change thrust upon them by circumstance.

Often, when people hit rock bottom and are ready and eager for a change, they are looking for an excuse to do so. If religion is presented as a mechanism for this change, it can provide the psychological motivation needed to practice self-control, find community and other beneficial work. Turning to religion can also provide instant fixes for all sorts of relevant issues. Attending church can provide immediate, consistent community. Reading the Bible and praying can help create routines and meditative states, which are good for brain health. And as we've learned, worship services and even time alone in prayer release brain chemicals like those experienced during an enjoyable meal, physical exercise or even some types of recreational drugs. So while Christianity may be a major factor behind someone's transformation, that doesn't prove the existence of a god, nor does it prove that Christianity is true. It is simply evidence of that person's ability to change.

"God doesn't reveal himself to you because that would take away your free will."

When I express to a believer that I've never experienced anything that was undoubtedly a God-encounter, the assertion above is a common argument they make in response. My question to them is always to ask about some of the most revered biblical figures: Did Moses have free will? God had no problem speaking to him through a burning bush in Exodus 3. What about Jacob? Genesis 32 claims that he physically wrestles God, and in verse 30, Jacob says, “I saw God face to face, and yet my life was spared.” In the New Testament, Saul, a man known for persecuting Christians, encounters Jesus in the form of a bright light and voice that impacts him so profoundly that he converts and begins preaching in the synagogues. Was his free will overpowered by that “Road to Damascus” experience in Acts 9 when Saul is blinded by a light from heaven and has a conversation with Jesus that ultimately leads to his conversion? And what about Jesus’s parents or his disciples who walked and talked with him regularly and are said to have witnessed his miracles? It’s interesting that the believers asserting free will as a defense have no complaints about the free will being taken from these biblical characters. In fact, we’re supposed to believe these characters are spiritual leaders and apostles worth following and respecting. Having more information about something, or more experience with it, doesn’t take away free will and the choices that come with it. This argument is really just a poor attempt to excuse God’s lack of evidence.

THE SHAME OF FEELING NOTHING

One of the features of crediting these experiences to a god is that when that god doesn’t appear to show up, the blame can be shifted to to the perceived shortcomings of the person, rather than the deity. While I often thought I was encountering the Holy Spirit, I also remember countless times when I didn’t feel anything. I’ve heard from many who grew up in evangelical culture and never felt the chills, awe or euphoria they were expecting to. As a pastor’s daughter who fully embraced her role, I was at every meeting, every conference and even attended other local church conferences to hear interesting guest speakers or worship leaders. I always went with the expectation of feeling God’s presence, but sometimes I felt nothing. Maybe the songs weren’t as moving, my mind was on something else or some other natural explanation. But the teachings I grew up with made it clear there was no excuse. I was missing out on God. This self-shame had been programmed into my head from an early age. I was taught that God’s presence is always available, and if you don't feel it, something is wrong with you. I was told that I must have left a spiritual door open for sin that created a wall between myself and the Lord (Isaiah 59:1–2).

Despite the embarrassment of having my sin exposed, I wanted to be honest, and when I didn't feel God's presence, I didn't want to pretend otherwise. I remember one day my mother, who was a worship leader in our church, encouraged me to raise my hands and visibly worship God. When I confided that sometimes I just didn't feel him, she explained that such things happened to her as well, and that sometimes our sin just gets in the way. Her solution was essentially "Fake it until you make it." She told me that sometimes "Our heart just needs a jump start," and that if I were to act as though I felt God, it would make space in my heart for me to truly feel it. So I began to implement that trick. I would raise my hands and sing with feigned enthusiasm until it felt genuine. I would close my eyes and pray fervently, repeating emotional statements like "Make me less of me and more of you, God" until I brought myself to tears or adopted some sort of posture that would paint me as reverent.

It always puzzled me that I was supposed to deny my feelings in certain circumstances but accept them without doubt in others. If my emotions and senses led me to feel like I was being impacted by the Holy Spirit, I was told to trust them and assume it was true. But if my emotions and senses told me there was nothing special going on, I must be walking in sin or in need of more faith. That train of thought was supposed to be followed, not questioned. If it was good, it was God. If it wasn't, it was a personal failure.

This form of manipulation takes something seemingly benign—not being spiritually moved, for example—and turns it into an attack against a person's identity. You felt nothing, so you're bad. Along with the constant messaging of how perfect God is and how undeserving we are of his presence, this psychological manipulation often drives people further under the control of evangelical dogma. These tactics chip away at an individual's self-confidence and trust in their own senses. They foster a new insecurity—that God may not be pleased with them and that the only way to resolve this is to attend more church services, give more tithes and offerings, raise hands higher in worship and further submit to spiritual leaders.

TRUSTING YOURSELF AGAIN

It's a strange and unique thing to be a person who once believed they had encountered God and now doesn't believe any gods exist, much less were ever encountered. I have a lot of compassion for anyone clinging to these experiences as a reason to maintain their belief. It is one thing to go through the painful process of realizing that others have lied, indoctrinated you or misled you on the facts surrounding God and Christianity. It's an entirely different sort of pain to confront the idea that your own natural feelings, sensations and mind helped convince you of something false. It not only fills you with self-doubt but leaves you with questions about things you were once certain of. If that bright light you saw as a child after you were in a car crash wasn't an angel, what was it? Did you even see it? If that number that keeps popping up isn't your sign that God is watching over you or that you're on the right path, how do you cope with the lack of validation? Is there nothing out there keeping you safe? If that time in worship that had you sobbing on your knees and feeling comforted by something external during a difficult time in your life wasn't "real," what was it? You may have incorrectly attributed a source to these events, but that doesn't have to make them less impactful or meaningful to you. Those chill bumps, tears, overwhelming emotions, dreams or other hard-to-explain sensations are what make you so beautifully human. They are a sign that you were present, you were vulnerable and your brain was doing what all brains do to bring you a sense of reward and comfort.

Applying skepticism to your current interpretation of past experiences does not have to mean discounting them altogether. I have many stories from my childhood where I was convinced that I saw something supernatural. One time, a bright light filled a room, causing me to believe there had been an angel. Another memory is of a dark, shadowy figure coming into my room one night and pulling my hair. Of course, I interpreted this as demonic activity. So many times, I opened my Bible to the perfect verse to describe my circumstances. Other times, my beloved number 22 made an appearance as my hotel room number or on a passing license plate right when I needed confirmation that I was on the right path. Now I look back 30 years later and recognize that these memories are often fuzzy and incomplete if I'm being completely honest and not attempting to turn them into a logical story. I view some of them as unexplained moments that I did my best to fit into the approved narrative I had been taught. And of course, these perfectly timed moments of encouragement or sightings of my favorite number still occur just as consistently when I'm speaking at atheist conferences or writing this counter-apologetics book. The difference is that now, I don't take it as a sign that God is pleased with my work. While I trust myself, I do not trust my past narrative of events because it was all experienced through a filter of expectation, confirmation bias and more. Moving forward, I've rebuilt trust in myself by utilizing skepticism as a method of protection against believing things without cause. Here are some skeptical questions to ask yourself about past or future "spiritual" experiences:

1. **What evidence do I have for this experience?** Evidence consists of facts that point to something being objectively true or not. Things that can be measured, counted, physically observed, tested and verified by others. Examining your experiences in order to determine what in the fog of unreliable memory or personal bias can be confirmed as fact will reveal the strengths and weaknesses in your interpretation of events.
2. **What questions would I have if this experience were reported to me by someone I was not predisposed to trust?** When we discount our personal biases and proclivity to trust ourselves implicitly, it can allow some good questions to come into play. Hypothetically exploring what your reaction might be if you were to hear this story from someone you did not assume was reliable will often bring forward skeptical thoughts that allow you to question your beliefs more thoroughly and honestly.
3. **If I knew without a doubt that the cause of this experience was not a god or supernatural source, might there be a natural explanation?** Occam's razor, the principle that the simplest answer is generally the best, is a great tool here. While that doesn't mean the most obvious answer is the correct answer, it's a great place to start looking. As the natural world is all we know and have tested, it makes sense to search there first when questioning our mysterious personal experiences. If we find a natural explanation for what we encountered, there is no need to jump to the "supernatural" as an explanation.
4. **Is there any chance my perception of an experience was impacted by vulnerability?** Taking account of personal circumstances can also help you discover potential discrepancies in your conclusions about your experience. How much sleep did you have? Were you sick? Perhaps a high fever was at

play. What was your emotional state? What were your expectations? The context of our experiences is a big piece of the story that shouldn't be overlooked.

5. What would it take to change my mind about my conclusions surrounding this experience? If the answer is "nothing," you've outed yourself for prioritizing a specific narrative over whether it's true or not. If you believe God audibly spoke a Bible verse to you while you prayed in your room but admit you would not change your mind about this even if presented with evidence that someone was playing an audio recording of that verse just outside your door, then you are committed to a story, not to the truth.

So much of religious dogma requires abandoning reality and oneself. Everything must be assigned to some role in the narrative. There is no room for nuance or even just saying "I don't know." These indescribable, deeply personal and seemingly supernatural experiences are innately human, and our understanding of them can be limited. While skeptics and atheists have developed a reputation of being dismissive toward this part of life, I find this form of spirituality to be one of the most potentially unifying, especially when approached with neutrality instead of an agenda that assigns meaning without evidence. How beautiful it is that our response to normal events like a sunset, the birth of a child, the sound of an instrument or being with like-minded people is to be overwhelmed with awe and wonder. This feeling is so great that many often relegate it to "God" or "magic."

And this is a universal occurrence. People across many cultures, religions and backgrounds experience these altered states of euphoria and emotional release. Attendees at concerts and raves (both sober and with the use of drugs) are an obvious example of people impacted by music, crowds, physical movement and emotional expectation. Marathon runners and other athletes experience this euphoria as well due to the change in brain chemistry while exercising, which is called "runner's high." There are many indigenous traditions throughout the world that combine things like fasting, dancing and group chanting to induce this. And while charismatic Christians like to believe their spiritual encounters are unique, Hinduism, Judaism, Islam, Sikhism and more all have traditions reporting these same sorts of trances, emotional states and physical sensations. The difference in these experiences is simply which combination of mind-altering mechanisms (e.g., music, crowds, drugs, movement) are at play and who or what the individuals credit for it.

Our predisposition for tribalism and certainty makes us quick to note the differences and points of separation in our encounters instead of finding unity. Instead of embracing our shared sensitivity to the world around us, we arrogantly claim that only our experiences are legitimate. It's never, "I heard a voice, and you did too! How interesting!" Instead, it's, "I heard God, my specific God. And you're either lying or wrong if you think you heard yours." Regardless of how uniquely personal these events feel to us, they are something most of us have in common, and the only differences tend to be what we credit as the source. The truth is that meaning found across these experiences is subjective. Recognizing this allows individuals to simply enjoy an experience for what it is rather than try to find some divine message in it. How much more special is that than being bound by whatever religion tells us to find meaningful or not?

CHAPTER 5

No Faith Healers, No Prophets

"All that glitters is not gold."
—WILLIAM SHAKESPEARE

When most people hear the terms "faith healer" or "prophet," they conjure up specific images. Perhaps of a suit-wearing televangelist, charismatically rebuking the "spirit of infirmity" in a crowd while roughly laying hands on the desperate and pronouncing them healed as they're shoved to the ground. Maybe even visions of President Trump's spiritual advisor Paula White-Cain, frantically speaking in tongues while declaring "angels from Africa" were on their way to secure Trump's presidential victory (which—surprise!—did not occur during that election). For me, these terms bring up memories of my father. Memories of him placing a hand on my head when I was sick as a child and praying that I would be healed. Memories of him sitting with politicians and leaders in South America to reveal the meaning of their dreams or prophesy God's plan for their lives and country. Memories of standing with him outside on the front porch as he declared that the incoming storm would turn away and produce no tornadoes. Healing and prophecy may sound wild and unfamiliar to the average person, but I grew up with them. Our family believed that Jesus meant it when he said, "whoever believes in me will do the works I have been doing, and they will do even greater things than these" and that "you may ask me for anything in my name, and I will do it" (John 14:12-14). We believed that "you can all prophesy in turn so that everyone may be instructed and encouraged" (1 Corinthians 14:31). And as a child, I was in awe of Jesus's words when he said, "if you have faith as small as a mustard seed, you can say to this mountain, 'Move from here to there,' and it will move. Nothing will be impossible for you" (Matthew 17:20). I believed it wholeheartedly. And yet, I never moved any mountains. It was a strange way to live, believing that technically and spiritually God could absolutely heal people and speak to them through us, and yet there seemed to be no rhyme or reason to when he would follow through on that biblical promise. Sometimes it worked, other times it didn't.

One of the first times I explicitly remember it not working was for a little boy I'll call "Eli." I'm not sure how my family became connected to his, but I'm sure it was through their reputation as charismatic pastors who believed Jesus still actively healed people, and Eli needed healing. He was 5 years old and had an inoperable, terminal brain tumor. Like any family would be, Eli's was desperate for him to be healthy again. Whether they asked my parents to come pray for him or whether my parents volunteered to, I'm not sure. But either way, I remember them going to Eli's home for hours on end to join his friends and family in praying for his healing. My dad, especially, spent a lot of time in their home praying and praying and said he truly believed God could heal Eli. Sometimes, I went with him. Partially because I wanted to do what I thought God wanted me to do, partially to try to be like my father and partially out of morbid curiosity. Would God really heal him? How would that play out? Instantly, like a magical transformation? Would God slowly shrink the tumor? What did someone that sick look and act like?

I was only 9 years old myself, and it was hard to imagine a fellow child dying. I remember walking into their house; several others were there to pray along with their three other children, yet the house was quiet except for the sounds of soft worship music. We went into the parents' room. I will never forget the smell. It was sour and stale, with a bit of sickly sweet. It was probably a combination of medical equipment, medications and whatever anointing oil someone had opened, but if you had asked me, I would have said it smelled like death. And then there was Eli, propped up in the center of their bed. His body was chubby and swollen from the steroids. He relied on intubation to breathe and a feeding tube to eat. But Eli's sweet blue eyes were very much alive and aware, seemingly taking in everything around him, blinking slowly as though struggling to stay open. I remember getting on the bed and sitting next to him, placing a hand on his arm as my dad began to lead us in prayer. Several other adults stood around, also praying and swaying to the worship music. Some reading Bible verses aloud, some praying in tongues, some pleading with God in tears. I remember feeling scared and awkward and wondering if Eli felt the same and wished he were watching cartoons instead. All of it made me uncomfortable and I worried God could sense my uneasiness. It was odd to experience what I now understand to be anxiety taking hold at a time when I was supposed to be expressing faith and facilitating God's supernatural capabilities. Eli died a few weeks later, and it left me feeling deeply scared. Why did God let that happen? Where was he? Did somebody do something wrong? Did I do something wrong? Naturally, I was sad and confused by this, especially since all of the adults had led me to believe Eli would be healed.

I was most traumatized by my dad's reaction. I remember him coming home from Eli's house that day with a face I can only describe as distraught and completely defeated. I had never—and have never since—seen him looking so shattered. He seemed genuinely shocked by the outcome, and what bits and pieces I overheard from his conversations with other adults revealed that he was. He and my uncle had even prayed over Eli's dead body, believing he would be resurrected, citing the stories of Lazarus and Jesus in their prayers as though this would somehow remind God that he raises people from the dead. I recall feeling disturbed just by the idea that my father had been in the room with a dead body. It was so much information to take in, and all of it conflicted with what I had been taught about God. He was supposed to be a healer, a comforter and the source of all good things. And yet all of this seemed very, very bad. I remember my dad eventually sharing at church that God had revealed to him that Eli, and all the prayers of faith people said for him, planted a seed that would bring about healing for others. I didn't understand how that worked. Why did it feel like a game God was playing with us? Was our mustard seed faith not enough after all? Why did an all-powerful god need seeds? And why did he need that seed to be the life of an innocent 5-year-old child? Why did we have to keep moving the goalpost? First it was praying for a miracle healing, then a resurrection and now a commission to go out and heal others? When did we get to just mourn the sad thing that happened? This belief in the power of healing seemed less and less about actual healing, and more like an attempt to ignore the realities of being human.

Life is full of difficulties that we are naturally averse to. Our aversion is how we survive. When faced with illness, we want a cure to be healthy again. When financial hardships occur, we want to know there will be money or resources coming our way. When a relationship turns sour, we want a fix for it or any easy out. When someone dies, we want more time with them. And sometimes, instead of facing these issues head-on and finding accessible solutions, we try to deny that they're happening at all. We look for ways to cope, and coping mechanisms sell. Many faith healers, pastors and self-proclaimed prophets have figured this out. We want to avoid suffering, whether physical or mental, and they promise to provide an instant fix to our ailments. Kenneth Copeland, who attributes anxiety and depression to "spiritual" issues, is known for blaming demons as the culprits behind disease and other natural occurrences.[1] He is said to have an estimated net worth of somewhere between $300 and $800 million, including multiple private jets.[2] Joel Osteen is known for telling his followers that God has "overflow" of financial blessing for them[3] and preaching the power of positivity and gratitude, all while pandering his teachings to the tune of an estimated $40 to $100 million personal net worth.[4] Perhaps the most famous modern faith healer, Benny Hinn, often seen preaching to large audiences while waving his hands or jacket over people and yelling "Take the anointing" and then inviting them to share their healing testimonies,[5] has reportedly gained his wealth through books on the topic and these healing services at packed stadiums. Whether or not these men genuinely believe they have these spiritual abilities is something only they know for sure.

---

1 "Question of the Day: How Can I Overcome Anxiety?" Kenneth Copeland Ministries. https://www.kcm.org/read/question-of-the-day/how-can-i-overcome-anxiety?language_content_entity=en-US.
2 "Kenneth Copeland Net Worth 2025." Cult Education Institute (May 25, 2025). https://culteducation.com/group/1010-kenneth-copeland-ministries/38340-kenneth-copeland-net-worth-2025-inside-the-lavish-life-of-the-450-million-televangelist.html.
3 Joel Osteen. 2023. "Get Ready for Overflow | Joel Osteen." YouTube (February 9, 2023). https://www.youtube.com/watch?v=CVlcCBOYqPU.
4 Rachel Dobkin. "Joel Osteen's 'Simple Things' Post Sparks Fury." *Newsweek* (June 27, 2024). https://www.newsweek.com/pastor-joel-osteen-simple-things-money-net-worth-1918465.
5 BringBackTheCross. 2010. "Benny Hinn - Raw Anointing of the Spirit (1)." YouTube (April 2, 2010). https://www.youtube.com/watch?v=xdUIqKJyD0Q.

IT'S SHOWBIZ, BABY!

Much like megachurch worship leaders, these popular evangelical figures are skilled performers that know how to work a stage. Even before you arrive at their services or turn on their TV program, you are primed with expectations of supernatural signs, wonders and wisdom from God, to be revealed by them just for you. Their target audience comprises the most desperate people. Vulnerabilities to scams include depression, loneliness, financial or other life stressors[6] and Hinn, Osteen and their peers benefit from this neediness in others.

When your primary audience is someone who actively wants and expects you to solve their problems and is coming to you out of desperation, most of your work is already done for you. Another feature is the cult of personality that megachurch ministers often create. Images of their smiling, impassioned or worshipful faces, often with outstretched hands, are found plastered on their flyers and book covers. Their names are in large, bold print, frequently with an authoritative-sounding title preceding them like "apostle" or "prophet" or "reverend." Other times, a less hierarchical title such as "brother" or "sister" is used to create an image of a down-to-earth, humble figure.

Physical appearance also plays a big part. Female evangelists such as Paula White-Cain, Jan Crouch and Tammy Faye Bakker are well known for their bold makeup, meticulous hairstyles and bright wardrobes. Their male counterparts, including Copeland, Hinn and Osteen, appear most frequently in expensive tailored suits. Many televangelists also appear to have undergone cosmetic procedures, with Joyce Meyers being one of the most famous to openly admit it. Possibly even more distinct than their looks are the individual preaching styles and the tone of voice they adopt. Benny Hinn uses a soft, almost hypnotic, breathy vocal style, then shifts into loud, confident proclamations following dramatic pauses and quiet moments for added effect. His physical gestures include lots of hand waving and blowing on the audience as though it was wind from God. Paula White-Cain plays up the energetic, emotional charismatic side with lots of repetitive statements and speaking in tongues. She shouts, paces, shakes her fists and even snaps her fingers. Joel Osteen plays the calm, cool, happy-go-lucky guy with

6 David Lacey et al. "The Cyberpsychology of Deception" EasyChair (September 13, 2024). https://easychair.org/publications/preprint/s5gh/.

a predictable demeanor that appeals to a broader audience. This is all part of their personal marketing and allows people to pick their favorite charismatic leader, much like teens have pop star idols. These are not just people, they're brands, and they need you to buy what they're selling.

My anecdotal experience from spending time in greenrooms with guest speakers at church conferences and healing events or at dinners at fancy restaurants post-event provided quite a bit of insight. On multiple occasions, I heard a popular revival meeting evangelist brag about people asking him to sign their Bibles and joke about getting to "lay hands" on attractive women to pray for them. None of his peers seemed shocked or averse to this, and several laughed along and shared similar stories. Other times, I recall leaders speculating how large of an offering they were going to get that night and later would talk about "God's provision" after ordering the surf and turf at the dinner paid for by the tax-free church that was hosting. My general experience with these men and occasional women was that they all had larger-than-life personalities, an air of elitism and an astounding amount of confidence in their abilities.

TACTICS AND TRICKS

As I'm not a mind reader, I can't tell you which evangelical ministers truly believe what they preach and claim. I'm sure there are some that are incredibly genuine in their practices, deeply believing that God can and does heal and speak to his people through their ministry. I'm also confident that many are fully motivated by what drives numerous people: money and power. Another likely option is that quite a few are a combination of the two. Perhaps consciously, they believe and would tell everyone including themselves that they are genuine, but subconsciously, they are motivated by the prospect of fame or fortune or both. Maybe some started off as wholehearted believers but eventually realized it was their performance, not their faith, that people were most influenced by and decided to let that take the lead. Something they all seem to have in common, whether it is deliberate, learned or accidental, is a reliance on at least some of these practices:

PAY-TO-PRAY The idea of sowing metaphorical seeds and reaping blessings is abundant in evangelicalism. Ministers are quick to use the Parable of the Sower (Mark 4:8) and other verses like Luke 6:38 and 2 Corinthians 9:6 to support the idea that *the more you give, the more you get.* They apply this teaching to financial giving, encouraging followers to give generously as a way to receive healing or a financial breakthrough. Another favorite story is in Luke 21, when an impoverished widow gives two coins and Jesus points out that her gift is more generous than what the rich give because it costs her more. You'll find that those teaching this level of generosity are always the ones on the receiving end. Prosperity gospel preachers such as Osteen often deliver positive, hopeful messages all about how much God wants to bless his people and provide them with finances, raises, cars, healing, houses and overall abundance. Prosperity doctrine is marketed as personal empowerment but always includes the idea that one must be charitable themselves to receive their blessings from God. What's important to note is that these pastors make their money from donations, book sales, speaking engagements and other methods fully dependent on their audiences—*not* a supernatural provision from a god. Some evangelists are less subtle. There are countless clips on the internet of preachers asking for donations, like the one of Jesse Duplantis saying that Jesus hasn't returned because people aren't giving enough,[7] all while sitting on an estimated net worth of $20 million.[8] Kenneth Copeland claimed criticisms about his two private jets were "persecution,"[9] and Jim Bakker hawked a "Miracles Happen" blanket in exchange for thousand-dollar donations on his self-titled show. Evangelical ministries have also been known to "give" away anointing oil, prayer clothes and other religious objects they claim will perform miracles in exchange for large donations. The Bible verses you don't hear these pastors quoting? Jesus's own words of "it is easier for a camel to go through the eye of a needle than for someone who is rich to enter the kingdom of God" (Matthew 19:24), "Do not store up for yourselves treasures on earth" (Matthew 6:19) and "Sell everything you have and give to the poor" (Luke 18:22).

CONFIDENT AMBIGUITY Most of these ministers have mastered the art of confidently proclaiming a whole lot of nothing. They use large hand gestures, point at worshipers in the audience and speak with booming voices.

---

7 Owen Morgan (Telltale). 2022. "Televangelists SHAMELESSLY Beg for Peoples Money." YouTube (May 8, 2022). https://www.youtube.com/watch?v=lBfD5Tz6Fuc.
8 Leonardo Blair. "Televangelist Jesse Duplantis calls poverty a 'curse,' says his wealth is because he's 'blessed'." *The Christian Post* (April 29, 2024). https://www.christianpost.com/news/televangelist-jesse-duplantis-calls-poverty-a-curse.html.
9 Owen Morgan (Telltale). 2022. "Kenneth Copeland Feels so PERSECUTED for Buying Private Jets." YouTube (February 27, 2022). https://www.youtube.com/watch?v=YY1eXU7DXZ0.

Their expression will be either smiling or stern, but always animated. They will act as though they are channeling God's very voice, sometimes even speaking as though they are him: "*TONIGHT I AM GOING TO DO A BIG WORK FOR SOMEONE HERE THAT NEEDS IT! THIS IS THE YEAR THAT I AM GOING TO SHINE MY FAVOR ON MY CHILDREN! BLESSINGS, OVERFLOWING BLESSINGS ARE HEADING YOUR WAY! I, THE LORD YOUR GOD, AM GOING TO HEAL SOMEONE IN THIS PLACE!*" No specifications are made, no falsifiable claims, just vague statements that sound exciting and allow listeners to apply subjective meaning to what's said. Often, there is a caveat assigned to the promise—*as long as you have enough faith, as long as you are right with God, as long as YOU have planted a seed.* Even if their declarations don't come true, they can always blame the wannabe recipient for having failed to do what was needed to "earn" God's blessing.

SENSE OF URGENCY Research has shown that people have "a tendency to pursue urgency over importance,"[10] and these preachers have certainly learned to capitalize on that. Phrases like "Don't let your blessing pass you by! Don't miss this moment!" and "Your healing is just an act of faith away!" create the illusion that time is scarce and there's an immediate need for the listener to do whatever the speaker asks. With this seemingly urgent task taking priority in the person's mind, it bypasses their ability to apply much skepticism or take the time to think about what's really going on. Another easy way for preachers to introduce this urgency is to talk about the "end times." They dramatically declare that Jesus is coming back soon, and we *must* be ready. Or they more positively note that God's kingdom is being established here on Earth if we just *act now*. They don't want you to pause and ponder, they want you to engage and get swept away in the moment.

PEER PRESSURE It is common practice for evangelical crusades and healing services to designate a time for the minister to share stories of previous healings that have supposedly occurred or to invite audience members to present their personal testimonies of either a previous healing God did in their life or a testimony about something that occurred earlier during that very same meeting. Another version of this occurs when the speaker is praying over the

10 Meng Zhu et al. "The Mere Urgency Effect." *Journal of Consumer Research*, Volume 45, Issue 3, (October 2018), Pages 673–690. https://academic.oup.com/jcr/article-abstract/45/3/673/4847790.

audience and, mid-prayer, announces, "God is healing people right now, he's touching people all over this room! Wave your hand if he's healing you, if you can feel his presence." Hands will go up, and the speaker will often then say, "He's got more where that came from! Keep standing for your blessing, we're going to see more hands go up after this prayer!" He'll pray again, and miraculously, more hands will go up. Group conformity is a powerful influence, and even without consciously applied pressure or reward from others, we tend to go along with the majority.[11] Seeing hands go up has a powerful visual effect and yet offers no answers as to *what* the healing was or if anything beyond an emotion was experienced.

PERSECUTION Some ministers will seek to inspire pity as a motivating factor, especially when it comes to asking for financial donations. They'll announce they are being "persecuted" for doing God's work. And absolutely anything they dislike can qualify as that persecution: unpaid bills, a fellow minister critiquing their theology, low book sales or, in Copeland's case, criticisms about his lavish lifestyle that were piled on after his infamous *Inside Edition* interview.[12] The goal is to always create a feeling of "us versus them," whatever or whoever "them" may be. Not only can this garner more support, but it also creates an unspoken warning to remain loyal and stay on the side of "us." If you're showing up, giving and actively engaging, you're on God's side. If you aren't, you're helping the enemy. This can also help create a sense of belonging for people that are looking to find community or feel they are part of something bigger than themselves.

"SIGNS AND WONDERS" Gold dust, feathers, gemstones and spontaneous clouds—all things that have been claimed to happen as a gift from God. The gemstone claim consists of service-attendees finding what they believe to be gemstones or crystals in church pews, on the floor or sometimes even spit into their hand by the preacher. However, when these gemstones are tested by jewelers, it becomes clear they are cheap cubic zirconia or even plastic. If God is truly raining down diamonds from heaven, he's not sending his best. Gold dust appearing in the air, on people's heads or hands or in their Bibles

---

11 Solomon E. Asch. "Studies of Independence and Conformity." *Psychological Monographs: General and Applied.* Volume 70, Number 9, (October 19, 1955). https://cynlibsoc.com/clsology/pdf/independence-and-conformity.pdf.
12 "Inside Edition's Lisa Guerrero Breaks Down Her Interview With Televangelist Kenneth Copeland." *Inside Edition* (June 7, 2019). https://www.insideedition.com/inside-editions-lisa-guerrero-breaks-down-her-interview-televangelist-kenneth-copeland-53440.

is another frequent supernatural claim. As a child, I attended multiple meetings where this happened. The speaker, Ruth Ward Heflin, would shake her head and gold dust would seemingly pour out of her hair. People would find gold dust on their hands and in their Bibles. I even brought a strip of tape and collected some of the dust from the floor to keep as a token. But when tested, this gold dust proved to be nothing more than glitter. What's interesting about all of these claims, feathers and clouds included, is that none of it has ever been found to have a supernatural or unearthly source. There is zero evidence linking these occurrences to a god; instead, available evidence exposes them as scams and false claims. But people are fascinated by it. They want to see it for themselves, like a circus show, and many evangelists have made careers out of traveling around, claiming they will bring these signs and wonders to your church.

BE HEALED IN JESUS'S NAME!... EXCEPT FOR AMPUTEES

During the hundreds of hours I spent in faith healing services or even praying for others myself, I began to notice God had favorites. There were certain kinds of ailments he was more eager to heal than others. And even the ones he did heal seemed to be more of a temporary thing. It was quite common that the person would be back for more prayer for the same issue. Our church had a lot of success with healing headaches, but the double amputee in the congregation remains an amputee to this day despite the many rounds of healing prayer we put him through when he was a child. I struggled to understand how a 4-year-old just "didn't have enough faith." What seems more likely than a god that picks and chooses between illnesses is that some conditions are simply more conducive to the placebo effect than others. And some of these healings are simply illusions carefully crafted by the "healer."

CHRONIC PAIN Endorphins, dopamine and serotonin all help ease pain. These chemicals are also released by increased heart rate, listening to music and interacting with other humans: All things people experience in these faith-healing environments. Add to that the power of expectation and you have someone primed for at least a moment of reprieve from their pain. This is also something the audience can't verify; they are basing it on that person's report. There's nothing stopping that person from lying or just lying to themselves and assuming the slightest bit of pain reduction must mean they're healed.

DIGESTION ISSUES Like chronic pain, this is not a visual testimony like an amputee healing would have to be. It relies on self-reporting. Digestion issues also fluctuate over time and even throughout the day. The placebo effect can be a real relief here and makes for a great testimony.

LEG LENGTHENING While God seems to struggle with amputees, he (or rather his faith healers) seems to have a fetish for healing uneven leg lengths. There are lots of video clips of evangelical ministers like Todd White performing these "healings."[13] I remember specifically being taught this practice when I attended ministry school in my 20s. I was told that if someone needed healing for back or leg pain, it's "very common" for people to have legs of uneven length that are actually the source of this pain. Never mind what their doctors have concluded the issue to be. I was taught to sit these people down in a chair and extend their legs, holding their feet in my hands. I was then supposed to identify which leg was shorter. I was told that sometimes you have to move the legs side to side until it becomes apparent. Then, I was supposed to pray and lightly tug at the offending leg. I was told that this supernatural limb growth would start pretty quickly and I'd need to physically support the person by scooting them along with the growth. Even then, I remember thinking that this seemed to just be readjusting someone's hip position to extend or retract the legs as needed. That's because that's precisely what it was. Many people, including the illusionist Derren Brown, have made videos breaking down this scam and exposing the multiple ways it can be done, including simply adjusting the shoe on one foot to extend it farther out than the other.

EYESIGHT/HEARING The majority of blind or deaf people are not completely unable to see or hear. Many blind people can see some shapes, colors or movements. And many deaf people can hear certain frequencies. But a skilled faith healer can invite them up and say "This person is blind, let's pray for them!" After prayer, they then offer some proof that the person can see something and claim they've healed them. This can come across as a true miracle to those

---

13 whizzpopping. 2009. "Todd White - More Healing on the Streets." YouTube (August 24, 2009). https://www.youtube.com/watch?v=Ek8p3m9HdZ4.

witnessing it, as long as they don't have all of the facts about what the blind or deaf person was already capable of before being questioned.

Something we also have to acknowledge is that many healings are reported by people actively undergoing medical treatment. But crediting doctors, while having also prayed to God for healing, now puts the person in the position of discrediting God. A common response is "God used the doctors to heal me," which I find to be incredibly insulting to the time, skill, education and hard work of the doctors. While so many of these reported healings can easily be exposed as the work of doctors, scams or placebos, science doesn't deny spontaneous healings and remissions. Unexplained recoveries can absolutely happen. But the important thing to note is that they are unexplained and none of the research into the cause of these recoveries has suggested a god was involved. And these spontaneous healings occur in all sorts of environments outside of religious meetings or prayer. There are plenty of medical mysteries, but they are called "mysteries" for a reason. What I find most fascinating is that there are no verified healings of amputees. A faith healer laying hands on someone who reports a diminished headache is not much to write home about, but a faith healer laying hands on someone missing an entire limb with an audience watching it grow back would be quite another. But something tells me we won't be witnessing that anytime soon.

COMMON ARGUMENTS YOU'LL HEAR

"His ways are higher than ours, so sometimes we don't understand why he doesn't heal."

Yet another example of God always getting a free pass and being completely unaccountable. Despite his claims that he is the "Lord who heals you" (Exodus 15:26), if he doesn't heal someone, that's just his way and we must submit. What "higher" reason could there be for allowing a child to suffer from bone cancer? And "higher" according to what standard? Certainly not one that benefits the person suffering. If we don't blame God when he doesn't heal, instead attributing it to his mysterious ways, why do we credit him when someone recovers and praise him like he *did* something rather than consistently labeling it his "mysterious ways"? This sort of universe, where God heals at the rate of chance, is completely indistinguishable from a universe without a god at all.

"I know God heals because he healed me!"

This is similar to the argument about personal prayers being answered in the previous chapter. It is quite incredible to believe that God chose to heal you while more than 100,000 children die of cancer every year. What about the person who was healed by a witchcraft ritual? Or the person healed after praying to a Hindu god? Is that evidence that their beliefs are true? Or is it possible that placebo, confirmation bias and other things are at play? To believe God healed you at all is already an extraordinary claim, especially if there are other likely causes for whatever you experienced. The cause may even be unknown. But to claim that your experience of a god amounts to knowledge of this god's character is one of the more arrogant assertions I can think of.

"God didn't heal them because they didn't have faith."

Why does this god have so many terms and conditions around his self-proclaimed identity as a "healer"? From my anecdotal experience, I can think of many times that I was experiencing illness or pain and believed so wholeheartedly that God would heal me that I was shocked when he didn't. I certainly *felt* as though I had faith. I watched my grandfather, the most faith-filled person I knew, slowly wither and die from Parkinson's. Bill Johnson, the pastor of Bethel church and the Bethel School of Supernatural Ministry, which I attended, centers his theology around the idea that God absolutely does heal people and his ministry school claims to "equip" students to practice these spiritual gifts.[14] And yet, his own son is deaf and his wife passed away from cancer. Did they just not have enough faith? This argument is really just blame-shifting. Once again, there is no accountability for God. It's never his fault, always his credit and *you* are the weak link.

FRAUDS EXPOSED

The evangelical movement is not a monolith. Instead, it is a patchwork of varying denominations and networks, connected so loosely that connection can often be denied altogether. This is a feature, not a bug. This multi-headed monster is able to function like a powerful force as needed, but if you take down one head, the rest maintain plausible deniability and can continue on unscathed. There is no system of accountability, no agreed-upon ethics.

---

14 "About BSSM." https://www.bethel.com/ministries/bethel-school-of-supernatural-ministry.

Because of this, evangelicalism is rampant with fraud, abuse and scandal. The most you'll get when these acts are exposed is a statement from a ministry condemning them while maintaining that this was some individual's fall from grace and not representative of God or Christian leaders. More often, you have peers calling for forgiveness and rehabilitation, claiming someone's godly gifts shouldn't be wasted just because they made a mistake. These "mistakes" are quite prevalent, though. Jim Bakker was a famous televangelist who was accused of sexual assault and then sentenced to 45 years in prison for fraud, which was later reduced to eight years.[15] He got out after less than five years and resumed his ministry work. Faith healer Peter Popoff went bankrupt after infamously being exposed for using a wired listening device operated in tandem with his wife to feign God-sourced knowledge, only to revamp his ministry years later by selling "miracle spring water."[16] Jimmy Swaggart[17] and Ted Haggard[18] both confessed to sex scandals involving prostitutes. Earl Paulk[19] and Mike Bickle[20] were both accused of sexual assault involving minors. Robert Morris, a megachurch pastor who served on an advisory board for President Trump, pled guilty to five counts of lewd or indecent acts with a child.[21] Unfortunately, these are just a few of the known scandals, and no doubt there are countless more still hidden. I personally know of two popular "prophets" under investigation for both "sexual sin" (which usually refers to gay people) and falsifying prophecies. One of them was exposed by his own children for finding personal information about audience members on Google and Facebook and claiming God gave him the information. The same hoax allegations have been made against the other prophet as well. Growing up as the daughter of an evangelical leader, I was privy to many whispers and rumors of affairs, drug use, "sexual sin" and other scandals. It seemed systemic, yet the issue was never treated as such.

---

15 Lauren Effron et al. "The scandals that brought down the Bakkers, once among US's most famous televangelists." ABC News (December 20, 2019). https://abcnews.go.com/US/scandals-brought-bakkers-uss-famous-televangelists/story?id=60389342.
16 John Dart. "Evangelist Popoff Off Air, Files Bankruptcy Petitions." *Los Angeles Times* (September 26, 1987). https://www.latimes.com/archives/la-xpm-1987-09-26-me-2461-story.html.
17 BBC News On This Day (February 28, 1988). http://news.bbc.co.uk/onthisday/hi/dates/stories/february/21/newsid_2565000/2565197.stm.
18 " Evangelical confesses to 'sexual immorality' in letter." CNN (November 6, 2006). https://www.cnn.com/2006/US/11/05/haggard.allegations/index.html.
19 "Granddaughter accuses megachurch leader of sexual abuse." Law.com (December 18, 2007). https://www.law.com/article/almID/1202552298860/?slreturn=20250922060431.
20 "Grieving Together." International House of Prayer (January 17, 2025). https://ihopkc.org/press-releases/press-center/press-releases/grieving-together.
21 Robert Downen. "Robert Morris, former Texas megachurch pastor and Trump adviser, indicted for child sex crimes." *The Texas Tribune* (March 12, 2015). https://www.texastribune.org/2025/03/12/robert-morris-texas-megachurch-indicted-sexual-abuse/.

"TOUCH NOT THINE ANOINTED!"

Aside from some of the more extreme cases that make headlines, most of these men and women are almost untouchable when it comes to scandal. Sure, they have scandals, but their most devoted fans ignore things like Osteen's initial mishandling of the Hurricane Harvey crisis[22] or White and Hinn's alleged affair.[23] Psalm 105:15, "touch not thine anointed," is often quoted as an excuse to gloss over unethical behavior amongst God's supposed servants. Many of us were taught that to question someone God has chosen is no better than questioning God himself. If we were to raise doubts about the integrity or ethics of their actions, we were aligning ourselves with the enemy and were being used to persecute the church. These scandals are also largely considered to be "internal issues," even when it is clear criminal behavior is at play and law enforcement should be involved. The "us versus them" mentality is so heavy that churches would rather do anything to hide their scandal than have to submit investigations to an outside authority. Victim-blaming is a tool often implemented in the case of sexual scandal. In any case of an affair with a woman, the easy thing to do is claim she is being used by the devil to distract God's leaders. It's not the man's fault, it's the devil and the woman. Many times, the doctrine of forgiveness is used to shield the perpetrator from accountability, claiming that they have repented, had a change of heart and been forgiven by God. After all, you can't question what God has forgiven.

PROPHETS FOR PROFIT

A wave of self-proclaimed prophets started gaining popularity amongst charismatic evangelicals in 2016 during Trump's run for the presidency. While riding the coattails of conspiracies like QAnon or the "Big Lie" Trump spouted about the 2020 elections, evangelicals such as Lance Wallnau and Kat Kerr saw the size of their audiences grow larger and larger. They tend to focus on political and social issues, capitalizing on polarizing issues that evoke tribalism. Their "prophecies" are mostly just vague predictions of

22 Tom Dart. "Why did America's biggest megachurch take so long to shelter Harvey victims?" *The Guardian* (August 30, 2017). https://www.theguardian.com/us-news/2017/aug/30/lakewood-church-joel-osteen-hurricane-harvey.
23 Cary McMullen. "Benny Hinn Sued for 'Inappropriate Relationship' with Paula White." *The Ledger* (February 18, 2011). https://www.theledger.com/story/news/2011/02/18/benny-hinn-sued-for-inappropriate-relationship-with-paula-white/26416486007/.

storms, or wars or metaphors so ambiguous that virtually any outcome could be implied. The more specific they are, the easier it becomes to expose them as likely charlatans. Greg Locke, Dutch Sheets, Kat Kerr, Jeremiah Johnson, Shawn Bolz, Kris Vallotton and others all prophesied that Trump would win the election in 2020. When the results proved otherwise, many doubled down[24] and, throughout 2021, after Biden's inauguration, continued to say Trump had won and would be reinstated that year.[25] This persistent narrative, while completely false, not only didn't end their ministries but strengthened them by aligning themselves fully with conspiracy theories and political extremism. Combining the already prevalent prosperity gospel teachings with the emotionally provocative and highly engaging topics of politics and social issues, these "prophets" have found an extremely lucrative outlet for their books, television and web shows and speaking engagements. Not only that, but they also gain power and popularity from their appearances at White House events, where they are pictured praying over President Trump. This parasitic relationship has created an entirely new evangelical monster that we have yet to see the full effects of. If nothing else, I hope the skepticism I encourage throughout this book is applied to this most perverted creature that attempts to use dogma as a mechanism to influence elections, encourage bigotry and sow distrust amongst fellow humans.

---

24 Julia Duin. "For Christian Prophets Who Predicted Donald Trump's Reinstatement in 2021, No Apologies." *Newsweek* (January 4, 2022). https://www.newsweek.com/for-christian-prophets-who-predicted-donald-trumps-reinstatement-2021-no-apologies-1665157.
25 Julia Duin. "The Christian Prophets Who Say Trump Is Coming Again." *Politico* (February 28, 2021). https://www.politico.com/news/magazine/2021/02/18/how-christian-prophets-give-credence-to-trumps-election-fantasies-469598.

CHAPTER 6

Divine Pain

"You may not control all of the events that happen to you, but you can decide not to be reduced by them." —MAYA ANGELOU

I WOULD LIKE TO PREFACE this chapter before we continue: If you fall into the category of someone who has experienced religious trauma, it is my hope that our examination of the following subject matter does not cause you to feel the pain of old wounds reopened. Rather, I hope it makes you feel validated and supported on your journey. Perhaps it will help empower you to put more words to what you have survived and feel less alone in what you have experienced.

If you fall into the category of someone who wasn't raised in a religious household or never experienced the negative impact it can have, it's my hope that your exposure to this information will inspire empathy and allyship toward those of us who have. While you may not have firsthand experience of these issues, at some point in your life, you will most likely come across someone who has, and maybe some of what you learn here will help strengthen that relationship.

If you fall into the category of someone who isn't really sure if you've been negatively impacted by religion and then find yourself relating to some of what you read here, I hope you feel motivated to explore more avenues of personal healing and growth. I am not a mental health expert, nor is any of this meant to diagnose a condition or provide instruction. It's meant to attest to the very real harm so many have experienced and will continue to experience as long as the fear-based, anti-science theologies and practices subscribed to by evangelicalism are allowed to continue. Religion does not exist in a vacuum, nor do its practitioners. The more popularized and socially acceptable a religion is, the more influence it has on culture. To ignore its impact, especially its negative side, is irresponsible at best and complicit with abuse at worst. My personal experiences do not even begin to scratch the surface of what some others have faced, but I hope by sharing what follows, I can expose how even some of the seemingly benign practices of evangelicalism can result in a lifetime of recovery and recalibration.

Talking about the technicalities of religious trauma and negative impacts of religion is one thing, but expressing the deeply personal ways this can take shape is like trying to plot red strings on a corkboard to map out a conspiracy theory or account for each wound that led to death by a thousand cuts. How do you explain to someone that what seemed "normal" in the moment was simply one red flag of hundreds revealing a culture that promised protection but instead consistently harmed you? How do you explain that the foundation of all your hopes, morals, comfort, safety and existence was the same thing that caused you the most damage? I did not realize the harm religion had caused me until I had already left it behind. I thought I had simply become intellectually honest: I had acknowledged my disbelief and was now moving on in life. Much of my life had been tied to religion—my family, community, work, creative outlets and more. What I didn't know yet was how many of my personal struggles over the years had been caused by or exacerbated by it. I thought I was one of the lucky ones who had made it out unscathed. It turns out that injuries inflicted by religious trauma aren't always so obvious. I still find myself discovering new ways my old religion altered my thinking or behavior in ways that make life more difficult for me than for someone who didn't experience those things. That said, I do not consider myself to be a helpless victim. I consider myself an aware survivor, brave enough to move forward in life and cognizant of the impact of past experiences on my present life. One of evangelicalism's most insidious aspects is how much harm it causes without leaving an obvious mark on the victim. Somehow, it avoids any responsibility for the damage it causes. And its adherents, who refuse to acknowledge its harmful nature, enable it to thrive and, in fact, allow its victims to simply blame themselves for any injuries they suffer.

It wasn't until after I left Christianity that I was able to start identifying the damage that had already begun to rear its ugly head. My symptoms began to manifest most forcefully in my early 20s, when I was still deeply religious. I was heavily involved with a local Bible study. I had a fulfilling job as a nanny, which I loved. I regularly attended church and enjoyed community with fellow believers. Suddenly, however, I found myself experiencing random physical sensations that would spiral into what I now know were panic attacks. Heart palpitations, powerful headaches, abdominal pain—every week, it seemed to be some new thing that had me convinced I was dying or close to it. Sometimes my anxiety over these symptoms got so intense that I would go to the ER, convinced something was physically wrong with me. A headache must be a brain tumor. Shortness of breath must be an oncoming heart attack. Stomach pains must be invasive cancer. I came to believe that any ailment was inevitably going to result in a worst-case scenario diagnosis. At the root of all of these concerns was an overwhelming fear of death. It never even occurred to me that these problems could be due to a mental health issue.

Over the course of a year, I had CT scans, x-rays, blood tests and ultrasounds just to reveal that I was fine. Finally, a doctor sat down with me and said, "I work with very, very sick people every day. You are very, very healthy. But you're experiencing something I commonly see in people your age: anxiety." I had never heard the term used in this context before, as something someone could *have*. Growing up, anxiety was just another thing on the list of weapons Satan could use against us. I didn't have anxiety; that wasn't possible. I loved Jesus, I followed his commands and I was doing everything I could to live a life that was pleasing to him.

Desperate for answers and solutions, I turned to my parents and other religious leaders in my life. The only answer they provided was a theological one: This must be spiritual warfare, and I should fight back. I was encouraged to spend more time in my prayer closet and read the Bible out loud. Whenever a trigger (chest pain, shortness of breath or other physical sensation) manifested, I was supposed to immediately become a prayer warrior and engage in spiritual battle with whatever demonic forces were at play. I found myself spending hours locked in a dark, tiny room, rocking back and forth, weeping and begging God to intervene and take away whatever this heavy feeling was. My voice was hoarse from repetitively reading aloud scriptures about God's peace. Some nights, I didn't sleep at all and could only lie there frozen with fear whispering "Jesus, Jesus" over and over again, as though it were a magic spell that would protect me from whatever this torment was. It didn't.

If this behavior sounds unwell, it's because it was. I was not okay. What I believed to be the devil attacking my mind were actually intrusive thoughts. What I believed were helpful prayer rituals were simply compulsions that further fueled my anxiety. What I believed was necessary repentance and confession to God for even the smallest negative thought or behavior was "reassurance thinking." My avoidance of "secular" music, TV or even friendship was not holiness; it was fear of spiritual contamination. All these things are common symptoms of something called scrupulosity—religious OCD. I didn't need prayer; I needed a therapist. I didn't need rituals; I needed to get outside and enjoy doing something just for the fun of it. I didn't need ancient religious writings; I needed books written by experts about self-growth and mental health. My religion was not only harming me, it was actively preventing me from getting the appropriate help.

This scrupulosity didn't just come out of nowhere. I was raised with it and practically taught to embrace it. Fear of eternal damnation acted as an incredible anchor to anxiety and fear. As a child, I was obsessively concerned that I might fall away from Jesus and find myself condemned. I also ruminated over thoughts of my loved ones being sentenced to hell and kept a journal with a list of their names so I could pray for their salvation and security in heaven. I felt it was my personal responsibility to intercede on their behalf and I was terrified that they could fall away someday. I was so young that I had barely learned how to write out their names, and yet already felt the weight of responsibility surrounding the eternal lives of my family members. I also had obsessive thoughts about sin and was hypervigilant about my own thinking, attempting to ward off even the slightest idea that could offend God. He was always listening, after all (Jeremiah 17:10). To ensure I never forgot, I wore a little bracelet featuring beads of different colors that told the message of salvation. There was a yellow bead to symbolize heaven and the streets of gold we would someday walk on (Revelation 21:21). A green one represented the spiritual growth we could experience if we followed Christ's teachings (2 Peter 3:18). A white one resembled snow—a symbol of our purity when cleansed by God (Psalm 51:7). A red one stood for the blood that was required to cleanse us (1 John 1:7). But the bracelet story began with a black bead, the color of my heart when poisoned with sin—sin

I was born with (Romans 3:23). Or so I was told.

I was constantly thinking about this dark soul of mine. I was so embarrassed and ashamed to know that I was sinful by nature. As a people pleaser, I wanted to be good and do right. I wanted those qualities to be part of who I was at my core, yet I was consistently reminded that the opposite was true: I was born bad and was worthless without God's sacrifice on my behalf. I was also deeply aware that while I had accepted this "cleansing," many had not and were tainted by sin. I was always afraid of being influenced or deceived by the devil through nonbelievers or even just lukewarm followers. A friend would play a song I wasn't allowed to listen to, and I immediately felt that God was disappointed in me or worse. When my female cousins wore shorts that I would never be allowed to wear, I judged them and felt self-righteous for my superior modesty. We were 10 years old. On Halloween, my parents turned off our lights, locked the doors and we watched movies in the basement to avoid trick-or-treaters. I remember feeling an intense guilt over my secret desire to wear a costume and participate in what I was taught to be an evil holiday. The us versus them thinking was in full effect, but my inability to consistently stay loyal to the "us" side caused chronic shame. The fear, guilt and anxiety drove me to ask God to remove the bad feelings and help me "be better." When the prayers didn't work, my anxiety would deepen and I would repeat the cycle. I accepted that this must be spiritual warfare and streamlined my compulsions into manageable, automated rituals. I had exact prayers for safety, for health concerns, for nightmares, for judgmental thoughts and for eating meals. These rituals absolutely consumed me, and it was only years after leaving religion that I became aware of how abnormal and exhausting it all was. Therapy, self-growth and the love and support of the people in my life now have made all the difference, but these ill-effects stole so many moments of peace and joy from my past. I would not wish the mental battles I experienced on anyone.

The idea that so many children are still subjected to the teachings that turned my own mind against me provides a powerful source of motivation to continue speaking out against indoctrination.

A SAMPLING OF SYMPTOMS

COMPULSIVE BEHAVIORS Compulsions are not acts that a person genuinely wants to participate in. These urges are nearly impossible to stop and are usually an attempt to soothe some sort of distress. In regard to religion, these compulsions can appear benign on the surface, but it's the unseen mental battle that negatively impacts one's mental health. Repetitive prayers can be a big one. I remember as a child feeling that I *must* pray for safe travels for my parents exactly as their plane took off every time they flew, or else they might crash. Ritualistic reading of Bible verses or religious devotionals and repetitively reciting scripture aloud can also be a compulsion. Reassurance-seeking through confession and asking for forgiveness can be a big one for some, leading them to divulge even the smallest "sinful" behaviors or thoughts to spiritual leaders or to God in prayer. I was taught that these fear-fueled compulsions were "conviction" from the Holy Spirit: supernatural feelings to guide my mind and actions to best serve Christ. The problem is that these compulsory behaviors were not serving my life well; they were anxiety-driven and sending me into cycles of shame and mental exhaustion. These sorts of urges can live on long after leaving religion, and your brain can keep taking you down paths of obsessive prayers to a god you don't even believe in. This can lead to another cycle, where one ruminates over the fear that "maybe these desires mean there really is a god and that's why I can't stop praying" or "maybe I still secretly believe and I'm just not being honest with myself." In everyday life these compulsions can look like prayers, as well as oversharing (as a form of confession), reassurance-seeking, obsessive checking or researching or extreme avoidance.

BLACK AND WHITE THINKING In evangelicalism, things either come from God or they're *bad* (Deuteronomy 30:19). There is no gray area. It's holy, or it's sin. You're saved, or condemned (John 3:18). Living for Jesus, or living for "the world." If you're not obedient to God, you're rebelling against him. Revelation 3:15-16 even goes as far as to say it is better to be cold or hot than to be lukewarm. This sort of thinking makes even the smallest things feel high stakes. You're not just entertaining a question about the Bible; you're entertaining rebellious thoughts. You didn't just worry about paying the bills this week; you doubted God's goodness. You're not just aiming to make decent choices in life; you're looking to make *the* choice that God wants. The pressure to do the "right" thing is immense, and this idea that picking anything else is the "wrong" thing can continue long after leaving religion. In everyday life, this can look like unnecessary moralization, conspiratorial thinking, addiction to certainty and intense highs and lows in self-esteem.

PERFECTIONISM In line with black and white thinking, perfectionism is one of the many idols of evangelicalism. It's not just an acceptable goal (which is already toxic) but it is *the* goal. To be a Christian is to be one who attempts to be Christlike, and to be Christlike is to be perfect. This absurd goal, based on a standard that does not even exist, creates a breeding ground for scrupulosity and shame. The standard can never be reached despite attempts to police your own thoughts, and thus the cycle continues into shame and more failed attempts at perfection. In everyday life, this attachment of self-worth to performance can lead to overthinking or obsessive thoughts, avoidance (because why do something at all if you know it won't be perfect), oversensitivity to criticism, inability to accept or ask for help, need for validation and, ultimately, burnout.

ANXIETY, PANIC ATTACKS AND SLEEP DISORDERS When your entire worldview includes ideas of eternal hellfire, standards of perfection, being born sinful, spiritual warfare, demons and ridiculous moral expectations, all while rejecting many healthy life skills and tools such as therapy and self-care, it's no wonder dysregulation often occurs. Chronic fear left untreated will absolutely result in these undesired outcomes. In everyday life, this can result in constant feelings of uneasiness or dread for no obvious reason, episodes of intense fear alongside shortness of breath and chest pain and constant nightmares or sleeplessness.

HOLY HARM At the heart of all religious trauma is that it is attached in some way to religion. A study on this topic found that "when religion is involved in the trauma itself maladjustment outcomes may be more severe, and recovery may be more complex."[1] Experiencing trauma is already known to cause varying stress responses that can appear as anxiety, panic attacks, sleep disorders and PTSD, but when you compound this with someone's faith, it creates a much more complex situation. Often, your faith is a core part of your identity. It is also the source of your community and has jurisdiction over every area of your life. Discovering that something so pervasive and "good" is actually harmful is like having the blood in your veins turn to poison. Everything is tainted. To make matters worse, many indoctrinated people have been discouraged from using helpful tools like boundaries, critical thinking and

1 Hannah Doctor. "Religion-Justified Childhood Maltreatment And Adult Psychological Maladjustment." UND Scholarly Commons (January 2023). https://commons.und.edu/cgi/viewcontent.cgi?article=6229&context=theses.

positive self-esteem, which allows the trauma associated with evangelicalism to take even deeper root. It's almost as if it's not just trauma you experience, but an assault by God himself. It is a betrayal of the deepest kind to commit yourself to something wholeheartedly and believe it is the "right thing" and then experience pain or damage because of it. Ultimately, my religious trauma manifested as OCD, perfectionism, anxiety, panic attacks and hypervigilance, but it can come in many forms and occur through different means for different people.

The pain that evangelicalism causes exists on a wide spectrum of experiences. Exorcisms, or casting out of demons, can be extremely disturbing for both the person they're centered around and even those observing the act. I remember being witness to many of these rituals as a child and it appeared to be humiliating and even violent in many ways. Those who are deemed "possessed"—sometimes as a result of having a mental illness—are made to feel as though they are literally hosting something evil within them. This can be psychologically damaging and offers zero effective support or treatment to the person.

Conversion therapy is another traumatizing practice within evangelicalism. Despite including the term "therapy," these are anti-science, religious methods that attempt to "convert" a queer person's orientation or identity. This is obviously harmful, and we'll talk more about it in the next chapter. Diet culture is prevalent in evangelical culture for many reasons as well. The idea that "your body is a temple" (1 Corinthians 6:19) is often cited as a reason to monitor your food and weight, and fasting is seen as a spiritual ritual that can bring you closer to God or allow you to hear from him more clearly. Women are also expected to be physically appealing to their husbands and fit a conventional standard of beauty. I remember being told in a pre-marriage counseling session that it was my duty to lose no more than 10 percent of my original level of beauty per child I gave birth to. Men are expected to appear hyper-masculine, and physical strength is part of that expectation. All of this can easily lead to eating disorders and dysphoria. Financial abuse is another wound evangelicalism can inflict. Many churches encourage tithing of 10 percent or more and shame those who do not comply, regardless of the person's financial situation. Pastors who preach "prosperity" tell their congregations that God will bless them according to how much they give, encouraging generous donations with the uninsured promise that they'll receive even more in the form of healing or even material gain. The evangelical obsession with gender roles often forces men into the role of financial provider and women into a position of financial dependent, making it difficult to leave abusive relationships. There is also abuse committed by clergy members, including sexual abuse. Psychological abuse using shame or emotional manipulation can occur, particularly when the abuser uses private information gained through confession or religious counseling. Spiritual abuse is perpetuated by clergy when they use religious teachings to justify abuse or control choices and behaviors of their congregation. Sometimes, evangelical leaders demonstrate narcissistic behaviors, believing themselves to be above accountability and worthy of special admiration and loyalty due to their closer position to God. They often use this grandiose persona to gain unquestioned allegiance, which often results in yet more abuse. These examples barely scratch the surface of the types of harm that evangelicalism can cause, and there is still so much research to be done and data to collect on exactly how detrimental these theologies are, not only to the individual but to society as a whole. Christianity hides behind the idea that it is untouchable and irreproachable, too holy for mere mortals to criticize. But anything worth devoting your entire life to is worth scrutinizing intensely, and when toxicity is revealed, it should be shouted from the rooftops as a warning to all who may come across it.

COMMON ARGUMENTS YOU'LL HEAR

"God didn't hurt you, people did!"

As an atheist, of course I agree with this. I don't believe any gods exist, much less caused me or anyone else harm. But this common response to religious trauma is an attempt to dismiss any accountability on the part of the religion itself. Instead of recognizing the role religion played in the harm someone experienced, many Christians would rather let their god-belief completely off the hook. The problem is that it is very relevant whether harm is attached to religion or god-claims, as the mere association of trauma with religion can result in a more complex and distressing outcome. To ignore the religious-based abuses committed by clergy, spiritual "authorities" or even rank and file practitioners of Christianity is to ignore a key part of the harm caused. Sure, God didn't hurt anyone—but those acting on his behalf and using teachings credited to him did.

"You're just bitter!"

It's not the word "bitter" that I have a problem with here; it's the word "just." People are allowed to feel their pain. Animosity toward something that harmed you is a natural—even healthy—response. While it can be helpful to heal and move past this anger, it is not necessary for one's criticisms to be considered valid. You don't have to forgive an abusive spouse before you move out of an unsafe home. You don't have to view an unfair boss through rose-colored glasses before quitting and finding a better job. You don't have to make peace with harm caused to you by a religion, a clergy member or a god-belief before you are allowed to distance yourself from it and critique it. You can be justified, reasonable, correct in your assessments and (not *just*) bitter. Anger toward people, institutions or beliefs that harmed us can be a tool to protect ourselves from being victimized again and motivate us to help prevent others from having similar experiences. To be human is to experience emotions, and separating ourselves from these feelings only serves to dull our testimonies, not bolster them. While feelings don't supersede facts, they can certainly coexist.

"You were weak and failed God's test."/ "God tests the ones he loves."

Why is an omniscient god issuing a test? If you know the outcome of something, you don't need to test for it. If an all-knowing god causes or allows a negative experience, he is inflicting harm, not issuing a test. God doesn't need to learn anything, and in fact these "tests" are often argued as being for *our* sakes, not God's. It would be more honest to say, "God inflicts suffering on the ones he loves to teach them a lesson," which sounds an awful lot like, "He only hits me because he loves me." When humans inflict harm on someone or something, we call it abuse, but when it's believed to come from God, Christians treat it as something holy. While this sort of belief can be used to justify all sorts of things followers may experience while still within the fold, it is often used to discredit those who have left and chosen to speak out about the harm they experienced. It serves as a way to both invalidate dissenters *and* act as a warning for current believers who are considering doing the same. The message is: If you speak up, we're just going to put the blame back on you.

"Don't throw the baby out with the bathwater."

Often, survivors of religious harm who no longer believe or practice a religion are told this as though they should "keep the good parts." But this assumes that there is a "baby" in the bathwater—something exclusively and intrinsically good about the religion. It undermines the individual's ability to determine for themselves what is and isn't a "good part." And in this case, the claimed "baby" *is* the harmful part that absolutely should be thrown out. When the core doctrines and beliefs of a religion perpetuate shame and fear, the whole thing deserves to be done away with. Anything positive found within religion can be reclaimed elsewhere without the toxic "baby." Victims do not owe systems their loyalty and deserve support in abandoning that which caused them suffering.

"That was false Christianity. True Christianity would never harm you."
There is no such thing as "true" or "false" Christianity. Christianity is completely subjective, as is demonstrated by the 45,000+ denominations it includes. Saying this is just moving the goalposts to protect the reputation of Christianity. But long-term, this has the opposite effect, because instead of identifying what is truly causing harm, the issue is simply waved away. Some of the most common beliefs held by Christians, such as eternal damnation, original sin and purity culture, are also some of the most damaging. Evangelicalism doesn't simply allow harm; it often calls for it. By dismissing religious trauma as "false" Christianity, the root issue is never addressed and abusers and abusive rhetoric remain in place. The Bible has been used for thousands of years to control, manipulate and abuse. This cannot be ignored.

TRAIN UP A CHILD

While evangelicals are known for their claims of being "pro-life" and caring about children, their actions often demonstrate otherwise. Spanking, or "corporal punishment," remains one of the most socially acceptable forms of abuse in the United States, with 50 percent of children 20 months or younger having experienced it,[2] and it's heavily encouraged, justified and normalized by many evangelical groups. Many of the stories I've heard from individuals who have left evangelicalism included trauma from physical punishment, so it's no surprise that a study from the 1990s found "adherence to Christian fundamentalism" to be "a significant predictor of reported use of corporal

---

2 Michael J. MacKenzie et al. "Who spanks infants and toddlers? Evidence from the fragile families and child well-being study." Children and Youth Services Review Volume 33, Issue 8 (August 2011). https://doi.org/10.1016/j.childyouth.2011.04.007.

punishment."[3] The book *To Train Up a Child* by Michael and Debi Pearl was very influential on evangelical parenting in the '90s, with IBLP (a large nondenominational organization) even endorsing it. Along with completely ignoring all the science on children's needs for healthy attachment, it encouraged physical violence against them, recommending exact ways to inflict pain and what materials or force to use at different times. James Dobson, a famous evangelical psychologist and founder of Focus on the Family, authored the popular book *The Strong-Willed Child*, which recommended corporal punishment and compared it to beating a dog. Many families I grew up around had designated belts, paint stirrers, branches and other "spanking" devices. In our family, we had a wooden spoon or spatula for when a hand didn't suffice. Another common way to use pain or discomfort as discipline was soap, hot sauce or vinegar applied to the tongue. This was especially used as punishment for speaking words that were not permitted.

Scriptures like Proverbs 23:13-14 are commonly used to defend this violent practice: "Do not withhold discipline from a child; if you punish them with the rod, they will not die. Punish them with the rod and save them from death." Many Christians interpret this as not only permission to hit their children, but a command that must be followed to save them from "death"—eternal torment in hell. The belief is that if you do not properly discipline your children, they will fall away from God and turn to sin instead. But the implication of a creator god that views physical pain against children to be an appropriate teaching mechanism is that this god designed them to be taught this way. It implies that an all-powerful, all-loving god decided to create children with brains that are improved upon when their caretakers inflict violence on them. Fortunately, we know this is not true at all. The research is clear that physical punishment "increases the risk of broad and enduring negative developmental outcomes,"[4] and no studies have supported the idea that it provides any positive impact on development. To follow religious teachings about corporal punishment is to directly disregard a child's well-being and everything we know about brain development and the effect of violence on children. At the root of these abusive teachings is the idea that obedience is the most important thing. The goal of this sort of Christian par-

---

3 James Francis Ross. "Christian fundamentalism and the reported use of corporal punishment." (Master's thesis, Iowa State University, 1994) https://behost.lib.iastate.edu/DR/Ross_ISU-1994-R733.pdf.

4 Joan Durrant and Ron Ensom. "Physical punishment of children: lessons from 20 years of research." Canadian Medical Association Journal (September 4, 2012). https://pmc.ncbi.nlm.nih.gov/articles/PMC3447048/

enting isn't to raise well-adjusted, happy and healthy beings who know how to think for themselves but rather to "train up a child in the way he should go" (Proverbs 22:6)—most often interpreted as obedience to God and parents and practiced as indoctrination. The same people practicing a religion that spouts "free will" as a value are the ones motivated to raise obedient robots. Instead of recognizing children as new humans that need help and guidance to learn the ropes of existence, these teachings view them as less-than and a liability that must be disciplined into submission. Interestingly enough, this abuse and its effect on the recipient is a perfect example of what evangelicalism as a whole does to its participants: Fear is the primary mechanism of control ("obey your parents or get hit," "obey God or go to hell"). Bodily autonomy is withheld, power dynamics are used to justify control and we are taught that love and violence have crossover—*I only hit you because I love you.* When a religion is centered around a god that orchestrated the violent blood sacrifice of his own son, it's no wonder cycles of abuse occur within the families that practice it.

WHEN RELIGION IS A THIEF

When I was 5, my favorite toy was a colorful cassette player with an attached microphone. I would blast *The Little Mermaid*, *Annie*, *Pocahontas* and *The Sound of Music* all over the house, singing along at the top of my lungs. Singing felt like switching my brain over to the most relaxed, joyful part of myself. Fear, worry and responsibility all seemed to float away. This obvious love of mine was quickly recognized by my parents and I was put into professional voice lessons. Suddenly, my private hobby was turned into my "calling." I was told that Jesus gave me my voice and that I should use it to honor and worship him. That meant singing lots of solos at church and lots of warnings against treating singing as a form of self-expression. It was supposed to be an offering to God, not something for myself. Suddenly, this "gift" that once gave me delight and escape became a burden. I suffered from severe stage fright, and when combined with the pressure of knowing this was "for God," it sometimes felt unbearable. But I still loved singing and music, and I was convinced that it was my duty to demonstrate my appreciation for it by using it for God's glory only. I sang in every Christmas play, performed solos at homeschool events and even won a local Christian radio station singing competition. In my early teen years, I was trained in worship leading and, along with singing at our local church, would also lead worship on mission trips and speaking events when my dad was preaching or speaking at a conference. I was heavily praised for participating in these ways. My parents were clearly proud of me and my "calling" and I was more and more relieved to have an activity at church that helped get me through the endlessly boring meetings I found myself attending as the pastor's daughter. As an oldest child who was expected to be mature for my age, I also enjoyed getting time with adults on the worship team and being invited to "hangs" with the band members. Some of them even expressed interest in working on music with me outside of church and the attention was thrilling. I loved feeling that I was participating in something important and that others thought I was good at it. Most importantly, I was delighted at the idea that I was pleasing God by fulfilling my calling and using the gift he gave me.

There was a darker side to this as well. Along with the stage fright, there was the off-stage fright of living up to the expectations that were put on me. I was taught that my visible position required me to be held to a higher standard than my peers. If I was going to demonstrate what it looks like to worship God on a platform, I must resemble that in the rest of my life as well. Along with the cool adult friendships came adult drama. As a teenager, I faced weird jealousy and competition from much older people who wanted my position. In hindsight, many of those friendships were incredibly inappropriate for someone my age to have. Over the years, starting from my first voice lessons, I also felt that I didn't get to choose music. It was chosen for me not just by my parents, but by God. I had the ability to sing; therefore, it must be what God wanted to use me to do. This gift very often felt like a burden. I couldn't just enjoy singing as a hobby; I had to "steward" well over it (1 Peter 4:10). This burdensome feeling only increased over the years, and by the time I found myself as a worship leader at a very large school of ministry, I was experiencing panic attacks before my sets would begin. These were called "attacks from the enemy" but were really just warranted reactions to the stress and anxiety I was under. I was also witness to extreme hypocrisy and spiritual abuse by worship pastors. The leaders telling me to pray away my stage fright were popping benzos before taking the stage Sunday morning and others were using their positions of authority to manipulate and control those under them.

That same year that I began doubting my beliefs and ultimately walking away from religion altogether, I found myself completely jaded about participating in music. Singing felt forced and meaningless, and I never wanted to be on stage again after being gaslit into thinking I was "worshiping" instead of what it really was: performing. For years, I had to grieve this loss. Something that was a big part of my life, that at times brought so much release and joy, was completely tainted. This loss of artistic expression is a common story I hear from fellow ex-evangelicals. Some lose the motivation or inspiration to paint, write, dance or play an instrument. Talents and skills that could have just been recognized for what they were instead are required to be used to serve the Lord. For some, this leaves them feeling lost when it comes to using their creativity outside of religion. They experience residual feelings of guilt from being taught that their "gifts" are for God, not personal pleasure. Creative expression is often so personal and linked with self-worth or identity, and the loss of it as an outlet can be devastating. It took me years of grieving this loss before it finally came back into my life due to the support of my partner. I finally allowed myself to make music simply because I found joy in doing so. Not everyone is lucky enough to reclaim their passions, however, and I would speculate that religion has deprived us of many creative voices.

HOW TO HEAL

There is no one-size-fits-all or instant cure when it comes to complex trauma. I don't believe that being negatively impacted by religion makes you broken or damaged goods, either. If anything, it's a sign that your brain did what it could to cope with what it was subjected to. That doesn't make the results any less frustrating or undesired. The good news is that there are so many tools for improving your quality of life and not feeling held back or like a victim of your own mind. Here are a few:

PROFESSIONAL THERAPY Unlike counseling from a clergy member, which is based on dogma and ancient scriptures, a good professional therapist stays up to date on the latest methods for addressing trauma and helping you develop the emotional skills to regulate yourself and feel empowered to move forward in life. There are even organizations that specifically vet and recommend therapists trained to work with those impacted by religious trauma. Somatic therapy, EMDR and Internal Family Systems are just a few of many different methods that professionals can employ based on your unique needs.

While religion often rejects science, science is unsurprisingly one of our best assets for living a healthy life.

COMMUNITY Loss of family and friends is one of the biggest blows many suffer when leaving religion. Even the lucky ones who are able to maintain some sense of relationship often don't find fulfillment in them. While many reference community as a positive aspect of Christianity, it's important not to fall into the trap of believing that this is something exclusive to religion. You can have an amazing community *without* religion. Not only that, but a healthier and more fulfilling community can be based on compatibility, shared values and choice rather than dogma. The difficulty is that this new community doesn't just appear out of thin air. Organized religion creates the illusion that it does, and hands us over friendships via church gatherings, bible studies, home groups, youth groups, volunteer services and more. It utilizes the "us versus them" mentality to fabricate feelings of connection with fellow believers simply based on the idea that none of you are a "them." In reality, good friendships take intention and cultivation. It takes time to build trust and establish healthy boundaries, something the church does not often teach and even discourages at times. When I left religion, I had to reevaluate everything I thought I knew about community and decide what it was that I wanted and needed. There were periods of loneliness and grieving what I lost, but the chosen family and friends I have now far exceed any of the community I had that was left behind with my religion. Great ways to find your new community are volunteer programs, political campaigns, hobby meetups, group activities (like sports or dance), neighborhood gatherings and even online venues. These are all ways you can strategically enjoy shared experiences with people who already have points of connection to things that are relevant to you.

SELF-CARE There are so many personal actions you can take to invest in your mental health. Educating yourself through books, podcasts and studies on trauma can be helpful for some. Embracing practices that encourage being present such as mindfulness, breath work, yoga and hiking or other physical and mental exercises can be beneficial as well. Many of these practices that center the body or nature are demonized by evangelicalism despite the proven positive effects on mental health. Creative outlets with no agenda or goal, like painting, writing, music and other handicrafts, are great ways to rebel against the lie that what you do must have godly significance.

HEALING IS NOT LINEAR I've learned to view it as part of my personal hygiene routine. Today I will brush my teeth, wash my face, do something that contributes to my mental health and extend grace toward myself when reminders of what I have survived attempt to disrupt my day. To this day, those compulsive prayers I developed as a traumatized child come to my mind every now and then—especially before a flight takes off or when I'm experiencing fear. But now, instead of playing them on repeat, I smile at the way my brain still seeks to take care of me, admire how far I have come and laugh at the silliness of it all.

One of the most important parts of my healing journey has been to befriend myself. My religion caused me to abandon myself over and over. My thoughts and fears were dismissed and supposed to be replaced with the "mind of Christ" (1 Corinthians 2:16). My dreams and hobbies had to align with God's plans, not fleshly desire (Galatians 5:16). Instead of acknowledging that part of being human means experiencing discomfort and hardship, I had warred against it and took it as a personal attack against me, never developing the appropriate life skills of acceptance and resilience. My whole life had been a rejection of reality and pining for the promise of an afterlife where I would be "perfect." When I first began to realize how damaging all of this was, I was heartbroken over everything I never even knew I had lost. So many experiences I would have loved to have had, so many creative outlets I would have loved to explore. I have since realized that while it's important to grieve the losses, there is still so much to enjoy and embrace. One of the most empowering parts of my journey has been getting to know myself without the restrictions of dogma—what music I enjoy, what movies I like, what hopes I have for the future, what types of friends I like to make. Now I can view myself outside of the lens of shame and unreasonable expectations. I can observe and appreciate my quirks and preferences without categorizing them into "sin" or "holy." I've learned that most of the facts about myself are completely neutral. I'm not all bad or all good; I'm a human who is constantly evolving. I can make choices without the worry that there are only two options—God's way or the wrong way. I can decide what my standards and goals are and, instead of dogmatically binding myself to them, reevaluate and shift them as needed whenever I gain more information. Evangelicalism forced me to see everything as black and white, but reality is a rainbow of nuance. Sometimes healing is simply sitting back and enjoying all the colors.

CHAPTER 7

S-E-X: The Evangelical Kryptonite

"In the part which merely concerns himself, his independence is, of right, absolute. Over himself, over his own body and mind, the individual is sovereign." —JOHN STUART MILL

FROM A VERY YOUNG AGE, I became ashamed and hypersensitive about anything remotely or potentially sexual. In our home, we had to close our eyes or change the channel if any kissing or romantic contact occurred, even if it took place between two characters in an animated children's film. When I was 5 years old and came home from a church children's event claiming I had a "boyfriend," I was informed that I was not allowed to have boyfriends and that I needed to wait until God told me who my husband was. I can't remember exactly how this was communicated, but it certainly registered as a shameful moment and a lesson to never tell my parents about crushes.

My parents reiterated this rule over and over whenever a boy would give me attention or when a friend would reveal that she had a boyfriend: "Now remember, Promise, we don't do 'boyfriend-girlfriend' in our home." This was taught to me along with Song of Songs 2:7, "Do not arouse or awaken love until it so desires." It was my responsibility to refrain from engaging in anything that would trigger emotional or romantic attachment to anyone until it was "time"—until I was of marriageable age. Not only this, but I was constantly told that anything I engaged in before marriage was a direct act against my future husband. Of course, no amount of shame or motivation could stop me from developing a crush or being attracted to someone else—a completely natural occurrence—but I certainly learned that I should keep these feelings to myself and just live, quietly, with the shame they caused.

Occasionally, I would gush about these crushes to my friends or in my journals. Soon enough, my parents informed me that they were reading these journals when I wasn't looking and again told me how my girlish behavior dishonored my future spouse. Deeply embarrassed—and more than a little traumatized—I renewed my commitment to maintaining a "pure mind."

At 12 years old, I experienced another deeply embarrassing moment. A friend arranged to host a pool party and invited me and some of our other churchmates to attend. They also invited my best friend, who happened to be a boy. I was so excited that we were all going to have a pool day together, and imagined the games of Marco Polo, mermaids versus pirates and underwater races we might have. The day before the event, my mom received a call from my best friend's mom requesting that I please wear an oversized T-shirt over my bathing suit. When my mom gently tried to pass the news to me, I became incredibly confused. I understood modesty was important, but I had just purchased a brand-new blue one-piece with little yellow flowers and gold trim. I was excited to wear it. Why did I have to cover it up with an ugly shirt? My mom explained that my friend's mom was just protecting the minds of her sons and husband from the sin of lust. Just hearing this (and even thinking about it all these years later) made my skin crawl. I was a young 12-year-old, having not yet gone through puberty. The girls at gymnastics class called me "Skeletor girl" because my frame was so skinny and board-like. My innocent mind could not understand what in the world I needed to protect my childhood friend from. Even so, I found it more disturbing that I might cause his father to "lust" after me—whatever that even really meant. How was it possible that my little girl body could victimize this man, a leader in our church, whom I viewed as a father figure? These thoughts disgusted me, but I targeted that disgust at myself instead of the adults responsible for those feelings.

With this as my prepubescent background, my parents did not need to do much to encourage my participation in evangelical purity culture in my teen years. I became a teenager in the early 2000s, a homeschooled Christian, as were all of my friends. I was raised to believe that "saving myself for Jesus" was the coolest aspiration. Every couple of weeks, I received *Brio* magazine, a *Focus on the Family* publication for teen girls that was supposed to be a Christian alternative to *Seventeen* or *Teen Vogue*. It featured modest fashion, trending makeup and hairstyles and articles with titles like "Judgment Day: Are You Ready?" It was also full of evangelical propaganda about saving sex for marriage, anti-abortion propaganda and testimonies from "ex-gays." One of the covers featured my favorite Christian pop star: Rebecca St. James, a young singer from Australia. Within her songs declaring love for God, she also pushed the message of abstinence. Her popular song "Wait for Me" was a lyrical fantasy, wondering what it would be like to meet her future husband for the first time and praying that he was saving his physical and emotional intimacy for her, just as she is saving herself for him. This soft messaging and romanticizing of abstinence was powerful propaganda—and certainly easier to ingest than the fear-based rhetoric I was used to. Purity rings were another form of that romanticization: a piece of jewelry worn on the ring finger of your left hand to symbolize a commitment to preserving your virginity for your future spouse. These purity rings even had a mainstream moment when popular stars like the Jonas Brothers, Miley Cyrus, Jessica Simpson and Britney Spears started to wear them. I had my own ring engraved with "For you I wait," which I found to be incredibly special and romantic at the time. Now, of course, I find it deeply disturbing that my 12-year-old friends and I were celebrated for publicly advertising that we hadn't had sex yet. Around the same time, I had a poster of the book *I Kissed Dating Goodbye* hanging up in my closet. The author, Joshua Harris, was a prominent evangelical voice (and has since apologized for his books and the harm they caused). That book, as well as several others he authored, centers around the idea that dating is a "worldly" practice that dishonors your future spouse and results in inappropriate premarital activities. Casual relationships were selfish and sinful. *Courtship* was the way to go. Through the instruction and discernment of your parents, you were to only enter into a romantic relationship if the goal was marriage. Ideally, there would be no physical touch; chaperones should be present and the relationship should glorify God with its example of adherence to boundaries.

Another common feature of this courtship culture is exemplified by

1 Corinthians 7:9: "It is better to marry than to burn with passion." This verse is referenced as encouragement to pursue a spouse as young as possible—essentially, *find someone quick before the horniness is too much to handle.* I know so many people, myself included, who rushed into marriage with the first person they dated in order to avoid sexual temptation. In some cases, physical lines were crossed and marriage was initiated as a form of "redemption" for the sin the couple had committed. As you can imagine, these marriages did not often result in healthy relationships. The purity culture popularized in the '90s was pervasive in evangelical culture. Parents didn't need to do much to expose their children to it—simply give them the most popular Christian books for teens, drop them off at a youth group meeting, order them a Christian magazine subscription and the rest was history. The goals of abstinence, stereotypical gender roles, homophobia, transphobia and sexual control were not only accepted but popularized.

THE DIRTY, ROTTEN GIFT OF SEX

The relationship evangelicalism has with sexuality is an incredible paradox of glorification and demonization. Sex is a gift from God *and* a temptation from Satan. It's dirty and wrong and should be avoided *and* starting on your wedding night, you should have a lot of it. Men are the stronger sex, worthy of leadership *and* they're so weak that women need to cover their skin to protect them from temptation. Single women should appear innocent and modest *and* once married, they should transform into sexual goddesses who never say no.

While sex is talked about as a blessing, it is easily the most vilified act as well. It's never approached as a neutral or natural part of life. It latches onto your identity—if you're a virgin, your value increases. If you have sex before marriage, you're damaged goods. If you're gay, you're broken. It also promotes shame and fear toward your own body. Natural urges and desires—even if they exist solely in the mind and are never acted upon—can be labeled sinful and lead to dissociation and rejection of oneself. Masturbation is deemed evil or simply not discussed, personal desire is vilified and anyone who isn't married is expected to be asexual in practice. The result is hypersexuality in the few circumstances that sexuality is allowed at all. I've heard countless stories from survivors of purity culture who married at a very young age purely to have access to sex. In many cases, they or their partners suffered from sexual addictions or compulsions once they finally had that access.

A common trope is that of a minister including comments about his "super hot wife" in the middle of Sunday morning messages. Men like Mark Driscoll and Steven Furtick are examples of pastors who report on their sex lives and how attracted they are to their wives as though trying to validate their biblical theologies. Instead, it comes off as nothing more than an attempt to "prove" their manhood.

Sex is not just permitted in marriage but treated as an absolute requirement. The day you marry, your sex drive and attitudes toward sex are expected to shift from Virgin Mary modesty to porn star-level enthusiasm, literally overnight. Men are praised for their high sex drives while women are taught to always be available. (Asexual people are completely erased in this scenario.) Relationships in which a wife has a higher sex drive than her husband are never mentioned, however, and while a woman is expected to be "available" to her husband at any time, she is still shamed if her sexual desires exceed those of her husband.

Children, especially young girls, are sexualized at an early age when they are taught that their bodies can be a temptation to grown men. The church claims to be preaching all of this in order to protect people from harm, saying that sex is sacred and worth treating as something very special. But evangelicalism is often opposed to sexual education, which is proven to decrease pregnancy in teens, delay sexual activity, reduce the number of sexual partners and significantly decrease STIs far more effectively than simply teaching abstinence.[1] Yet again, evangelicals choose dogma over what science shows as being effective. If purity culture were about teaching important things such as consent, personal responsibility and safe sex practices, perhaps it would be of some value. But instead, it does the exact opposite: It teaches you that your body is not your own and that it belongs to God and your spouse. It shifts the blame to victims and paints a picture of temptresses and uncontrolled monsters. It shames people for their sexuality. It's not actually about protecting anyone or preventing harm and promoting proven well-being; it's about control and manipulation. Being educated and empowered about your own body promotes and encourages autonomy, and personal autonomy is a fundamental threat to the hierarchy of evangelicalism, which requires complete submission in order to maintain power.

---

1 Comprehensive Sex Education: Research and Results." Advocates for Youth. (September 2009). https://www.advocatesforyouth.org/wp-content/uploads/storage/advfy/documents/fscse.pdf.

THE MYTH OF VIRGINITY

From the glorification of Jesus's mother, Mary, to modern-day obsessions with abstinence, the concept of virginity has long been associated with Christianity. But a concept is all that it is. Virginity is not a biological state, there are no medical indicators for it and, despite popular belief, the hymen is not a marker for whether someone has had sex or not. Hymens can break for a range of reasons that have nothing to do with sex and can also remain intact during sex. Some people are even born without them. Conveniently, for the patriarchal tendencies of evangelicalism, virginity is not a construct that can easily be used in regard to men. It also completely dismisses the legitimacy of sex that does not involve penis in vagina, invalidating queer relationships and anyone who has other sexual preferences or anatomy.

Historically, virginity was seen as a tool to confirm heirs and even prevent disease. But these archaic beliefs are completely irrelevant in modern times. It's a grotesque way of reducing someone, usually a woman, to a mere physical act. Virginity also doesn't take into account the importance of consent and the trauma caused by sexual assault. An individual's value does not decrease if someone else violates their consent, but the concept of virginity sends the opposite message. In my youth group, when I was around 12, the pastor gave all of us a piece of gum and told us to chew it for a few minutes. He then directed us to gather around in a circle and told us to pass the chewed piece of gum to the person next to us. Immediately, we objected with a flurry of "ew's" and refused each other's gross offerings. The pastor then told us that this is what it's like if you have sex before marriage—you're destroying something that you're supposed to offer to your future partner as a clean and untouched gift. Some youth groups used the metaphor of a crumpled-up piece of paper or a rose with plucked petals, pointing out that you can never remove the creases in the paper or put the rose petals back on the flower once the damage is done.

None of these disturbing metaphors takes assault into account or tells us what to do if we "messed up." The message of these teachings was, and is, fear, and the goal has always been control. We were taught to look at our bodies as a form of currency, something that could diminish or increase in value depending on what we did with it. It's dehumanizing at its core and the impact it has on those who are taught this belief is heartbreaking. It encourages sexual dysfunction, shames and condemns normal and healthy attraction, teaches queer people that their sexual expression has no value and pits men and women against each other.

The truth is that your value is not defined by your sexual experiences. Your humanity and worth aren't linked to abstaining from sex until a religious ritual is performed and a legal piece of paper is signed. There is nothing more or less moral about someone who has or hasn't had sex. Consensual, responsible sexuality is not shameful—but attempting to convince someone otherwise is.

COMMON ARGUMENTS YOU'LL HEAR

"Biblical marriage is between a man and a woman."

"Biblical" marriage, you say? Which biblical marriages are we advocating for exactly? I have a feeling that modern-day evangelicals are not advocating for polygamy, slave marriages (well, maybe some are), concubines or marriages requiring widows to be remarried to their deceased husband's brother or father. The idea of a lifelong, committed, heterosexual, monogamous relationship built on love is a recent idea, as marriage motivated by romance wasn't encouraged until the 18th century. Before that, including the time periods when the Bible was written, it was an arrangement to secure economic and/or social standing. Men in positions of power also used it simply as a means to acquire women they wanted to own and have physical access to, or someone to provide heirs for them. The idea that the Bible provides any worthwhile instruction or ideas about modern-day marriage is just another example of the cherry-picking that religious people use to support a specific agenda (like submission of women or bigotry toward LGBTQ+ people). Only acknowledging the heterosexual aspects of these relationships and not the enslavement, abuse and power-grabs they were rooted in requires turning a dishonest, blind eye toward the modern-day irrelevance and unethicalness of "biblical" marriages.

"God wants us to stay pure for him; our body is his temple."

Imagine being the god of the universe and caring about what consenting humans do with their genitals. Humans are not buildings or temples that can be defiled. We are complex individuals with unique identities and experiences. A god that can be hurt or negatively impacted by the physical activities, or even the thoughts, of its creations is a weak god. This extreme metaphor that views the human body as an object designed solely to reflect the glory of its creator completely denies bodily autonomy and dehumanizes the person inhabiting it. Of course, this is the goal: to convince the person that they do not own themselves and exist purely to please God. However, with no evidence of any gods, and therefore no evidence of what a god could possibly want from its living "temple," clergy and religious institutions have an opportunity to assert their agenda over individuals. Your body is yours, not a house for gods.

"Marriage was created by God."

The idea of marriage predates the Christian god by thousands of years and historically has acted as a cultural or governmental contract, not a religious one. Modern marriage is now much more centered around romance and choice and is a subjective cultural practice defined mostly by the people entering into it and whatever terms they agree to with their government. It's common now for people to write their own vows, create unique ceremonial traditions or skip ceremony altogether and make marriage whatever fits their lifestyle. Marriage is created by and for humans, whether as a public display of commitment, a convenient social arrangement, an emotional act of romance or simply compliance with social norms.

"Modesty protects others from sin."

This teaching is nothing more than preemptive victim-blaming. It also completely ignores the need for personal responsibility and relies on controlling the external influences of others instead of internal regulation of self. Sexual attraction based on physical attractiveness is completely natural and normal. Demonizing it instead of teaching how to appropriately appreciate it encourages objectification. Ironically, modesty culture's attempt to reduce sexualization actually does the opposite and increases sexualization of the human body. It asserts that simply having human body parts makes you inherently sexual and dangerous to even look at. Modesty is also forced more aggressively on girls than boys, causing them to bear an unequal amount of pressure. Most importantly, it does not actually prevent harm to the person practicing modesty. Predators are not deterred by pieces of fabric. But shaming people, especially women, for simply having a body and wearing what they want teaches them that their worth is tied to attire (or the lack thereof) instead of their personhood.

"Sex acts create soul ties."

We'd need to prove a soul exists to even begin to give credit to this claim, but we can still address the idea behind it. While sex can be a meaningful, sacred act, it is not limited to that. There are no magical chains that form between you and another. There are many ways that people bond and form deep, emotional connections and, while sex can be one of them, there are many other ways as well. Problem-solving, setting or achieving joint goals and even building things together can encourage the same brain chemistry that occurs during sex.[2] But you don't hear people warning against bonding with someone you've trained for a marathon with. The idea that sex creates a god-given connection between two people is simply more fearmongering, as opposed to bodily autonomy and the nuances that can occur in sexual relationships.

"Homosexuality is a sin."

We could spend the entire book debating whether or not the Bible condemns homosexuality, but plenty of people have already done that. And as we have established, the Bible doesn't have one consistent message about anything. A book that offers advice for owning others as slaves, encourages rape and treats women as conquests is not one that I care to trust when it comes to issues of gender conformity and sexual behavior between consenting adults. What I do find interesting is that while Christians have developed a reputation for their anti-gay views, Jesus was never recorded as saying anything on the matter. If this issue were so fundamental to Christianity, you'd think their god would have clearly addressed it. Evangelicals have long persecuted queer people, acting as though they commit the greatest of all sins, yet their god is so vague on the matter that it's widely debated throughout Christianity. Labeling an entire person's identity as a "sin" is a disturbing level of policing others. This is not some innocent, personal religious practice—Christians cause real harm and damage to innocent people by claiming their bigotry is somehow acceptable because it's grounded in religious dogma.

**"When it comes to gay people,
we should love the sinner and hate the sin."**

This is awfully close to the concept of agreeing to disagree, and to quote author Robert Jones Jr., "We can disagree and still love each other unless

---

2 "Dopamine: The pathway to pleasure." Harvard Health Publishing. https://www.health.harvard.edu/mind-and-mood/dopamine-the-pathway-to-pleasure.

your disagreement is rooted in my oppression." You cannot hate someone's queerness without also hating them. It's not a hobby; it's an expression of the entirety of who they are. You don't get credit for loving someone while simultaneously hating their identity. The saying "love the sinner, hate the sin" is not even from the Bible. It may have originated in a letter written by St. Augustine, which was later rephrased in English by Mahatma Gandhi as "Hate the sin and not the sinner." But evangelicals have popularized it in recent years as an attempt to spiritualize their prejudice. It's a Trojan horse of shame and nothing resembling actual love.

QUEERNESS: A SUPERPOWER

Evangelicals' abuse and hatred of queer people has long been part of their reputation. After the Stonewall uprising (a momentous turning point for queer Americans fighting for their rights) in 1969, the "moral majority" evangelical leaders of the '70s, Pat Robertson, James Dobson (the same guy who advocated for hitting children) and Jerry Falwell, began a movement to push "traditional" values in retaliation. Their version of Christianity is not the self-contained Sunday morning type—it's a political stance that seeks control over believers and nonbelievers alike.

Evangelicalism employs a system of hierarchy to maintain control over its followers. Some sects of Christianity overtly adhere to and preach this hierarchy, while others apply it more subtly. Fundamentalism overtly places children at the bottom, women above the children, men above the women and children and God reigning over all. What happens if you don't obviously fit into one of those roles? What if your sexual or gender identity doesn't fit into the binary expectation of conservative Christianity? I believe this is why evangelicals find LGBTQ+ people so terrifying and why so much of their ire is directed at their very existence. Simply existing outside of heterosexual norms is an act of resistance against fundamentalism. Toxic practices of religious submission and gender roles fall apart in the face of queerness. How do fundamentalists control what they cannot categorize within their system of power? If you don't identify with one of their two acceptable genders or if your chosen gender isn't the one you were assigned at birth, you cannot be contained by the social cage they designed to hold you. A gay couple with children is a threat because neither parent can be defined as second in command to God. How do evangelicals apply their rigid system of order to a nonbinary person? Similarly, an asexual person is a threat because "sex is a gift from God," which evangelicals need to hold over your head in order to control you.

To address the challenges presented by queer people to their ideas of social order and control, evangelicals have waged a reputation war against them. They call them perverted, baselessly associate them with predatory behavior and equate their identity with an immoral lifestyle that goes against God's expectations of humans. The horrific practice of conversion therapy, which reframes outright abuse as a method of healing, has inflicted immeasurable harm, especially against young people. Families disown queer relatives and even abandon children. They claim they "love" LGBTQ+ people so much that they have no choice but to warn them about their sin and try to save them from hell. They are simply "speaking truth in love." In that regard, I love evangelicals so much that I have no choice but to call them out on their blatant bigotry, which causes them to miss out on relationships with their friends and family (and sometimes even reject their own identity). They have no evidence for their claims about sin or hell, and use fact-less faith as an excuse to avoid confronting the fear at the root of their prejudice. Instead of questioning why heteronormativity has been pushed by the church and examining the idea that they're being used by politicians to wage culture wars, they double down and cloak their hatred in self-righteousness. Their fear has made them pawns for billionaires who are busier playing god than actually pretending to worship one. The modern evangelical church has failed society in many ways, but I believe this is one of its greatest offenses.

NO "I DON'TS" AFTER "I DO"

Marriage is viewed as deeply sacred in evangelical culture. You are told that God has set aside one specific person for you and that if you follow the rules and save yourself for them, your relationship will be blessed. Sex is made out to be the mecca of all romantic acts, and presented to you as a physical and spiritual connection. You are led to believe that your very identity will change, not just from virgin to non-virgin, but from an individual to a unified entity. If you're a woman, you're taught that your body will someday be a gift for your husband. If you're a man, you're taught that if you can behave yourself before marriage, you'll reap your reward as a husband. What they don't teach is consent, nor do they warn against marital coercion. This harmful dynamic of sexual entitlement should truly be called what it is: rape. Instead, it's taught as "biblical submission." Sex is a duty to be fulfilled. Michelle Duggar, a prominent figure in American fundamentalist culture and mother of 19 children, calls it being "joyfully available."[3] Not only should your body be available to your husband on demand, but you should submit to him, happily. 1 Corinthians 7:3-5 is what is most commonly used to justify this:

"The husband should fulfill his marital duty to his wife, and likewise the wife to her husband. The wife does not have authority over her own body but yields it to her husband. In the same way, the husband does not have authority over his own body but yields it to his wife. Do not deprive each other except perhaps by mutual consent and for a time, so that you may devote yourselves to prayer. Then come together again so that Satan will not tempt you because of your lack of self-control."

While it sounds like it's requiring the same of both husband and wife, this verse is taught in the context of rigid gender roles: Men are the sexual ones, and women are not. I was taught that if I did not satisfy my husband by staying "joyfully available," he may "sexually wander" and ultimately it would be my fault for not relieving him of temptations. This teaching is harmful for obvious reasons, such as lack of consent, but it also traps people in abusive relationships. Divorce is frowned upon and in some circles simply not allowed—if the marriage isn't working, you should pray more, submit your relationship to God and continue fulfilling your marital duties. Even if those duties entail being abused.

These teachings on submission and gender roles are not just harmful to women. Men are required to take on positions of authority and domination when it comes to decision-making and finances, which can create its own trauma when they don't naturally meet the stereotype of "godly husband." Emotional suppression is a common outcome, as husbands are expected to be the stoic spiritual leaders. Instead of spouses enjoying an equal partnership, where they naturally settle into the roles they are best suited for or agree to share responsibilities equally, they are forced to view each other within a hierarchy of power and dominance. This imbalance can cause such resentment that it diminishes or destroys the friendship and vulnerability required for a healthy marriage.

3 Michelle Duggar. "Michelle Duggar's Marriage Advice for Newlyweds," The Duggar Family (October 8, 2015). https://www.duggarfamily.com/2015/10/michelle-duggars-marriage-advice-for-newlyweds/.

A successful marriage in evangelicalism is measured by time rather than the health of the relationship or the satisfaction of the people within it. "What God has joined together, let no one separate" (Matthew 19:6) is interpreted to mean that no one is permitted to end a marriage—not even the people within it. Because of this, evangelicalism often compares relationships to a battle. The mandate is to stay in the fight and never surrender. Couples are often credited for having experienced "battle wounds" and staying together. If you're together for 35 years, it doesn't matter if the relationship makes you miserable. You've been a good little soldier and God is pleased with you. Of course, when couples are encouraged to marry as young as possible (often to make their sexual activities permissible) and have children quickly as well, you end up with relationships that feel like a war instead of a mutual endeavor.

This system claims to be all about family but fails to look after the well-being of the individuals involved. Adults are stuck in lifelong loveless marriages. Children are exposed to poor examples of partnership and often bear the brunt of their parents' emotional frustrations. Divorce, which could end this pain and lead to healthier, happier relationships for all parties, is dismissed out of hand. Evangelicals may feel they've checked the appropriate boxes for marriage by adhering to such dogmatic principles, but if the goal is to have autonomous lives and experience an emotionally healthy, fulfilling relationship, these principles actively work against it.

What I believe to be at the root of this evangelical reaction to sex are two fears: fear of individuality and fear of personal satisfaction. If you're empowered to be yourself, to learn your likes and dislikes, to say "no" and "yes" instead of "whatever God wants," evangelicals will accuse you of trying to become your own god. But this is simply what others would call taking personal responsibility. Individuality and freedom of choice threaten any institution that needs you to believe life must be lived on its terms. Personal satisfaction and pleasure (and I don't mean only in a sexual sense) empower us to enjoy the present and experience joy and happiness. Evangelical culture considers "pleasure" to be a rejection of God and holiness, signifying the embrace of a hedonistic, selfish lifestyle. It teaches that loving yourself is wrong (2 Timothy 3:1-4).

But pleasure is simply indulging in the joyful satisfaction of the present moment. It's being completely entranced by a beautiful sunset, night sky or rain shower. It's the awareness of how delicious each and every bite of your favorite treat tastes. It's the giddy feeling of a conversation with a close friend who understands you. It's the feeling of connectedness at a concert when the whole crowd sings along as one. It can also be sex, of course, but it's so much more than that. Losing our freedom to experience the innocent pleasures of life cuts us off from one of the most beautiful, effective tools for healing anxiety, depression, pain, grief, anger and more. The forced rejection of pleasure required by fundamentalism is an overt attempt at maintaining control. If we are taught to reject pleasure, then we can easily be manipulated into thinking we lack what we need to survive. When we are trained to believe that we do not belong to ourselves, that our identity must fit a gender binary or that our value exists in the history of our sexual activity, we lose the best thing we have to offer those around us: our individuality. It can be intimidating to know that at the end of the day, you are truly responsible for yourself. Religion seeks to lessen that responsibility by outsourcing it. The beautiful truth is that you belong to yourself, and the privilege of all that entails is worth the challenges that come with it.

CHAPTER 8

The Angry Atheist

"A person who does not believe in the existence of a god or any gods."
—DEFINITION OF "ATHEIST," MERRIAM-WEBSTER.COM

AS AN EVANGELICAL CHRISTIAN, I believed in all kinds of things: Angels, demons, talking animals, seas being split down the middle, people rising from the dead, walking on water, God...the list goes on. What *didn't* I believe in? Atheists. Of course, there were people who called themselves atheists, but that was just out of rebellion and hatred for God. My indoctrination had limited my ability to comprehend that there was a chance someone simply lacked belief in a god. I thought there were only three options: 1) they believed in the right god (which was obviously my God), 2) they believed in the wrong god(s) or 3) they were lying about not believing. My theory was that these so-called "atheists" must have been deeply disappointed by God or their church or maybe other believers. Something heartbreaking must have happened to them to harden their heart. Instead of addressing their pain, they were rejecting God completely, rebelling against their creator out of spite and resentment. It didn't occur to me that perhaps these individuals were genuinely unconvinced due to logic and reasoning.

Although I thought I had developed this idea of a false atheist on my own, it was heavily influenced by the spiritual leaders and the theology I had been exposed to up to that point. Romans 1:18-22 is often used to claim that God has shown himself even to the "unrighteous" and that they "are without excuse" because of this. In other words, God is self-evident, which means disbelief is unwarranted. Therefore, the punishment for one's refusal to believe is just. This is what inspired my idea that nonbelievers had to have been hurt by something so awful that they simply couldn't believe. It was also argued that morality doesn't exist without God and that people would do horrific things if they weren't afraid that some deity would hold them accountable. Atheists who behaved themselves surely had an inkling that their judgment day was coming. Like many things in evangelicalism, fear is a big part of undermining nonbelievers.

For many religious people, the knowledge that someone doesn't believe in their god threatens the integrity of their own beliefs. If something they hold as truth can be questioned or deemed fallacious by someone else, it puts them on the defensive. And given how hard it can be to defend Christianity, this is a position they prefer not to be in.

Even more of a blow to their foundation of faith is a person who once considered themselves a fellow Christian, then began to doubt their faith before abandoning it entirely. This kind of departure weakens core evangelical doctrines, such as the threat of hell and belief that God has revealed himself to all. For many, it could instill a profound concern: *If this once-devout Christian stopped believing, maybe it could happen to me too.*

When I first stopped believing, I was hesitant to put labels or even words to it. So many stereotypes and prejudiced ideas about "godless" people lingered in my mind. Since I steadfastly clung to the idea that I was just someone who didn't believe in any gods, it was a bit of a shock to finally realize I was a full-blown atheist. I was watching a YouTube video of respected atheist activist (and now dear friend) Matt Dillahunty explaining why he's an atheist. His response was simple: "I'm an atheist because I don't believe that there's a god." That may not sound revelatory, but at the time, it changed everything for me. *I don't believe there's a god...I'm an atheist.* Of course, in reality, I had been one for a while, but my bias against the term and my misunderstanding of it had prevented me from identifying with the title "atheist." It was a scary pill to swallow because at that point in my life I didn't personally know any atheists, but I did know the stigma and negative connotations that came with the word. I was not alone in my fears. In a survey of nonreligious people in the U.S.,[1] 47.5 percent of participants "felt pressure to pretend that they are religious." Not just pressure to hide their atheism, but pressure to act as though they're an active believer. I grew up being taught that as a Christian in the U.S., I would face persecution and need to build strong faith to avoid publicly denying Jesus when pressured to conceal my religion. Never once did I find myself in a situation where I had to hide my beliefs, yet now, as an atheist, I am deeply aware of the risks I take when sharing my position. Stigma against atheists is not a conspiracy; it's all too real. One study describes them as "one of the most disliked groups in the United States" and indicates that they were less likely to be allowed "to sport a symbol of their beliefs in the workplace" than Jews, Christians or Muslims.[2]

Think about that. Walking about with a cross around your neck—a literal torture device that's been redefined as a symbol of sacrifice by the faithful—signaling that you believe in a supernatural being that rose from the dead? Totally cool. A necklace with an "A" symbol identifying yourself as free from any religious beliefs? Inappropriate. Politically, American atheists, agnostics and other nonbelievers are extremely underrepresented. In 2021, the religiously unaffiliated (atheists included) made up 46 percent of the U.S. population and yet only one member of Congress identified as religiously unaffiliated. At the same time, 90 percent of the members of Congress described themselves as Christian. Congressional meetings are opened with prayer, presidents are permitted—and expected—to appeal to God's authority and 45 percent of Americans believe the U.S. should be a "Christian nation."[3]

Though technically unenforceable due to federal protections, multiple state constitutions still ban anyone who denies the existence of a god or supreme being from holding office. Someone who does not believe in any gods is deemed unfit to hold office, while people who are linked to "End Times" beliefs (trials and tribulations that bring about the second coming of Christ), like Pete Hegseth, Marjorie Taylor Greene and Ted Cruz, hold positions of authority. Somehow, it's acceptable to have a "Secretary of War" whose theology asserts that world war in the Middle East is necessary for God's plan. Yet

---

1 "United States Secular Survey." https://www.secularsurvey.org/executive-summary.

2 Beth Ellwood, "People are less tolerant of atheists expressing their beliefs at work compared to Christians, Muslims, or Jews." PsyPost (August 2, 2021). https://www.psypost.org/people-are-less-tolerant-of-atheists-expressing-their-beliefs-at-work-compared-to-christians-muslims-or-jews/.

3 Patricia Tevington, "A closer look at Americans who believe the U.S. should be a Christian nation." Pew Research Center (October 27, 2022). https://www.pewresearch.org/short-reads/2022/10/27/a-closer-look-at-americans-who-believe-the-u-s-should-be-a-christian-nation/.

the U.S. has never had an openly atheist president because those candidates are immediately deemed "godless" and therefore untrustworthy or immoral. Another study showed that atheists living in towns that are more conservative and religious "experience a heightened sense of danger because of their non-belief."[4] According to another survey ranking warm (positive) feelings versus cold (negative) feelings toward religious groups, atheists received the "coldest" rating on average tied only with Muslims.[5] This same survey revealed two other conclusions of note. First, when the person questioned about their attitude toward Christians, Jews, Muslims, atheists, etc., reported that they knew someone from one of those groups, they gave a warmer rating to that group than those with no such personal connection. Second, it showed that those who actually knew the definitions of atheism and agnosticism assigned warmer ratings to that group than those who didn't. It's no surprise that education and familiarity help overcome unease. With 62 percent of Americans identifying as Christian and only five percent as atheist in 2024,[6] indicating fewer opportunities to interact with an atheist, it's no wonder there are so many misconceptions. Unfortunately, it is a self-fulfilling prophecy: The stigma of being an atheist can cause substantial anxiety and often prevents people from being open with their views and engaging with people who believe differently than them. This lack of representation exacerbates the stigma.

All that said, other statistics reveal a much kinder view of atheists in the U.S.: They are more likely to find satisfaction with their community and personal life than those who are religiously affiliated. They are also just as likely to be involved in volunteer or community service groups.[7] Even so, Christians are still viewed more charitably.

With all this negativity surrounding a term that simply delineates someone as a nonbeliever, why did I decide to take on the label? In short, I value freedom and well-being. Being able to live a life free from religion without being rejected by family or society for doing so falls under that. Despite my igno-

---

4 Leonardo Blair, "Many American atheists hide their unbelief due to social stigma in Christian culture: study." The Christian Post (June 15, 2023). https://www.christianpost.com/news/many-american-atheists-hide-their-unbelief-due-to-stigma-study.html.
5 "What Americans Know About Religion." Pew Research Center (July 23, 2019). https://www.pewresearch.org/religion/2019/07/23/feelings-toward-religious-groups/.
6 "2023-24 U.S. Religious Landscape Study Interactive Database." Pew Research Center (2025). https://www.pewresearch.org/religious-landscape-study/.
7 "Religious 'Nones' in America: Who They Are And What They Believe." Pew Research Center (January 24, 2024). https://www.pewresearch.org/religion/2024/01/24/are-nones-less-involved-in-civic-life-than-people-who-identify-with-a-religion/.

rant and arrogant evangelical feelings toward atheists, I was able to change my mind and realize how silly my prejudices were. I believe education, normalization and familiarity can help reduce prejudice in others as well. I lived under a doctrine of shame and fear my entire life because of religion. I have no intention of suffering through that again, no matter what label I choose for myself, nor do I want to see anyone else experience the same.

WHAT IS AN ATHEIST?

Like most words do, this one has subtly changed in meaning throughout time so there is still a lot of discourse over what the term means today, especially when used colloquially. During the Enlightenment, philosophers like Baron d'Holbach and Denis Diderot gave atheism the reputation of being more of a hard assertion *against* theism rather than a soft denial of it. Moving into the 20th century, philosophers such as George H. Smith, Antony Flew and Richard Dawkins began to define the term atheism more clearly by separating different levels of disbelief into categories such as hard versus soft or positive versus negative. Positive atheism claims that gods do not exist, whereas negative atheism is an absence of belief altogether without a claim attached.

Regardless of the different categories, what remains true is that an atheist does *not* believe in any gods. That, to me, is the most important piece of information and the definition I am using when I say "atheist": a person who lacks belief in the existence of gods or deities. Whether they would move beyond a basic rejection of god-claims into an assertion that gods do not exist is a follow-up question that would then reveal hard or soft atheism. While it may seem like semantics, there is a major difference between "I do not believe in a god" and "I believe there is no god" when formally discussing the subject. For me, my positive or negative atheism very much depends on whether we are discussing a specific god or not, and how falsifiable (something testable that *could* be disproven if untrue) that claim is. If you tell me there is an invisible, undetectable god that does not engage with life as we know it, then I would withhold belief and remain atheistic toward the claim but also would not assert that such a god doesn't exist because there would be no way to prove it one way or the other. But when someone claims there is an all-loving, all-powerful, all-knowing creator god that exists in a world where a thousand children die every day simply due to lack of clean water,[8] it's pretty easy for me to say that that god doesn't exist—unless we redefine the word "love" to something less kind. Either way, as Matt Dillahunty explained so clearly, if you don't believe in any gods, you're an atheist.

Similar to my story, plenty of nonbelievers are technically atheists but may say something like "Well, I just don't like labels," or "'Atheist' just sounds so certain!" As a wannabe edgy teenager, I also didn't like labels, but then I realized they're not sacred contracts—they're just words we can use to help define ourselves and communicate who we are to others more efficiently. Atheism does not assert certainty, nor does it prevent you from changing your mind. If I were given evidence of the existence of any god, I would be a theist. My current position as a disbelieving atheist does not stop me from becoming a believing theist, just like my position as a believing theist did not prevent me from leaving the faith. Just like when an evangelical Christian claims "I'm not religious, I just love Jesus!" going out of one's way to avoid the label "atheist" is no less of an effort to dodge any stigma associated with the term. While there may be prejudices to face when using the term, there are many more benefits to reap, like normalization and accurate representation.

It's understandable to want to avoid the false assumptions about the label, but the only way to minimize those assumptions is to prove them wrong. All of this being said, if you feel more empowered to simply communicate your position by saying, "I don't believe in any gods" instead of "I'm an atheist," I respect your choice to do so, even if I wish you'd join the fight for accurate representation.

EVANGELICAL ATHEISM?

There's nothing I was more uncomfortable with as an evangelical than the mandate to evangelize (Matthew 28:18-20). As a teenager, it felt so awkward to talk to strangers (or, worse, people I knew who were nonbelievers) about religion. Many times, our youth group would send us off in groups to the mall or some other public space to ask people if we could pray with them and share the gospel. The expectation was that we would come back and share "testimonies" or success stories of how the conversations went. The funny

---

8 "Burden of disease attributable to unsafe drinking-water, sanitation and hygiene: 2019 update." World Health Organization (June 28, 2023). https://www.who.int/publications/i/item/9789240075610.

part is that as this all took place in the South, where pretty much everyone we talked to was already a Christian. At those rare times when we were rejected, we would immediately chalk it up to "persecution." Meanwhile, I still felt so uncomfortable getting into other people's personal space, uninvited, with such an aggressive agenda.

Now I face accusations from religious people claiming that I'm an "evangelical atheist," that I'm no different than them in my passion to push my beliefs on others. It's an interesting thing to consider: What's the difference between atheist activism and evangelical proselytization? For starters, Christians go door to door, have churches on every corner, run youth programs in schools and post billboards threatening hellfire. As the most populous religion in the U.S., their messaging is everywhere. And the message is "Choose Jesus or miss out on heaven." They believe in one, exclusive truth, which has all sorts of moral and, in many cases, political expectations. I'll speak for myself when I say that my activism is not looking to convince anyone of a specific story that has some eternal consequence attached to it. I simply want to champion freedom of thought, freedom to ask questions and freedom to doubt without shame. There is no dogma I want to peddle; in fact, my goal is to challenge the dogmas that are in place. I want people to learn how to think, not be told what to think. I want them to feel empowered to ask good questions, resist manipulation and coercion and get comfortable with not always having the answers. My value for consent remains, to the point where I hope those who have been indoctrinated hear or see something that sparks their critical thinking. The right question from an earnest seeker can set a mind free. So how do we equip ourselves to challenge the current dogma? To engage in conversations that have the potential to inspire someone toward freedom? We stay curious. We ask good questions, we don't fear doubts and we get good at skepticism.

SKEPTICISM'S TOOLKIT

Skepticism is the idea that belief should be withheld until there is sufficient evidence, and while there are different philosophies about it, for me, it is simply an approach to figuring out what is true. It's more about challenging knowledge claims than simply questioning or doubting everything all the time. Not every situation, thought or choice warrants questioning, nor would that be a reasonable way to live. I do not wake up in the morning and ponder if the floor will be under my feet when I get out of bed. Overanalyzing relationships (unless given evidence to consider) is also a potentially damaging trap that's best avoided. Reasonable trust is all that is needed for low-stakes or everyday situations. Skepticism is best applied on a scale that matches the claim being made. Claims about science, philosophy and ideology that impact the way you define reality should absolutely be tried and examined; you should conclude that either they are accurate, warrant further investigation or should be dismissed altogether until a reason is given not to. Here are some simplified examples of the thought process tools that skepticism offers:

"I DON'T KNOW...YET" This was the first tool I found myself in need of. Dogma does not allow for ignorance and instead often replaces it with arrogant assertions. In my evangelical days, saying, "I don't know..." felt almost blasphemous, unless it ended with "...but I know God does and I trust him!" Being able to acknowledge when you don't have enough information or understanding of something leaves room for an answer to become available later on.

THE SCIENTIFIC METHOD This is a "process of observing, asking questions and seeking answers through tests and experiments."[9] It involves observing something, asking a question about it, creating a hypothesis to provide a possible explanation, experimenting and testing to see if that explanation could be true, then using the data that's been gathered to draw an educated conclusion about the thing you've observed. Perhaps the most important aspect of the scientific method is that it allows peers to repeat the process and critique the findings. Scientific studies are peer-reviewed to check for mistakes and hold the work accountable for its claims.

EMPIRICAL EVIDENCE This is what the scientific method sets out to analyze. It includes what can be observed, measured and tested. It's not a feeling or an anecdote or even rational reasoning, but something grounded in observable reality.

BURDEN OF PROOF Being aware of where the responsibility lies when it comes to providing evidence for a claim should be the basis for examining

---

9 The Editors of Encyclopaedia Britannica. "scientific method." Encyclopedia Britannica, September 12, 2025. https://www.britannica.com/science/scientific-method.

ideas, beliefs, etc. The easiest way to determine this is by identifying whether the claim is a negative or a positive. Someone who says "Fairies exist, prove me wrong!" is making a positive claim. Therefore, they need to provide evidence. Some easy tips for appropriately assigning the burden of proof would be to say, "What is your evidence for that?" "How did you reach that conclusion?" or "Why do you believe that?"

OCCAM'S RAZOR If you have two competing conclusions, the correct one is likely the most obvious or simple one. While it's certainly not a law to abide by, it's a helpful guideline for avoiding unnecessarily complex assumptions. For example, my husband and I live in the same house. I stay in bed and he gets up to make coffee in the kitchen. I hear the sound of someone humming in the kitchen. The voice sounds like my husband. Is it a) an alien that has taken over my husband's body and is now about to bring me poisoned coffee or b) my husband humming in the kitchen like he does every morning? If you answered b), you're applying Occam's razor correctly.

STEELMAN This is an incredibly important skill to develop if you want to remain intellectually honest. Take a person's argument or claim and rephrase it in the strongest, most convincing form that you can. Think of anything you can that would bolster their point and make sure you fully understand what their opinion is. In essence, it's giving the counterargument the benefit of the doubt. If you really want to engage in a genuine conversation with someone and comfortably agree or disagree with their claim, then it benefits you to know the strongest points of their argument so you can focus on those instead of wasting time on irrelevant parts of the conversation or potential misunderstandings.

FALSIFIABILITY Before you can even determine if something is true or false, you have to know if it is even possible to find that out. In other words, if the assertion was not true, would there be a way to know? If I say "An intangible, invisible pink unicorn lives under my bed," there would be no way for you to observe, test or measure that claim, which would make it unfalsifiable. Unfalsifiable claims can't be proven or disproven and should be an instant flag for dogma.

DON'T FALL FOR THE FALLACIES

To have a productive conversation when it comes to things as universal yet as personal as politics, philosophy and religion, I believe certain values must be maintained throughout. These include 1) the value of what is true 2) the value of communicating clearly and honestly and 3) the value of attempting to understand what the other person wants to communicate. One of the biggest stumbling blocks to any of those three values is logical fallacies—failures in reasoning. You may be well-versed in what logical fallacies are and how to spot them, while others may be learning about them for the first time. Regardless, I find it helpful to refresh yourself on different logical fallacies often in order to train yourself to recognize them when they come up—whether in your own argument or in an argument being made against you. The faster you recognize these failures in reasoning, the quicker you can course correct and focus on the values of what is true, what you want to communicate and what is being communicated to you. The following section provides a cheat sheet of the most common fallacies used in religious arguments. There are many of them, and arguments often contain more than one. While this list covers some of the most frequent offenders, it is not comprehensive, and I highly encourage a side quest to learn about other logical fallacies that aren't addressed in this book:

AD HOMINEM* Making personal attacks against the character, personality, physical appearance, emotions or other personal attributes of the presenter in lieu of addressing the argument itself. It is often hidden as a passive-aggressive attempt at labeling emotions (the "angry atheist" trope) to distract from the inability to address the actual reasoning.

Look out for: Assertions about the other person's motives, circumstances, appearance or intelligence. Addressing the person instead of the argument. "Well, *YOU*..." is often a red flag.

Evangelical examples: "You're just bitter and hurt," "You just left so you could sin," "You've been deceived by Satan."

Counteract with: "Aside from your thoughts about me, do you have a response to my argument?"

***Important to note:** This is no longer a fallacy when presented with an argument.

GOD OF THE GAPS This is exactly what it sounds like: A gap in knowledge or understanding that gets replaced with "God." This can sound like, "Well, where do you think everything in the universe came from?" or "I didn't die in that crash, so it had to have been God who saved me." In the past, this sort of thing might have sounded like, "The bright light that sometimes comes from the sky to the ground when it rains must be a weapon from a god!" or "This person has random episodes of shaking and convulsions; they must be possessed by demons!" We've since determined, of course, that these examples simply describe the effects of lightning and symptoms of epilepsy, respectively. Not having a natural explanation for something (*yet*) or being ignorant of the information that *is* available is not sufficient reason to assume a supernatural explanation.

Look out for: The lack of an explanation for something (or ignorance of a proven explanation) resulting in the assertion of a supernatural answer to the question, and any arguments claiming "god" as a source that would be ruled obsolete if a natural cause were identified.

Evangelical examples: "Science can't explain..." "The universe is so complex that..." "Well, how do you think the world came to be?"

Counteract with: "If someday a natural cause were to explain this, would your god-claim still hold up?"

PRESUPPOSITIONAL FALLACIES A presupposition is something assumed true at the start of something (in this case, a conversation). Spotting when this is actually fallacious can be tricky at first. When someone's argument contains an assumed (but not proven) statement, you can be duped into arguing something unnecessarily. For example, if someone says, "Mermaids are the most intelligent sea creatures because they're half human," they're asserting that mermaids are real but are skipping past that entire claim by acting as though it's true in order to get to their next claim, which is that they're the "most intelligent." Circular arguments, or "begging the question," is another type of presuppositional fallacy. Circular arguments assert that A proves B, and B proves A or that A simply proves A.

Look out for: Assumptions that have not yet been agreed upon in the conversation.

Evangelical examples: "The Bible is the word of God because the Bible says so," "This all had a creator, so it must have been a god."

Counteract with: "How do you know that your assumption is true?"

STRAWMAN Picture your argument being represented by the figure of a man. Let's say your argument is "I don't believe a god created the universe" and it's displayed on a sign around the figure's neck, waiting for someone to make a counterargument. Then picture someone walking up to do so, but instead turning around and making a separate figure of a man out of *straw*, upon which they hang a sign that says "I believe everything came from nothing" and start arguing against that instead of the statement you actually made, all while acting as though they are one and the same.

Look out for: Exaggerating a position, oversimplifying and removing key nuanced points, using extreme situations as examples, misquoting or not quoting altogether.

Evangelical examples: "I can't believe you think this all just came from nothing," "How silly to believe we all came from monkeys."

Counteract with: "Would you mind telling me what you think my argument is so I can see if I've communicated it in a way that you understand?"

FALSE DICHOTOMY This is falsely presenting only two possible options. Implying that if one thing is not true, then a second option must be, even when other possibilities exist. This binary thinking is prevalent in, and a major marker of, evangelical thinking, primarily because nuance is not helpful to indoctrination or fear tactics. But it's not exclusive to evangelical thinking and is a big one to watch out for in your own thinking, too.

Look out for: Using either "THIS or THAT" language, oversimplification of the topic.

Evangelical examples: "If you don't worship God, you worship Satan," "You're either going to heaven or hell."

Counteract with: "How do you know those are the only options?"

SPECIAL PLEADING Think "rules for me, not for thee." The argument is based on a double standard: specific logic applies to everything else but is conveniently ignored for their own position without any appropriate reason.

Look out for: Expressions like, "Well that's *my* truth," "But it's different when it comes to this," or "It just is, that's why."

Evangelical examples: "All things have a beginning, except for God," "Taking a life is wrong, unless God does it," "God isn't bound by anything."

Counteract with: "What's the reason you would give your claim these exceptions but not mine?"

APPEAL TO EMOTION* One of the favorite tools of evangelicalism: make someone feel something. Fear, self-righteousness, shame and outrage are all ways you can trigger someone into agreeing with you, unquestioned. This is the tactic of fire and brimstone preachers who passionately and sternly describe the horrors of hell in order to scare their audience into conversion. It's also the tactic of prosperity gospel pastors who smile and joyfully declare that God's going to bless you—if you just give some money over first—playing on your desire to have positivity in your life.

Look out for: Strong language, lack of facts.

Evangelical examples: "God is real and that's why you feel empty without him," "Your sin breaks Jesus's heart," "You're going to feel meaningless without religion."

Counteract with: "Do you think emotions alone are a good reason to believe something? Do you have other reasons you think I should believe this is true?"

***Important to note:** It's when emotion replaces facts that it becomes a fallacy. Discrediting someone's argument because it *included* emotion is an ad hominem.

EQUIVOCATION Somehow, at the beginning of their argument, a word means one thing, and then the word's meaning shifts. It begins with one definition and later takes on a completely different one, while the person using the argument acts as though the two are the same. It's a clever way of trying to hide one argument behind another agreed-upon claim. It's a misuse of language that conveniently works in favor of their argument.

Look out for: Ambiguous words, emotional language.

Evangelical examples: Arguments using the words "faith," "spirit," "soul," "salvation," "truth." "You have faith in science, I have faith in God," or "Real freedom is found in freedom with Christ."

Counteract with: "Can you please clarify what you mean when you use that word?" "Can we agree on a definition for that word so I can understand your point?"

APPEAL TO AUTHORITY Arguing that something is true based on the opinion of someone in a position of leadership, knowledge, fame or other role of authority that has made the same assertion or agreed with it to some extent.

Something is either true or it isn't, regardless of who does or doesn't agree.

The claim should have its own source of merit and not be dependent on a noteworthy figure aligning with it. Citing experts is great, but only when the citation refers to a qualified authority that has evidence to back their conclusion.

Look out for: Name-dropping of experts from an irrelevant field, quoting authorities without context, vague references to "scientists say..." "scholars say..." or "So and so was brilliant and *they* believe!" *without* supporting evidence.

Evangelical examples: "The founding fathers believed in God!" "Biblical scholars say the entire earth was flooded!"

Counteract with: "What was that person's reason for believing that?"

APPEAL TO RIDICULE Laughing, mocking or otherwise dismissing something as absurd instead of engaging with the argument. Think of it as an ad hominem toward the argument, not the individual. It's probably the fallacy we atheists are most prone to when engaging with theists. Sometimes it's difficult to hear threats of burning in hell, claims about talking animals and regurgitated talking points like "*But just look at the trees, they had to have a creator!*" without erupting in laughter, but that's not actually addressing the point. Mocking an idea does not actually expose its issues. If you're going to call something absurd, explain why.

Look out for: Oversimplifying, comical comparisons without counterarguments.

Evangelical examples: "Believing in evolution is ridiculous!" "It's crazy to think we didn't have a creator!"

Counteract with: "What is it about my position that you disagree with and why?"

APPEAL TO IGNORANCE Assuming that lack of information about one thing means another thing must be a certain way, or asserting that no evidence to the contrary must make something true (or false).

Look out for: Uncertainty reinterpreted as certainty, lack of evidence.

Evangelical examples: "You can't prove God doesn't exist, so he must be real," "Science can't answer ________, so it must be God."

Counteract with: "Would you agree with that statement if it were a claim made about a god other than yours?"

POST HOC The assertion that one event must be the explanation for a subsequent one. But correlation does not prove causation. Coincidental timing is purely coincidental until proven otherwise. If I hold my breath every time I drive through a tunnel and the tunnel doesn't collapse on me, it's not because I held my breath as there is no evidence for that. There *is* evidence that the tunnel was designed *not* to collapse.

Look out for: Event sequence as the only evidence, oversimplified explanation.

Evangelical examples: "I prayed that my headache would go away and then it did," "I gave my life to God and then everything got better."

Counteract with: "What is your evidence that the first event caused the other one?" "How did you determine that this is the only possible cause?"

WHATABOUTISM/RED HERRING This is just a plain old deflection. Bringing up something unrelated to their assertion in order to shift the blame or argument to something else. Relationship therapists will tell you this is a common one in arguments between couples—one party brings up a valid concern about the other party and instead of having that concern addressed the first party is met with, "Yeah well you do that too" or "I did *this*, but what about all the times you did *that*?" Another, potentially valid, criticism does not negate the topic at hand.

Look out for: Topic change, failure to respond directly to a question, using "What about...?" questions instead.

Evangelical examples: "What about schools? They have abuse scandals too!" "What about atheists? They've done horrible things throughout history too!"

Counteract with: "We can absolutely have that conversation, but can you please address mine first?"

NO TRUE SCOTSMAN This is one of my least favorite fallacies, due to how often it is used, yet so easily dismissed. The original example of this is credited to philosopher Antony Flew, who told a story of a man reading about someone who committed an atrocious act and responded with claims that he must not be a Scotsman because a Scotsman would never have done that. Then, when provided information about a Scotsman who indeed does those atrocious things, the man's argument changes to "Well, no *true* Scotsman would do that." This fallacy is an attempt to hold a characteristic as true ("All men have muscles"), by arbitrarily redefining the group to exclude any examples to the contrary ("Well, all *real* men have muscles").

Look out for: Claims about someone being a true, real or false version of something without providing a reason why.

Evangelical examples: "If you left the faith, you were never a true believer to begin with," "People who commit harm in the name of Jesus are not real Christians," "It's no wonder you left that church; it was full of false teachers."

Counteract with: "What's a reliable way for us to determine the difference between a true and a fake?"

COMMON ARGUMENTS YOU'LL HEAR

"I don't have enough faith to be an atheist!"

Christian apologists Frank Turek and Norman L. Geisler used this fallacious phrase as the title of their 2004 book, which was (unsurprisingly) full of fallacies like God of the Gaps, special pleading and strawman arguments. It has become the most popular strawman argument against atheism that I hear, and boy, is it a flimsy one. First, the blatant use of "faith" as a derogatory term is inconsistent with the typical Christian glorification of it. Evangelicals believe that "without faith it is impossible to please God" (Hebrews 11:6) and use "faithful" as a laudatory term, and yet in this declaration about atheism, they completely reverse that. It takes zero faith to lack belief in something. I don't have faith that Zeus, Tapio or Jesus are supernatural gods—I simply don't believe it. Turek's attempt to shift the burden of proof here (which is very much on the person asserting a belief) is even more dishonest when combined with his personal definition of faith: "trusting in what you have good evidence to believe." [10] Tell me how "I don't have enough trust-in-what-I-have-good-evidence-to-believe to be an atheist" makes any sense? He continues with "If they say they disagree with the proposition God exists, they're an atheist," which makes his proposition of a faithful atheist even more nonsensical, based on his own definitions. No one needs faith, trust or assertions about anything to disagree with the proposition that a god exists. I find it incredibly telling when someone throws this comment at me, though—it's the one time theists seem to understand the ridiculousness of religious faith and why it's a terrible reason to believe something.

---

10 Frank Turek. "What is Faith? And Why Everyone Has It!" CrossExaminged.org (October 1, 2021). https://crossexamined.org/wp-content/uploads/2021/10/WhatIsFaith-IDHEFTBAAPodcast10.1.21.pdf.

"Atheists use faith every day for all kinds of things, why not for God?"

If we're using "faith" consistently as a religious term, then no, I don't use faith every day. I use *trust*. I don't have faith in my car starting. I trust that my car will start because I know it has gas in it, I know I've kept up with its maintenance and I have evidence that it has started every other time I pushed the ignition in the past. I don't have faith that gravity will keep me on the ground, I have empirical (observable, testable, documented) evidence that it will. I don't have faith that my partner loves me. I have a consistent shared history of him expressing love for me through words, actions and prioritization of my well-being. I don't have any evidence of a god's existence, but I do for the other things I mentioned. I have both practical and evidentiary reasons to trust the things I do, I don't have reasons to believe in god.

"You're just angry at God."

By definition, an atheist cannot be angry at any gods or deities. At least not in a literal sense. To be genuinely angry at something, one would have to believe that thing exists. I cringe when I hear testimonies from Christians about how they once were a "militant atheist that hated God!" There's your testimony right there—you still believed in a god, you were just struggling emotionally. The nuance that anyone making this accusation toward atheists is missing is that an atheist absolutely can be angry at god-*claims*, and yet have no feelings at all about "god." For example, while watching a movie featuring a problematic villain, I can criticize this character and express negative emotions about the idea of them while not actually believing they exist. Similarly, when reading the Bible, I find it impossible to *not* feel anger at the idea of a god that would wipe out almost all of his creation in a flood (including infants and animals), especially given that real people actively worship this character in the present day. The implication that atheism is an emotional position rather than one reached via logic seems much more like a projection coming from Christians rather than a rational argument. It is a complete dismissal of an atheist's actual position, which is not based on emotion, but but simple disbelief. If I were presented with incontrovertible evidence that the Christian god exists, I would believe in it, but I would also be an angry theist, feeling a lot of anger about such a horrific monster's existence. Luckily, there's no reason to think such a monster actually exists. Humanity wreaks enough havoc on its own, including the harm it causes with religion. My anger is righteously aimed at the injustice, indoctrination, abuse and lies caused by people, not gods.

"Atheists are obsessed with talking about God."

Personally, I am not obsessed with talking about any particular god. I am obsessed with exposing the harm perpetuated by religion and encouraging free thought, which often means having to address god-claims as well. This has much more to do with my passion for helping others escape indoctrination and almost nothing to do with atheism. In my experience, most atheists are content to avoid the topic of religion entirely and prefer to live and let live. Unless religion comes up, you would probably never know that someone was an atheist. But in the U.S., where 68 percent of people are Christian,[11] the topic *does* come up. It may seem to evangelicals that all atheists are discussing religion all the time, when in reality, it's only the atheists they're engaging with on any given day. This is a sampling bias, because of course they aren't accounting for all the atheists who don't broach the topic. When atheists *do* talk about religion and god-claims, it is in response to the very real impact these beliefs have on our own lives and the function of society. Were the U.S. more populated with Muslims than Christians, and were atheists to criticize *that* god-belief, I doubt you would hear many evangelicals complaining that we are "obsessed with talking about God." I dream of a day when I never have to engage in conversation about any gods, but until religion stops being used to justify behavior that hinders and harms the well-being of myself and others, I'll continue speaking out.

"Everyone believes, deep down."

This assertion positions the speaker as a mind reader, claiming they know what you *really* believe. It's dishonest and baseless—the verbal equivalent of putting their fingers in their ears, closing their eyes and saying "Nuh uh!" It's also a conversation-stopper. Continuing to engage with someone who is just going to make up their own story about what you believe and essentially call you a liar for claiming disbelief is not a worthwhile cause.

"You were never a real Christian if you walked away."

I have found that one of the most difficult things for a believer to accept is that someone could have genuinely believed and yet no longer does. This "no-true-Christian" assertion also relies on the idea that there is such a thing as a "real" or "true" Christian, and there isn't. It's also a convenient, circular

---

11 "How Religious Are Americans." Gallup, (March 29, 2024). https://news.gallup.com/poll/358364/religious-americans.aspx.

claim that if you've left you were never a *true* Christian to begin with because true Christians don't leave. This theological claim is usually rooted in 1 John 2:19, which says, "They went out from us, but they did not really belong to us. For if they had belonged to us, they would have remained with us; but their going showed that none of them belonged to us."

Again, this is nothing more than generalization and false dichotomy fallacies, regardless of it being in the Bible. The same book is often used to defend the opposite theology believed by many Christians, which is the idea that you can never lose your salvation (or, "once saved, always saved"). More important than trying to convince someone of your sincerity is to realize how irrelevant it is. My response to people who say this sort of thing is that for 20-plus years, I sincerely believed that Jesus was the son of God, that he died for my sins and rose again and that I was called to be a follower of his, and that I no longer believe any of that. I call that being an ex-Christian or former Christian. If they feel the need to define my experience with a different word, they can have at it.

"Why don't you leave Christians alone?"

As an atheist, I have never gone door to door asking if I can enter a stranger's home to share the good news of disbelief. I haven't stood on a street corner with a megaphone telling people that they will face eternal torment if they don't believe what I believe. Sure, in my own space, I speak freely, but I don't presume to force my belief or lack of belief on anyone. Yet the common rhetoric is that atheists are harassing Christians. I can only speak for myself, but I don't force my activism on anyone. I'm not leaving my book in hotel nightstands or standing outside of churches yelling at children that "GOD DOESN'T EXIST!" Anything I do is purely in response to religious assertions. I would love to stop speaking about atheism, to never again engage in debate. But religion does not exist in a vacuum. Until adults stop telling vulnerable children they need the blood of a savior for a condition they were born with that will send them to hell, until spiritual, physical and sexual abuse is no longer committed by religious leaders, until there are no longer billboards saying "believe or burn," until "men of god" stop profiting off of the "least of these" (Matthew 25:40) while jetting off in their tax-free planes, until someone provides evidence that any gods even exist...I will not "leave Christians alone."

"There are no atheists in foxholes."

Except that there are. There are veteran organizations made up of secular and atheist military members and testimony from soldiers that maintained disbelief after combat.[12] As for what this statement is claiming—that when faced with difficulty people turn to a god—I find that this only supports my belief that Christianity is fueled by fear. You never hear testimonies of people living in lovely circumstances, feeling content and happy in life and then converting to religion. The stories are about feeling lost, needing help or facing a crisis. All of this is evidence that humans will turn to whatever coping mechanisms they have easy access to (drugs, alcohol and, yes, religion) when they don't know what else to do. Someone praying on their deathbed isn't evidence of a god; it's evidence of fear and desperation. Something evangelicals are happy to associate their god with.

"God lets us choose freely, and you chose to be an atheist."

Belief is not a choice. You can't just decide to turn it on or off. Go ahead and try it...choose to believe that this book is actually a loaf of bread. You could act like that's true, set it on a cutting board and slice yourself a nice piece, even do your best to chew and swallow down some pages. But this is called acting, not believing. Regardless of your actions, you're either convinced that it's a loaf of bread or you're not. Even in a life-or-death situation (as Christians tend to claim it is), you can't force a belief. If someone were to put a gun to my head right now and demand that I believe in a god, of course I would lie and say that I do to save my life. But if I were hooked up to a 100 percent accurate lie detector test, it would reveal that I was lying, even at gunpoint. I've had many conversations with theists who claim that belief is a choice, which makes me wonder if they're simply saying that in order to paint atheism as pure rebellion against their god, or if they also don't believe and are just going through the motions due to fear, indoctrination or some other perceived obligation.

"You were indoctrinated by liberals."

I was a pastor's daughter. I was homeschooled using a Christian curriculum for grades K-12 and was part of a Christian homeschool group. For much of my childhood, I was not allowed to listen to or watch or read non-Christian content aside from the rare classics that were thought to promote Christian

12 Brian Wansink and Craig S. Wansink. "Are there atheists in foxholes? Combat intensity and religious behavior." Journal of Religion and Health, 2013 Sep;52(3):768-79. https://pubmed.ncbi.nlm.nih.gov/23760855/.

or conservative values. I read the Bible every day, prayed to Jesus every day and all of my friends and family were Christians. To suggest that liberalism had any role in my leaving the church is laughable. Comparing political affiliations or social stances to religious beliefs is both a false equivalency and unnecessary. Plenty of political conservatives are nonreligious, and plenty of political liberals and leftists are religious. This accusation is yet another admission, though. Even if only subconsciously, it is an acknowledgment of the power of Christian indoctrination. Without this power, Christianity would likely struggle to exist today, if at all, as "most people who currently identify as Christian were raised as Christians." Equally relevant, "most who have left Christianity no longer identify with any religion."[13] So where is this supposed doctrine that we apostates have blindly switched to? The truth is that the majority of people who identify as nonreligious do so because they doubt the religious teachings themselves,[14] not because they hold to some opposing doctrine.

CURIOSITY CALMED THE CAT (THE EPISTEMOLOGICAL APPROACH)

Debate has its place in society and has historically been a benefit to philosophy and critical thinking. But it is significantly more useful for the audience than it is for the people representing their opposing stances. In an argument, it is expected that there is something true to be discovered, and often, that ends up putting some of the claims made in the category of "wrong." No one likes being wrong; it literally takes a toll on the brain, so much so that we develop cognitive dissonance in order to avoid the discomfort.[15] While it may spark some thoughts that eventually lead to a change, arguments are one of the less gentle ways to induce that.

Something I had to learn as an ex-evangelical was to let go of the need to "save" everyone around me. That meant I had to pick a new value for engaging in conversations about topics I find important and potentially divisive. I had

---

13 Kirsten Lesage et al. "Around the World, Many People Are Leaving Their Childhood Religions." Pew Research Center (March 26, 2025) https://www.pewresearch.org/wp-content/uploads/sites/20/2025/03/PR_2025.03.26_international-religious-switching_report.pdf.
14 "Religious 'Nones' in America: Who They Are And What They Believe." Pew Research Center (January 24, 2024). https://www.pewresearch.org/religion/2024/01/24/why-are-nones-nonreligious/.
15 Thea Buckley. "What Happens to the Brain During Cognitive Dissonance?" Scientific American, (November 1, 2015). https://www.scientificamerican.com/article/what-happens-to-the-brain-during-cognitive-dissonance1/.

to decide if I just wanted people on "my side" or if I actually valued humans experiencing free thought. Did I want to evangelize like in my religious days, or did I want to inspire them to think freely? I decided on free thought, because if I don't value the personhood of whomever I'm talking to more than whatever conclusions I've reached about life, then I'm no better than those who indoctrinated *me.* But how do you engage someone in conversation when the ideas they're entertaining border on delusional? How do you prioritize facts and reality with someone who completely ignores those things? And how do you do so without the conversation spiraling into an emotionally heated situation?

As we'll discuss in the next chapter, it's great to keep boundaries as needed with family, friends and coworkers when it comes to sensitive topics, but sometimes you may *want* to engage. However, I would first encourage you to check in with yourself about *why* you want to engage. If it's coming from an emotional place of defensiveness, take this as an alert that engaging may not be beneficial. Being able to justify your position or feeling as if you have a responsibility to do so is not the same as having an emotional *need* to do so. If a conversation topic or question has you feeling anxious, or in a hurry to get words out, or frustrated at your inability to get the *right* words out, I believe it's a clear sign that you need to build confidence. Topics that feel deeply personal (and are deeply personal) understandably can make us emotional. That's not always a bad thing, but sometimes it can diminish the quality of the conversation you're trying to have if emotions start to take precedence over content. The first step is to let go of your own need to be heard—there's a time and a place, but if you're truly looking to help others think critically, you have to focus on *their* thinking, not your own.

The best tool I have found for cultivating productive conversations in everyday life is curiosity. Socratic questioning and Street Epistemology (a conversation method focused on inspiring critical thinking) are both excellent methods for making every conversation a fruitful one. In essence, the idea is to politely question the other person's belief or claim and not only discover for yourself why they believe this but also help them better understand as well. It involves fostering a respectful environment without a hostile tone, asking how confident they are in their belief or claim, figuring out what reasons or evidence they have, determining together if they're good reasons and then reevaluating their confidence level. It's not about convincing them they're wrong or offering counterclaims. It's simply about inspiring them to examine not just *what* they believe, but *why* they believe it.

REPUTATION: ATHEIST'S VERSION

It was a sunny morning just after Thanksgiving and I was riding in the passenger seat blasting the *Lion King* soundtrack while my husband drove us to Disney World. I was in a great mood to say the least. And then texts started coming in, one after the other, asking if I had seen "the video" a popular right-wing media company had posted featuring *me*. I felt my heart go into my throat, already preparing myself for the trolling and harassment this attention would drive my way. I opened the YouTube link to see a thumbnail picture of my face between *The Daily Wire*'s Michael Knowles and teen heartthrob turned Christian apologist Kirk Cameron. The title in bold font said "ANGRY ATHEISTS." I laughed. I am many things, but an angry communicator I am not. I didn't even look angry in the picture; the closest screengrab they could get of me looking "angry" was an awkward shot of me caught in mid-sentence. The video was Michael and Kirk reacting to multiple atheist videos, mine included. Of course, there wasn't an ounce of anger in my tone, face or argument, but nothing gets views like clickbait titles that rely on stereotypes. Interestingly enough, once I put out a response video pointing out the ad hominem, the thumbnail image was changed to feature someone else. But why is this Angry Atheist portrayal so common despite it generally not being accurate? As previously mentioned, your average American who has a poor view of atheists doesn't actually know one. They get their information from TV, books, podcasts and, yes, *The Daily Wire*. Even more disturbing is the messaging that evangelicals and conservatives are being fed. Billy Graham is reputed to have said that marrying an atheist makes "the Devil" your father-in-law.[16] As Pat Robertson said on *The 700 Club*, "People who are atheists, they hate God, they hate the expression of God, and they are angry with the world, angry with themselves, angry with society and they take it out on innocent people who are worshiping God." [17]

And in his book *The New World Order*, Robertson dramatically asked, "How can there be peace when drunkards, drug dealers, communists, atheists, New Age, worshipers of Satan, secular humanists, oppressive dictators, greedy moneychangers, revolutionary assassins, adulterers, and homosexuals are on top?"

16 Pat Robertson. "Should a Christian Marry an Unbeliever?" CBN. https://cbn.com/article/marriage/should-christian-marry-unbeliever.
17 "Ask the Atheist: Activist and Comic to Field Believers' Tough Questions." Center for Inquiry (June 22, 2018). https://centerforinquiry.org/press_releases/ask-the-atheist/.

In 2017, a new conspiracy cult commonly referred to as "QAnon" emerged, fanning the flames of evangelical dualism. Followers are convinced there is a satanic cabal made up of social elites like the Obamas, Clintons, Mark Zuckerberg and even Tom Hanks. This deep state group supposedly runs a sex trafficking ring that involves pedophilic and cannibalistic activity, amongst many other wild claims, including the primary belief that Donald Trump is the chosen one to lead the underground fight against this evil. Despite the ridiculousness of the conspiracy claim, 27 percent of white evangelicals believe it,[18] and 7 out of 10 QAnoners believe "God has granted America a special role in human history."[19] The conspiracy is very much rooted in the idea that there is good and evil, and you are either on the "good" side (God and Trump) or the evil side. This way of determining good from evil suggests that atheists are part of the pedophilic, child-blood-drinking, devil-worshiping side. I experienced this accusation firsthand when I criticized an evangelical family member's ties to the conspiracy and was met with the assertion that my problems with it *must* be because I was opposed to "life, liberty and justice."

Of course, this modern disdain for atheists is nothing new. During the Inquisition, men like Lucilio Vanini were accused of atheism and, when found guilty, were tortured and killed for it. In Nazi Germany, Hitler spoke of the "atheistic movement" and that he had "stamped it out." During the Cold War, the U.S. government was quick to propagate the idea that this was not just about political differences but a battle between godless communism and God-fearing America. To support this idea, "under God" was added to the Pledge of Allegiance in 1954. Two years later, "In God We Trust" was made an official national motto. These were efforts made to further contrast the warring governments and highlight the good guy Christian versus bad guy atheist (which we'll get into more later). This long, strong history of placing atheists on the opposing side of God himself has paved the way for all sorts of negative stereotypes. The popularization of the angry atheist is a more modern take. Why is it that this characterization has caught on despite the lack of empirical evidence that atheists indeed are "angry"?

In addition to centuries of stigmatization, largely due to religious and political agendas, I believe there's another aspect at play. The most popular

18 "QAnon Beliefs Have Increased Since 2021 as Americans Are Less Likely to Reject Conspiracies" PRRI, (June 24, 2022). https://prri.org/spotlight/qanon-beliefs-have-increased-since-2021-as-americans-are-less-likely-to-reject-conspiracies/.
19 Ibid.

atheist voices that make their way to U.S. audiences tend to be straight, white men. Before I go on, let me be clear that this is not a criticism of the voices that have profoundly paved the way for skepticism, reasoning and atheism. The work of "the Four Horsemen," Richard Dawkins, Daniel Dennett, Sam Harris and Christopher Hitchens, positively influenced and freed the minds of many, myself included. These men have boldly put a voice to many truths. In his book *God Is Not Great*, Hitchens described organized religion as "violent, irrational, intolerant, allied to racism and tribalism and bigotry, invested in ignorance and hostile to free inquiry, contemptuous of women and coercive toward children." In *The God Delusion*, Dawkins describes the god of the Bible as "a vindictive bloodthirsty ethnic cleanser, a misogynistic, homophobic racist, an infanticidal, genocidal, filicidal, pestilential, megalomaniacal, sadomasochistic, capriciously malevolent bully." Dennett is credited with saying, "There's simply no polite way to tell people they've dedicated their lives to an illusion," and unfortunately, I believe that's an accurate statement. To a religious person who is unwilling to evaluate these criticisms honestly, the assertiveness of the atheist may come across as anger. And the media loves anger and hostility. Controversy sells and atheists are typically only featured in debate formats or viral clips featuring scathing rebuttals to religious claims. Atheists' emphasis on logic is perceived as coldness and their valid confidence in their criticisms as arrogance, stoking the accusations of anger. They are characterized as oppositional and are particularly entertaining when seated across from a religious apologist, as people love to watch the intellectual sparring. Of course, this doesn't just apply to atheism and religion. Historically, we humans love competition, feuds and battles. From sports to reality TV to the ancient Roman Colosseum, we enjoy observing conflict. Atheism makes for excellent conflict not because of what it is, but because of what it lacks. It's not a set of tenets, it's not a worldview, it's not an assertion of anything. It's a lack of belief in gods. It *is* an opposition. But atheists are not solely comprised of a disbelief in gods. We are complex humans like anyone else. Some of us are more oppositional in nature, some more soft-spoken. We have hobbies, hopes and dreams. We have families and friends, careers and passions. Some of us are funny and some of us are serious. We're far more diverse than the image of an older, white man engaging in relentless debate might suggest, and even those who fit that description are, as Walt Whitman might say, made up of "multitudes." But the media prefers to highlight atheists when they're arguing in the gladiator ring, and of course that practice highlights the atheist stereotype, which, in turn, makes the gladiator ring much more accessible to those men.

But, as noted, the stereotype does not represent who we are. Many nonbelievers live quietly because they *have* to. Some are reliant on families or churches, stuck in small towns due to career or other circumstances, where expressing doubt or dissent is a risk to the quality of their life. For them, their atheism is not a sword to wield, but a private position they've taken. A position reached after years of struggle, loss and hard work. I have heard their nuanced stories, layered with emotion. Their disbelief is just a fraction of who they are. It's not the sort of thing people get to hear about atheists because it's not what sells. Missing these stories has skewed our culture's perception of atheism. The combat is all they see, so they call us militant. We rarely see atheists when they are being warm, artistically talented, emotionally intelligent, silly or nontheistically spiritual.

Women, LGBTQ+ individuals, Black and Indigenous people, immigrants and other marginalized people are also underrepresented in atheism. Many communities view atheism as a betrayal, and to be "out" as an atheist can mean risking relationships, employment or even physical safety. While their voices are valuable, it's understandable that many choose to stay silent. The ones that do speak up usually do so unsupported, and it comes at a great cost. Many atheists from these groups, including me, report death threats, bigotry and generally hateful rhetoric at a much higher rate than their white, male peers. The persecution I was told to expect for being a Christian ended up being what I actually receive as an atheist instead.

I believe that is changing, though. As more of us speak out and make space for others to do the same, our stories will soften and challenge the strawmen that have been built up against us. That's why it's important to build personal confidence. Yes, debate and criticisms of religion should and must continue; they are an important aspect of progressing as a society. My own personal work is devoted to opposing the harmful lies and dangers of evangelicalism. But the foundation to all of this comes from being at peace with your own story. There is something deeply powerful about being able to confidently share your position not out of defense or justification but to help shed light on the humanity of being an atheist. Part of representation is pulling back the curtain and in doing so, naturally undoing some of the stigma surrounding atheism. While science and academia have been a haven for atheists, many in politics and other fields are less able to openly disbelieve. As more of us begin to live authentically, the more multifaceted the face of atheism will become, which will directly challenge the myths about our morality and our outlooks on meaning and purpose—not just on debate stages, but in our lived experiences. I deeply appreciate the loud and controversial versions of us, but I also value those who have other things to offer. When more people feel safe enough to live openly as atheists, we can *all* feel more peace. We should be able to do more than resist—we should thrive.

I was once bound by religion, abused and controlled by it. I was told my goal should be to sacrifice all that I have to God. I was commanded to be a shell of myself. To be a robot, a "bond-servant" of Christ. I never want another human being to suffer from the effects of that abuse. My atheism is not charged with anger but rather disdain for injustice and abuse. Illogical and harmful beliefs should be criticized, with the intention of setting more minds free. More stories should be shared about the harm religion causes, without fear of persecution. This is why I will continue to speak out against Christian nationalism and the attempt to create a theocracy in my home country or any place else evangelical extremism tries to sink its teeth into. I am not opposed to individuals consenting to religious lifestyles and practices in the privacy of their own homes and consenting communities. I am opposed to those individuals making the rest of us bow down to their beliefs, pay for them, give up freedoms for them and generally cater to whatever their unproven faith demands. I am against their use of religion to justify hatred and condemnation of others. I am against children being indoctrinated, lied to and abused while threatened with the most terrifying punishment imaginable.

As so many have said before, the truth is not afraid of questions. Any beliefs worth having are worth scrutinizing. I'm not here to convince anyone of any specific way, belief, philosophy or path. I'm here to challenge you to ask if you have good reasons to believe what you believe and to encourage you toward free thought. Not bound by dogma or commitment to certainty, but the freedom and humility to say "I don't know" and the curiosity and skepticism to embrace the journey of being present and thoughtful. No gods, no masters, simply worshiping nothing. A lack of chains, a lack of dogma and a lack of belief—space for what *is* hides in the freedom from what is *not*.

CHAPTER 9

Tiny Little Funerals

"The pain passes, but the beauty remains."
—PIERRE AUGUSTE RENOIR

WHAT THEY DON'T TELL YOU about leaving a harmful religion is how much you might miss it at times. You will miss being part of a family or community or doctrine, however toxic it may have been. Your life may have been built around these things. You will miss feeling like you belong. You will miss the shared belief, like an inside joke with friends. You will miss the ride-or-die of tribalism. You will miss the false utopia. The false certainty. I imagine it's similar to being a recovering addict—constantly holding space for the loss of a particular brand of high you (hopefully) will never experience again. There is so much goodness when you leave, of course. That makes it all worth it. I have found that the integrity of embracing reality is much better than even the most comforting lie. But often, freedom feels a lot like loneliness. A lot like being on an island. As if you were a tree uprooted from a sickly forest. You mourn what was thought to be true but never was and never will be. This grief is normal and healthy, if you befriend it. It's the evidence of how true you were then and how true you are now. A god may not have shown up, but your grief is proof that you were always fully there.

I attend multiple funerals every day—momentary ceremonies in my mind, held in remembrance of something permanently lost. It can be sadness for the praise I will never get from my family for my accomplishments. Sometimes, it's for the friendship I will never again have with my dad or the peace I can't give my mom, who worries about my eternal soul. And sometimes it's for the common ground my siblings and I once shared around religion. Now I stand alone, separate from all of that. A picture, an event or a conversation can send a wave of powerful sadness over me. The disappointment is impossible to escape. It used to feel like suffocation, like drowning, like the bad feeling would never end. Every time an emotional wave would hit, I would wear myself out trying to swim out of it. I would try to reassure myself: *Your family is proud of you, in their own way. Your mom and dad love you; nothing has changed that! You and your siblings still have so much fun together!* I was searching for comforting thoughts to distract myself from how I really felt. I had upended the family status quo, which is just one of the big losses my escape from evangelicalism cost me.

Growing up, I was told stories about my mother's mother, who had passed at a young age, and how exciting it would be to meet her one day in heaven. When my grandfather passed away from Parkinson's disease after decades of slowly becoming a shell of himself, I was reminded that I would next see him in eternity, where he would be healed. I lost those promises along with the guarantee of a paradise waiting for me after this life. I lost an eternity. I lost an entire god. As delusional as it was, the indoctrination had perfectly shaped my cognitive biases, fears and desires to be loved, transforming me into someone who was convinced she had a relationship with Jesus. I was trained to believe that much of my inner dialogue was actually God speaking to me. When good things happened, I thought it was an intentional act of kindness from someone who knew the best and worst parts of me. When I was scared and needed comfort, I believed something bigger and more powerful was out there watching over me. Now, none of that was true. Who was I now, without all of that?

There was something else even more difficult to think about: Who could I have been if religion hadn't declared me a sinner, even as a child, with intentionally impossible standards designed to reinforce my feelings of worthlessness with each failure? Who *could* I have been without the constant fear of spiritual warfare and thoughts of my loved ones burning in hell? If I had grown up in a culture that taught consent, valued personal autonomy and didn't approach sex with shame, could I have better faced some of the heartbreak and trauma?

Maybe instead of getting married at 19 to the first person I was allowed to date, I would have stayed in college, had some normal relationships and taken my time to figure out who and what I wanted in life. Maybe I would have been able to grow up a little bit slower and enjoy some of the fun parts about being a twenty-something instead of being shamed by my church for getting divorced. Maybe I would have felt empowered to explore, get to know myself, maybe even pursue a career because it was of interest to me, not because it was God's calling. There's an entire version of myself that was stolen. This "Pascal's Wager," which is often thrown around by theists, couldn't be more wrong. The idea that believing in God costs you nothing and potentially earns you eternity, while disbelief may cause you to lose everything, is a total lie. Evangelicalism cost me *my* identity—I lost myself in it. Leaving religion gave me the gift of *me*, but it also meant starting over from the very beginning. It was like escaping from a burning building. I was thrilled to make it out alive, but my home was burned to the ground, with all of my precious belongings turned to ash. Two things were true: There was a new life and freedom to be celebrated *and* there were losses to mourn.

Processing or even acknowledging the loss did not come easily or without work. I was indoctrinated to be incapable of coping with loss. If there are five stages of grief, Christianity only teaches the first: denial. The entire premise of evangelicalism is that this world is temporary, but that you can experience eternity if you go along with God's will (1 John 2:17). In the Christian worldview, death is the beginning of eternal life and the end of what was consistently taught to me as the uncomfortable part of life (John 11:25-26). We Christians just had to get through the trials and tribulations of this materialistic world and then we would get our reward (John 16:33). In other words, death is just a transition to a better place. Ironically, the religion that gives us a feeling of certainty about so many things we actually can't be certain of avoids the one certainty life actually offers: death.

Every single one of us will, at some point, know the feeling of losing something precious—maybe it's a pet, a friend, a family member, a house or even an experience we deeply desired but never had. I believe this is what makes evangelicalism so appealing to those who practice it. It plays on the fact that our brains work hard to avoid thinking about mortality.[1] We don't want to have death on our minds; we want to focus on living. But there is a healthy balance between obsessing over mortality and denying it altogether. Religion has often been advertised as protection from death and loss. It offers an afterlife, reunions with lost loved ones and divine plans to convince us that something better is coming and that there's no reason to cry over spilled milk. All will be made right in the next life.

But all of these promises come at the cost of rejecting reality. In theory, avoiding grief or negative emotions sounds great, but ultimately, it's impossible. We are all confronted with loss, death and grief at some point, and covering it up with a religious curtain does not make it go away. If anything, it limits our ability to experience the full spectrum of being alive. How can we fully embrace the joys and wins of life if we aren't equipped to handle the griefs and losses as well? Today, we have access to healthier life skills and more effective medical treatments and support than ever before. We have tools like trauma-informed therapy, advanced digital platforms and devices that enable us to connect with those who support us, at any time from virtually any place on Earth, and science-based literature that allows us to face reality with accurate information. We don't have to pretend that loss doesn't happen. Truly acknowledging the finality of death and the certainty of change is what gives value to this one life I have. It is my motivation to be present, pay attention and take in all that life offers. It is the hope I need when I'm afraid a moment of pain will last for eternity. It gives me the strength to face life's most difficult moments, to ensure the life I have is one worth living. It is what makes me human.

The false promise Christianity offers to avoid death can weaken our stomach for the topic, but we are still capable of facing sorrow. If we want to grow and thrive, we must be willing to do the emotional work of being human. That means learning how to sit with sadness, how to process grief and how to keep living with openness in a world where all things end. It's not easy, but it's worth it (cliché as that may sound). Accepting the end of something doesn't deny the meaning that thing or person holds. Accepting grief provided the meaning to life I was afraid would vanish when I lost my belief: Life matters *because* it ends.

---

1 Y. Dor-Ziderman et al. "Prediction-based neural mechanisms for shielding the self from existential threat." NeuroImage Volume 202 (November 15, 2019). https://www.sciencedirect.com/science/article/abs/pii/S1053811919306688.

THE THINGS WE LOSE

The death of a loved one may be the most obvious loss we have to struggle with, but grief extends to a myriad of things, especially for those who have left religion.

IDENTITY When you're an evangelical, there's a lot of emphasis on "finding your identity in Christ." Your identity is defined by terms like "child of God," "God's chosen" and "follower of Jesus." If you're known for anything, it's supposed to be something that points others back to God. A common prayer I heard growing up was "More of you, God. Less of me." Your faith is so enmeshed with your everyday thoughts and practices that walking away from it feels like having to rebuild from the ground up and discover "*Who am I without my faith?*" Many former evangelicals have told me that they felt like children upon leaving their faith in their 30s or 40s because for the first time in their lives, they had to figure out their own interests, values and personality traits that had previously been suppressed. This new freedom is incredible, but it often requires grieving the loss of one's past self.

FAMILY Some people who leave religion are completely shunned by their family and lose all access to them. Some of us, for better or worse, don't lose those relationships completely, but all of us have to grieve the loss of what these relationships once were. We grew up with these people, sharing our first inside jokes and creating positive memories together. For some, these are also the people who abused us or turned a blind eye to abuse.

Complex family issues and dysfunction are not exclusive to religious homes, but being a black sheep in an evangelical family carries its own unique complexities: tense conversations, even when you desperately want to connect. Holiday dinners that turn awkward or triggering, when all you want is to experience that old comfort of belonging. No longer feeling comfortable being yourself in the place you first called home. The shock to the system of finding yourself on the outside of an exclusive community you once belonged to. It's a lot.

For the first few years after I left the faith, I couldn't believe how different everything was. The people I had spent my life with were now accusing me of "being under the influence of witchcraft." My own family members, the ones I had prayed and worshiped with since I was a child, now believed I was going to suffer in hell for all of eternity. I wanted so badly to be close to them, to feel like I was still part of "the team." But I also knew I could never go back to that, certainly not in the same way, not when they believed what they did. I felt like a kid who had left the house, learned an important truth and could no longer get back in because of it. I could only look in the windows and watch everyone else at the dinner table, passing food and telling jokes.

I wanted to be angry and hurt but felt like I was solely to blame since I was the one whose beliefs had changed. My relationships with each family member also changed drastically. What they were to me before, what *I* was to *them*, no longer held true. I lost the family that I had, like so many of us do, but grieving them made more space for the found family I have now.

COMMUNITY The most convenient thing church has going for it (although often toxic in its own way) is that it offers instant community. Humans are social creatures; we need to be around others. Organized religion says, "Here are some friends who believe and follow the same worldview as you! And we're going to organize regular hangouts for you all!" There are meal trains for people who are sick or welcoming new babies, childcare for the overwhelmed single mom and even regular home groups enabling families to spend time together over a meal. You often have people checking on you—asking how you are, remembering your prayer requests and staying up to date on what's happening in your life. That shared system of community and support is undeniably diminished—or even gone completely—once your beliefs change.

PURPOSE/CAREER So many of us built our life plans, sense of meaning and even jobs around our faith. Some have devoted years of their lives to seminary school, overseas missions, volunteer or paid church and ministry work, clergy member positions, worship leaders, children's pastors, the list goes on. Aside from the obvious logistical, financial and technical hardships the change of faith can bring about because of this, it can be incredibly disorienting to lose the foundation of everything you built your life on. No longer believing in a god doesn't mean you didn't truly love certain things about being a pastor or missionary or whatever other role you may have had or aspired to. Some ex-evangelicals have to grieve the loss of worship bands they spent years bonding with, entire congregations they pastored or even countries they moved to as missionaries.

TIME Speaking of years devoted to religion, time is often something that is grieved. Some of us lost entire childhoods to religion—years of life robbed by indoctrination. Fear of "worldliness" and "demonic influence" compelled our parents to deny us normal, healthy life experiences. As silly as it sounds, little things like trick-or-treating, high school proms, dating and other activities we watched our peers engage in showed us the simple pleasures we were missing out on.

AFTERLIFE Something doesn't have to be real for you to miss it. It can be a traumatic life change to let go of the idea that you'll see your family, friends and even pets in a perfect afterlife. Not only does this have implications on how grief may feel for you during future losses, but it can also require you to re-mourn loved ones that have already passed, this time without the hope that you'll see them again someday. It is a massive loss.

TRADITION/RITUAL Religion is full of repetitive, intentional moments[2]—gatherings to sing and learn together, holidays, prayers, communion and more.

When we lose these things, we grieve for them, too. Grief is not something to be ashamed of or to fix. It's an expression of being human. There is nothing too trivial to grieve, and there is no hierarchy for sadness. In many ways, grief is just an indicator of how much something meant to you. No one gets to tell you what is or isn't allowed to make you sad. It's okay to mourn the loss of what you believed was real and found value in, even if you no longer do. It's also okay to grieve the loss of things that you *don't* want back. Emotions are complex things, and you'll find yourself grieving over losses that you did not anticipate.

EXPERIENCING JOY DURING LOSS

Another thing about grief is that it ebbs and flows. You don't have to feel unbearable emotions 24/7 in order for you to label a loss as meaningful. You are allowed to have happy moments, too. Happy moments don't take away from the value of your grief. They don't make your pain less valid. They don't

---

2 Nicholas M. Hobson et al. "The Psychology of Rituals: An Integrative Review and Process-Based Framework." Personality and Social Psychology Review (2017). https://faculty.haas.berkeley.edu/jschroeder/Publications/Hobson%20et%20al%20Psychology%20of%20Rituals.pdf.

discredit whatever hardships you are experiencing. You don't have to pause your compassion for others. We need joy like we need food, water, air and sun. There will be moments of heaviness and moments of lightness. You can experience it all, shamelessly.

COMMON PHRASES YOU'LL HEAR

NOTE: While previous chapters have focused on how to respond to arguments/claims, this one is more about helping you process them internally.

"Everything happens for a reason."

No. Horrible things happen, beautiful things happen and everything in between. That's life. Trying to put reason behind abuse or loss can be advertised as looking for the silver lining, but sometimes those silver linings are made of lead and accepting the rain clouds as they are results in *less* suffering. If you've experienced something that caused you grief, you can give yourself permission to sit with the emotions of sadness or anger or whatever they feel like. You don't have to look for some hidden lesson or conspiracy to explain why things could have been worse if this bad thing hadn't happened instead. Some things are just painful. The bright side isn't that the bad experience has some good in it. The bright side is that there are *also* good experiences and you don't have to deny your present discomfort to experience them.

"This world is not our home."

As a teenager, I would comfort myself with Hebrews 13:14, "For this world is not our home; we are looking forward to our everlasting home in heaven." My excuse for feeling anything negative or experiencing difficulties was that I just wasn't made for life on Earth; I was made for heaven. Everything would make sense once we got to eternity. This was a common teaching I heard growing up, but it was just another way to bypass reality—to avoid being present in one's life.

"They're in a better place now."

I understand the sentiment of this phrase, and in some circumstances, I can even agree with it. I don't believe we go to any "place" when we die, but for some who have been suffering from illness, pain or infirmity, death must be a relief. The "better place," in this instance, may be as simple as no place at all.

"You'll see them again someday."

I would love for this to be true, but we have no reason to believe it is. Dismissing the finality of death prevents us from fully appreciating our lives. As far as we know, this is the only life that we get. Death comes for all of us and that makes the time we have with each other precious. My life has only gained value, joy, peace and depth since reaching this conclusion. Because it is our very finiteness that gives the present value, not the baseless promise of the infinite. The temporariness and fragility of life are what motivate me to make the most of the time that I have and to hopefully add some value to the lives of others, too. Instead of waiting for a funeral or an afterlife, I do my best to communicate my appreciation for my friends and family here and now. Instead of saying, "Well maybe someday," I now say "yes" to exciting risks and adventures as often as I can. I have no idea what tomorrow will bring or what parts of it will be up to me. I do and enjoy what I can today.

WAYS TO WELCOME GRIEF

FEEL IT Instead of pushing uncomfortable emotions and sensations away, make designated space for them in your life without feeling an immediate need to address or "fix" them.

Schedule time for it: One of my favorite therapists introduced the idea of scheduling time for grief. Sometimes that meant literally scheduling a good cry in the car on my calendar or assigning a specific song as a designated time to sit in an emotion. Doing so gave me more autonomy and choice over the grief, instead of feeling like it was ruling my life. I was guaranteeing myself the time to fully feel.

Express it through art and activities: If you're someone (like me) who overintellectualizes their feelings in an effort to avoid actually feeling them, art and action (preferably without words) can be a great way to encourage more feeling and less thinking. Rage rooms, finger painting, crafting collages and even dance can all be effective methods to release some emotional steam.

Visualize it: The aforementioned therapist also taught me the art of building a "grief room" in my imagination. She directed me to design a room in my head—a cozy, safe space to which I could send myself, where I could just sit and be sad, light an imaginary candle, express an inner monologue for whomever or whatever I was missing and grieve in comfort. This was one of the ways I discovered I could attend "tiny little funerals" anytime I needed.

PUT WORDS TO IT Sometimes, feeling the feelings comes easily, but identifying them is more difficult. Words can be a perfect way to validate what you're feeling.

Name the feelings: Make a list (or even say it out loud) describing the things you're feeling. Maybe your chest feels tight, maybe your brain feels foggy, maybe you're able to recognize that you feel disappointed or confused. Whatever it is, try your best to describe it.

Record a voice memo: Verbal expression, whether you're going to listen to it later or not, can be a great way to release some grief and help you process it in real time.

Journal: Recording how you feel, how your day is going, what's bothering you in life and what's causing you to look forward can help reveal patterns of thought and action over time. Identifying and understanding these patterns can help you heal even further.

Write letters: Maybe there are things you wish you could say to someone or wish you *had* said. Maybe you want to write a letter to your past self or even your future self. Getting those things out of your head and onto paper can help you let go of the "what ifs."

MOVE WITH IT Our body takes on the stress of grief and trauma before our mind even knows what's going on. Physical movement not only helps release endorphins but also can relieve some of that tension.

Go on grief walks: Cry if you need to, play your saddest playlist and put yourself in nature.

Stretch your body with yoga or dance: This is a great way to be present with your body and bring yourself back to a more grounded place instead of sitting with that grief lingering in your head.

Breathing practices: Breath work can help calm your nervous system and regulate your body when it's feeling overwhelmed with emotion.

RITUALIZE IT Rituals and tradition aren't exclusive to religion. Consistent, intentional practices can help us find meaning and feel more engaged with the present while memorializing something from the past.

Memory altars: Designate a space in your home to whatever it is you're grieving. Maybe feature a photo, mementos and a place to light a candle or whatever else helps you take a moment and embrace the memories you want to honor.

Grief box: Fill a box with items that remind you of a time, person or other loss. Revisit it as desired, or even bury or burn it if doing so will help you heal and recognize the finality of the loss.

Celebrations: My family has a tradition of honoring loved ones who have passed away by eating that person's favorite treat on their birthday. For one, it's Coke and M&M's, for another, it's dark chocolate, and for another, Krispy Kreme donuts. It's a fun way to honor their memory. Find your own traditions and ways of remembering that involve something fun and celebratory.

REST WITH IT Emotions, whether expressed or not, can be physically exhausting. It's so important to give your body the care it needs to experience not just the uncomfortable emotions but also the fun ones.

Cancel plans: It's okay to reschedule things in order to give yourself time to be present with grief or recover from it. Sometimes saying no to plans is an act of self-care.

Naps: Never underestimate the power of a good nap. It not only gives your mind a break but also boosts brain health and improves mental performance.[3]

REACH OUT WITH IT Maybe most importantly, let others in. Your grief is unique to you, but experiencing grief in general is not.

Therapy: Finding a professionally trained therapist to help you process difficult emotions is a worthy investment. A therapist can provide a safe, shame-free space to feel your emotions without any pressure to have them figured out.

Support groups: It can be incredibly validating to sit with people who have experienced losses similar to your own. Knowing that you're not alone in your experience is huge.

FAMILY FEUD: RELIGIOUS EDITION

While it can be deeply healing and helpful to mourn the family and the relationships you once had, you also get to decide if you want to develop new relationships with those people and how those will look. I grew up in a very tight-knit family, which is not atypical of evangelicals. Second only to our loyalty to God was our loyalty to each other. While we experienced the typical

---

3 Isabelle Gerretsen. "Why power naps might be good for our health." BBC (January 28, 2024). https://www.bbc.com/future/article/20240126-why-power-naps-might-be-good-for-our-health.

sibling fights and teen arguments with our parents, we generally agreed on major issues and beliefs. Christianity was truth to all of us and it massively impacted how we viewed reality. Discussions about religion at the dinner table were calm and friendly. Maybe someone said a prayer or my mom prompted us to say what we were thankful to God for, but there was never any tension around the topic.

It wasn't until I left religion that I had an inflammatory conversation about the subject with my family, and the shock of that was real. From then on, whenever the topic came up, my heart would start racing, my voice would quiver with emotion and I felt as if I were one word away from completely erupting in tears or anger or both. Someone would ask a critical question about my position and I had no idea what to say back or how to defend myself. All the profound revelations I had about my past beliefs would seemingly disappear from my head. It was embarrassing. This inability to communicate made me feel like I was doomed to engage in conversations that were either toxic or disappointing. Unfortunately, being around family triggered my insecurities, reignited past dysfunction and made every conversation feel high stakes. My departure from religion led me to realize that without the proper tools to regulate my emotions or the self-confidence to maintain my inner peace, I could not engage with most of my family members. This meant stepping back and limiting contact with them while I did some work on myself in therapy.

Once I had figured out how to set boundaries, it was time to reengage. Now *I* decide what things are worth discussing, when it's better to stay silent and which family members are emotionally safer to have tough conversations with. These boundaries can change and grow with each individual relationship. I've learned that I don't always have to explain myself and that I can maintain my values without having to debate them. What is the secret to making this work? My family is emotionally intelligent enough to respect my boundaries. If you're constantly forced into conversations or situations you're not comfortable with, it's time to examine your relationships and take action.

Do you keep them in your life? It's important for me to acknowledge that not everyone gets to make this choice for themselves. Some are shunned by their families the moment they alter the status quo, while others may have to maintain contact because of financial, cultural or even physical safety reasons. But for those of us who have the privilege to decide, it is primarily an analysis of emotional cost. You have to weigh your options honestly: Are these relationships supportive of me and my well-being, or harmful? Does this relationship offer more peace, or more disruption? It's okay to reevaluate your conclusion as often as necessary. Ask yourself, "Does this relationship make my life better, or am I just getting through it?" It's also okay to create some space without completely cutting people off or to take a break and give yourself time to process things like I did. You don't have to say yes to every family event, and you don't have to engage in every group text chat. Boundaries don't have to be permanent either. They're just tools that you can adjust as your needs change in order to give the relationship a chance at the healthiest possible outcome.

What boundaries will you set? First of all, let's be clear about what a boundary is, since religion doesn't typically provide a lot of information about such an empowering tool. Setting a boundary is not about controlling other people; it's about communicating what you will or won't tolerate in your personal life. Telling someone, "You can't yell at me!" isn't a boundary, but communicating that "I'm not comfortable with yelling and I will exit the room (or conversation), if you raise your voice" and then following through if they cross that boundary is a great way to maintain a relationship while not allowing the behavior you've called out. Boundaries are a tool for creating a positive relationship, not ending it. Figuring out where you need to draw these lines in order to have good interactions with your family is vital. It's important to keep mutual respect and require no more than you're willing to give. For example, if I'm going to their house and they want to say a prayer before the meal, I don't mind sitting quietly while they do that. However, if they're at my house and I'm serving dinner, I'm not pausing for a prayer or catering to that. They're welcome to do that silently on their own. If I'm not in the mood to hear prayers or religious talk, I stay home.

Will you share your positions with them? One of the most important aspects of evangelicalism is that you evangelize. Your life is supposed to be a living testimony of God's greatness, and you are to share the gospel with anyone who needs to hear it. Keeping your beliefs private goes against everything you're taught. It's no wonder that many of us who change our beliefs and leave the faith feel a responsibility to share the reasons behind our departure. But you do not owe anyone transparency about your religious beliefs (or lack thereof). I'm often asked by people just leaving the faith how they should tell their family, and my first piece of advice is to evaluate if that's even safe to do. For younger people who are still living at home, their lives could be badly impacted if they reveal that they no longer believe. Some are dependent on family for childcare, their job or even their career. For some, it might even put their safety at risk.

It's a privilege to be in a position where you can be completely honest about your differences in faith and not worry about unwanted repercussions. Keeping your atheism to yourself can be an act of self-care, to protect you against anything from emotional drama to homelessness. Now, on the flipside, some may feel deeply uncomfortable hiding this part of themselves. Maintaining a relationship with family while not being fully transparent can feel empty. The key is to figure out which option is going to empower you to live a life on your own terms: keeping the status quo and not sharing your personal beliefs, or disrupting expectations and being upfront about your change.

COMMON ARGUMENTS YOU'LL HEAR

"Family is the most important thing."

Religious homes often put an emphasis on the importance of family and can use this to make members feel guilty for not maintaining loyalty. This requirement of dogmatic loyalty can be used to keep family members from challenging dysfunctional dynamics, revealing unfavorable family secrets or exposing abusive parents or other family members. As someone who grew up in a very family-oriented household with people I love dearly, I think family is deeply important. But not at the cost of your own mental health or safety or peace of mind. And guess what? Family does not have to be determined by blood. You can have autonomy over who is in your inner circle, who gets to be close with you and share familial moments. Chosen family, in my experience, can be just as fulfilling as "real" family, if not more so. Bonding with people over who you are now, and being fully accepted by them? Now that's family.

"You're breaking your family's heart."

You're not responsible for coddling the emotions of your family. They are allowed to experience their own pain and grief, but it's not your obligation to base your identity on what makes them comfortable. At the beginning of my process of leaving evangelicalism, I found myself frustrated with the idea that my family was hurt or upset by my deconversion, but I realized it's one of the things that gives us common ground. As much as they are heartbroken by my apostasy, I'm also heartbroken about the institution and theology they support. I'm heartbroken that they are trapped in cycles of indoctrination that they now choose to perpetuate. I can empathize with their sadness, experience my own heartbreak and still honor my journey.

"I'll be praying for you."

So many people ask me how to respond to this sort of comment. The answer is completely up to you. What do you have the capacity for? My personal advice would be to determine if it's coming from a genuine, caring place or if it's spoken more as a threat or condescending statement. When I think someone is just saying this due to their indoctrination, I give a smile and thank them for the good intention. When it's someone who repeatedly does this, I find it's sometimes worth taking a moment to let them know that, as a non-believer, I don't find prayers to be helpful or effective. While they're welcome to pray for me, it would be more impactful if they found another way to communicate their support. I don't really care if someone prays for me or not. If it brings them peace or even a feeling of superiority, that's their own situation, not mine. What I *will* reject, however, are offers to pray *with* me or "*over*" me, as some evangelicals would say. I'm not going to spend my time sitting there while someone makes me a part of the religious practice I walked away from. That's a boundary I can politely set, saying, "I appreciate that you want to pray together, but that's not something I care to do. You're welcome to do so on your own time."

"God will bring you back."

Hearing this can feel incredibly invalidating and triggering. It undermines the intellectual honesty and hard work that have gotten you where you are. It dismisses the real harm you experienced, and it asserts that you don't have autonomy. My response to this is simple: A god that loves me would never "bring me back" or "win me over." A god that loves me would respect my mind and integrity and would reveal themselves through evidence.

BORN AGAIN

How do you find yourself in the midst of this grief? After you've wrangled the parasite of indoctrination from your brain, just to realize the residue will never be completely scrubbed away? After the friends and family you thought would be a constant presence in your life slink away or shut you out due to fear or anger? After the words that promised a framework for belief and answers to all of life's questions no longer hold up to scrutiny?

Truthfully, you don't find yourself, because you didn't go anywhere. You were there all along, hidden under piles of dogma and expectation and shame and attempts to direct your "free will." You get to know yourself. You do new things. You do old things. You take care of yourself and ask, "How do I feel?" You find places and people that accept you as you are. You feel things that are good and bad, and you say, "Of course I feel that way!" and you learn how to welcome and dismiss all of it as needed. You don't find yourself, you tell yourself "I'm so sorry I ignored you." Yes, grieve who you thought you knew, mourn what was a familiar character. But do this to make space for the person who has observed all of this from the start and is still here striving to keep doing so.

Life after leaving religion really feels like a death of sorts. It feels like an entire reality ceasing to exist. And the grief is never-ending. Leaving religion is a welcoming sadness, but healing requires making peace with it. It feels like tiny little funerals, candles for past memories, constantly mourning the death of certainty, of an afterlife, of a god and of the parts of you that believed in those things. There are ghosts to this grief, too, often in the shape of a parent or sibling or friend who used to share a church pew with you. These ghosts will haunt you; some kindly, and some with threats of hellfire and death. But with all of them living in a different reality from you. So you will grieve for them too. More tiny funerals.

My hope is that you find something lighter in that journey than all the years you spent trying to escape it. The grief is beautiful because the grief is a sign that you are free to discover *real* happiness in the here and now. *This* is resurrection. Welcome to the actual land of the living: It's not anticipation of escape or a carrot on a string just out of reach. It's a joy that can be found in the here and now. Enjoy getting to be.

CHAPTER 10

Good and Godless

"And now that you don't have to be perfect, you can be good."
— JOHN STEINBECK

WHAT IS THE POINT of all of this—of life, pain and joy—if there isn't a god with a set of rules guiding all of it? Guiding all of *us*? While I was losing belief in an actual Eden, where man was crafted from dirt and woman from bone, I found comfort in the scientific observation that we're mostly made of bits of stardust. Billions of years ago, supernova explosions expelled into space the elements that would later be me. How cosmically romantic, how mystical and grand this sounds. But I learned that *everything* is made of stardust. Rocks, plants and animals. The neurons in a mother's brain that fire off sensations of love and affection when she holds her baby for the first time. The vibrations produced by an orchestra that travel through a concert hall. The pleasant scent wafting from a bouquet of flowers. Stardust, all of it. But it's also what comprises deadly diseases and cancers. It's the matter making up the brain of the worst serial killers that have ever lived. It's in the weapons humans use to commit violence against their neighbors. This rendered the stardust less magical for me, and neutral at best.

Coming from a black and white belief system, which taught that everything *good* came from God, and anything *bad* did not, made this new reality seem a bit too gray for me. I also learned something about our place in the universe that didn't help matters. The knowledge that if you laid out the history of the universe along a timeline of 24 hours, humanity's existence only comprises the last three seconds. Three seconds, that's it. The stunning Milky Way with its vastness and swirling stars and planets is one of billions if not *trillions* of galaxies. Earth is just one little blip on an immeasurable map. The idea that humans can do anything notably quantifiable in the grand scheme of things is absurd. For most of my life, I believed the creator of the universe knew *me*. Now I was nothing more than a momentary dust mote floating through space.

Despite facing the facts and accepting the terms, I still found myself hopefully curious. I wanted to know the meaning of it all. What was my purpose in life outside of religion? I shelved those questions the moment I felt their weight. I pushed them aside and embraced my new life, assuming I would figure it out eventually. I had gone my whole life with the answers all laid out for me and the mental muscle I needed to wrestle with these big questions about life was still weak and easily tired.

As an evangelical, I believed my life purpose had been assigned before my birth (Ephesians 2:10): I was to glorify God (Isaiah 43:7), live according to his will and eventually join him in heaven where I would spend eternity worshipping him (Revelation 7:9-12)—just like every other human was supposed to do. If there was going to be anything unique to my life, it would still be according to God's plan (Jeremiah 29:11). Meaning was also assigned by God. I thought there might be a better way to spend my time on Sunday mornings (reading a good book or spending time with friends, perhaps?) than clapping and raising my hands to the same worship songs I did the Sunday before, but if God found that practice meaningful, so must I. With this outsourcing of my worldview to religion, I had never contemplated my existence, my personal hopes and joys or what made me feel purposeful. I was completely unequipped to take the reins of my own life. All I knew was this one way that had been decided for me by my faith, given to me by my parents and the culture I was born into. Evangelicalism does not have space for, and often condemns, self-exploration of any sort. You're not encouraged to dream about your future unless that dream is rooted in "God's will". Personal autonomy serves one purpose—to glorify God with sacrifice (Romans 12:1-2). Yes, you have free will, but you had better use it to give yourself, your ambitions and your personal identity over to God. Doing so mitigates the complexity and uniqueness of each human life, offering an across-the-board solution to nuanced situations. It treats humans like simple life-forms that are as satisfied with one banal life-task as worker bees are with their honey-making. We're significantly more capable of complex thinking and tasks,[1] giving some explanation as to why most of us are not satiated by just one source of meaning. We typically enjoy an array of meaningful things in our lives, like family, career and material well-being.[2]

One of the most dangerous consequences of the belief that there is only one primary objective for humans (following God's will) is the intense tribalism and sense of superiority that develops. If you don't live your life according to evangelical expectations, you are less-than at best and an immoral monster at worst. This is the same thinking that brought about some of the most infamous atrocities in human history, like the Crusades and colonialism, which brought ruin to Indigenous peoples through enslavement, genocide and forced conversions. Even though we know such things are wrong, many who derive their purpose and meaning from religion are all too often ready to accept such outcomes. There's a sense of relief that comes with adhering to your cultural dictates, even when those dictates are deplorable. You have the satisfaction of believing you are doing the "right" thing, without having to think about what you're actually doing. You simply follow what you're taught. And you get to indulge in the satisfaction of knowing the answers to the big questions everyone else is trying to answer: "What is the meaning of life? What is our purpose?"

Perhaps for some, especially those who never grew up with religion, meaning and purpose comes intuitively. But in my personal experience, when you no longer fill in the blank with "God", you will inevitably be confronted with emptiness and uncertainty. For me it happened on a random February morning, just one year after leaving evangelicalism. Tears poured out of my eyes as I sat in a fetal position on my bed, holding myself, rocking back and forth in an attempt to soothe the intensity of what I was feeling. I was experiencing extreme loneliness and the weight of a toxic relationship that I had gotten myself stuck in. I was also recovering from a life-threaten-

1 Anne Trafton, "Study finds a striking difference between neurons of humans and other mammals." MIT News (November 10, 2021), https://news.mit.edu/2021/neurons-humans-mammals-1110.
2 Laura Silver et al. "What Makes Life Meaningful? Views from 17 Advanced Economies." Pew Research Center (November 18, 2021), https://www.pewresearch.org/wp-content/uploads/sites/20/2021/11/PG_11.18.21_meaning-in-life_fullreport.pdf.

ing ectopic pregnancy loss and operation, which had left me mentally and physically exhausted. Life was heartbreaking, and I felt hopelessly lost.

My mind was in a very dark place, so I began searching my thoughts for something positive to hold onto. In the past I would have turned to God in a moment like this, accused myself of being self-centered and swallowed back my tears before diving into scripture or worship. This approach to solving my issues pushed back the pain temporarily, only for it to come back stronger each time. But that was then. I didn't believe anymore. I didn't think there was some deity promising comfort during hard times. And suppressing my emotions, as I'd been taught to do, was no longer a viable solution. Here I sat in personal crisis, confronted with a reality that resembled hopelessness. Was this the "god-shaped hole" I had been warned about my whole life? I had done everything I could to continue believing in God, but could no longer do so. Was I now damned to feel empty and alone because of it? My chest felt heavy, like my heart was going to drop out of it. Mental anguish somehow transformed into a physical pain that shot through my nerves and ended in my fingertips. I wanted to scream but couldn't seem to catch my breath to let out anything other than sobs. Years of repression, anxiety and passivity all spilling over. Fighting against the shortness of breath, I became aware long enough to place my hand on my chest and tell myself to breathe. Those long, deep breaths gave me something to focus on, a goal. I felt my body start to relax a bit and I allowed myself to acknowledge the burning questions I had kept pushing off. I had suffered through worse feelings than this as a Christian, and with fewer coping skills. Acknowledging that gave me strength. It was as if I was finally brave enough to face the complexity of my own thoughts and walk toward the pain instead of avoiding it.

I feel like dying. In the past, I would have rebuked myself for such thoughts, and identified them as an attack from "the enemy." But now that I no longer believed in the influence of demons, I couldn't continue to avoid the scarier thoughts that plagued me. *What do I actually want*?, I asked myself. *I want to live*, I answered.

That epiphany doesn't sound very groundbreaking, I admit, but suddenly I felt empowered by a sense of autonomy. My evangelical upbringing, rooted in the idea that this existence is just a waiting room for heaven, had never allowed me to take charge of *being* alive. I was taught to view my humanity as a literal curse, not as an extraordinary experience. The only thing that had been extraordinary about me, in my evangelical view, was whatever I could attribute to God. This belief kept me disconnected from myself and my *life. THE* extraordinary experience. Now here I was acknowledging that I didn't want to be a bystander or a victim of my existence or a conduit for someone else's agenda. I wanted to be fully engaged with my life, even in this moment of psychological distress. It wasn't an awakening; it was simply an awareness of what was already there inside me. My thoughts continued. As a Christian, I would have had an inner dialogue with the God character I had created in my head. Now I was forced to have it with myself, no longer censoring thoughts or feelings or conditioned to respond a certain way. Instead of feeding myself the same, tired Bible verses and theology time and time again, I had to sit with what I really believed. And what was that? What did I believe about life? I knew what I didn't believe, but it was time to face the unfilled blank. I was craving meaning and purpose in the midst of hardship. I needed a path forward and maybe more importantly, I *wanted* it.

That experience didn't result in me sitting in bed until I had it all figured out. I would still be sitting there if that was the case. It was only the start of a conversation I desperately needed to have with myself. It was an acceptance of my humanity and all of the limits and foibles that come with it. I had accepted that I really wanted to live, and while I still wasn't sure what I meant by that, I wanted to find out. Journaling was something I had done my whole life, often addressing my entries to "Dear Jesus" (I thought he was reading everything I wrote, being an all-knowing god and everything). Now I could just write for myself, sort out my thoughts and befriend them instead of treating them like demonic influences or permanent constructs. Over the course of that year I did figure out a lot. I made lists. Lists of what I value. Lists of what makes me feel purposeful. Lists of what simply brings me joy. I asked myself what I think it means to truly be alive. Despite how alone on this journey I felt, I was not the first to ask these existential questions. Philosophers, kings, priests and artists have all attempted to identify the answers. So I read the books, watched the documentaries, practiced the meditations and listened to the gurus. I learned a lot of things that I still value to this day, but the most important thing I realized was that I didn't need to have the answers. In all my seeking for this illusive *meaning* and *purpose*, I was taking on some of my past dogmatic traits. I was once again falling prey to the idea that there was some disease I needed to cure. I wanted there to be a correct answer to my questions, so that I could confirm I was on the "right" path. I was so used to attributing the events of my life to external sources, I thought there must be one for this new stage of being as well, even if it wasn't a god. Freedom from this finally came once I realized that dependence a third-party (regardless of what that might be) to give my life meaning and direction was nothing more than a trap—a distraction that kept me focused on finding answers rather than simply living.

EVERYTHING IS MEANINGLESS AND NOTHING MATTERS...UNLESS YOU WANT IT TO

Despite religious assertions, there is no handbook on how to be a human. Some have put a lot of thought into the idea and share their conclusions, which can be helpful. Observing the paths of those who came before us can offer insight on living as well. But no one has ever lived the exact life that you will live with the brain and body that you have. Ultimately, *you are on your own*. As someone who very much believed I was never alone, always in the presence of a god, I fought this fact tooth and nail. Being left to my own devices was intimidating, as I had been taught to "lean not" (Proverbs 3:5-6) on my human understanding of things. I have since found that I am the one who has to answer for the life I create. I'm the expert on designing it (as much as one can in a world that largely decides things for you).

I want to be clear that I don't think there is a one-size-fits-all philosophy for living. While we humans can be very similar, it is our slight differences and unique experiences that result in each of us having drastically different outlooks on life. What I share in this book, and specifically this chapter, is purely what works for me. What I care about is that you find what works for *you*. I share this in the hope that by letting you in on some of my journey, it offers inspiration for forming your own perspectives and motivations in life. Whether that includes some or none of mine is for you to determine.

For me, the first step to finding meaning in my life was to accept that there isn't any. There isn't an objective source assigning meaning to what we do or why. Life isn't some big test that you might receive an A on if you behave just right. A common accusation that comes up toward those of us that don't believe in objective meaning is that we will descend into nihilism and end up hopeless and depressed. But I had already experienced hopelessness and depression as a devout believer. I remember being taught, through scripture (2 Peter 3:10-13 and Revelation 21:1) and evangelical rhetoric, that this world didn't really matter. This earth was just a test, a holding cell for the eternal kingdom of Heaven to come. The things I actually enjoyed about life were, at best, distractions and, at worst, demonic influences or false idols. I remember hearing, "You can't take it with you" in reference to beloved objects or people that I would be unable to take with me to heaven. There wasn't anything grounding or life-giving about this belief. It took *away* meaning and discredited the very tangible parts of life I found value in. If the danger of nihilism is that it paints life as ultimately worthless and void of meaning, evangelicalism is the closest I came to embracing that. Any negativity I experienced from nihilism post-religion was due to a lie I had been taught to believe: that meaning had to be objective.

Nihilism has many different philosophical interpretations and applications, but at its foundation is the position that the universe has no objective meaning, purpose or value. I agree with this, so much so that I can easily call myself a cosmic nihilist if that helps to better communicate my position on how I view the grand scheme of things. My experience of meaning is that it isn't some static, fixed concept. It grows and adapts with me and it's pliable and changeable as needed. At times I find most of my meaning in the relationships around me and the moments I spend being present with others and learning more about life through them. Sometimes it's found in my work, in experiencing the satisfaction of accomplishment or skill and feeling like my efforts and contributions are positive influences on those around me. Sometimes, meaning just comes from existing on this extraordinary planet. Observing a beautiful sunset or moonrise. Laughing unreservedly at something that hits my sense of humor just right. Enjoying the process of cooking a good meal and the delicious experience of eating and savoring it. Most of the time, I find meaning in the tension between all of these things—in navigating the highs and lows of life. It's something dynamic that I participate in by choice, over and over.

I've also found meaning in integrity—in matching my values with my actions. Not because someone or something told me to, but because I've done the work of figuring out what matters to *me*. *Why* does it matter to me? And do I have good reasons for that? Revisiting these questions allows my character to grow, as I learn more about myself and the world around me. The answers can and will change, too. What mattered most to me 10 years ago, even five years ago, has taken on a new shape over time. What some might have considered a volatile or inconsistent way of finding meaning was really just me, changing and growing for the better. Now, when I think about what brings my life meaning, I don't look for some eternal, all-knowing source to confirm or inform those beliefs. I look at the faces of my beautiful friends and family, I look at the fruits of my labor and the impact my work has had on others, I look at the personal growth I've achieved and how far I've come as an individual. And I look forward to the new things I'll find meaning in over the years to come. When nothing matters cosmically, anything can matter personally. Life is a playground of opportunities, many of them positive ones. The good isn't chosen for me, I choose the good.

COMMON ARGUMENTS YOU'LL HEAR

"There's no hope without a god."

In evangelicalism, hope is often the idea that you can expect something positive in the future, specifically hope in God's promises and plans. But with no evidence that there is any reality behind those assurances, this is just false hope. It's comforting in theory, but it isn't grounded in truth. Still, the idea that being without religion means being without hope is a false dichotomy. I have hope for all kinds of things. Hope that my husband will make me a cup of coffee in the morning, as usual. Hope that we'll spend the holidays this year with good friends and family and food. Hope that more people are being freed from indoctrination every year. The difference is that my hope is grounded; it has reason to expect these positive future events.

"People need religion to have meaning in life."

This is demonstrably untrue, and for many people meaning *can't* be found in religion. There are millions of people living their lives with purpose outside of religion. The problem is that evangelicals work to convince others that they need religion to have purpose when they don't. In a multi-country survey about what gives meaning to their lives, most people answered family, career, well-being and other similar things. Religion was barely a blip with just 2 percent of people mentioning it. However, when answers from US participants are accounted for separately, that number went up to 15 percent (the highest of any country surveyed), which reveals the unique hold religion has on Americans.[3] We humans give meaning to religion, not the other way around and yet so many of us have been convinced otherwise. This is just another layer to the ultimate con that costs you your relationship with reality. If it can convince you that your existence requires objective meaning, it

3 Silver, "What Makes Life Meaningful"

can convince you that you need religion. The truth is that objective meaning doesn't exist, and real meaning exists on your own terms, not those of a god.

"Everyone has a God-shaped hole."

Humans experience all sorts of emotions, desires and needs that we have trouble putting into words, such as anxiety, depression and loneliness. Christians take advantage of this and assert that it must be because we need God. It's emotionally manipulative and preys on people when they are at their lowest: "*Of course you feel bad, you don't have Jesus*!" But what happens when mental health issues are addressed and suddenly that feeling goes away? Or when someone discovers a new hobby that gives them a sense of excitement? Or when community is established, which fills the emptiness from before it existed? Suddenly the "God-shaped hole" has been satiated by things that are *not* God.

GOOD FOR GOODNESS' SAKE

When comparing secular morality to the evangelical solution for determining right from wrong, there is a clear winner. On one hand, you have a frame of thought that acknowledges reality—that there is no ultimate judge dictating laws for us. Secular morality is based on reason and logic, agreeing on objectives for humankind. Things like empathy, well-being, harm-reduction and consent. Such a system believes in this present life and focuses its attention solely on that, not on a distant hope for an afterlife. Perhaps most importantly, subjective morality is able to evolve and improve upon itself. The more we learn about how to take care of each other, the better standards we can set. On the other hand, you have evangelical morality, which is based on blind obedience rather than logic and reason. It pits people against each other, not for causing harm, but for simply believing differently. The ultimate goal of these moral requirements are not to improve our lives in the here and now, but to gain access to heaven and avoid hell. It's also rigid and unchangeable.

There are Christians who have done both horrific and wonderful things, just as there are atheists who have done horrific and wonderful things. Clearly the threat of hell is not enough to protect us from evil actions, and the promise of heaven is not necessary to encourage good ones.

COMMON ARGUMENTS THAT YOU'LL HEAR

"You just want to sin and get away with it."

If I wanted to sin and get away with it, I would have stayed a Christian. I could commit whatever atrocities I wanted, and so long as I had a genuine moment of repentance, I could believe that God had forgiven me, granted me access to heaven and relieved me of my transgressions. Sin is a religious construct though; an idea that there is an objective mark that has been set by an external force, and to miss it is a failure worthy of consequence. As an atheist I don't believe there is any force setting or keeping track of moral standards. I don't want to "sin and get away with it." I want to learn and do better for as long as I live. I want myself and others to be accountable for how we impact each other in the here and now, not after we're dead.

Despite Christian claims that atheists are immoral or still rely on God to make moral choices when deciding between right or wrong, atheists believe more strongly in "not hurting others" than religious people do. And where atheists rank logic and reasoning as more important to their decision-making, Christians find it better to "stay out of trouble" when deciding between right and wrong.[4] The Christian accusation that godless morality avoids accountability comes off as nothing more than a projection. Leaving it to God simply enables Christians to avoid accountability in the here and now.

"Without objective morals, everyone gets to decide for themselves what's right and wrong."

The problem is that objective morality does not exist. We can have objective goals we base our morals off of, but there is no moral set of laws floating around in space, much less an objective source to hold us to them. People are deciding for themselves every day what's "right" and "wrong", Christians included. If you ask two Christians what their moral stance is on the death penalty, gay relationships or war, I guarantee you will hear different answers. They can claim that they adhere to a single, objective source for their morality all they want—but just like the rest of us, they are using their subjective experiences to determine what they believe to be moral or immoral.

"You can't value human rights without acknowledging a god."

Sure you can, and here I am doing that now. If human rights were a value

4 "Religious 'Nones' in America: Who They Are And What They Believe." Pew Research Center (January 24, 2024), https://www.pewresearch.org/religion/2024/01/24/how-do-nones-think-about-morality/.

of the Christian god, why is the movement of free speech, freedom of religion, equality for all sexes, genders and races and bodily autonomy a modern idea? Why is the book attributed to God full of slavery endorsements, the subjugation of women, violence against innocent people and divine genocide? And if he had the foreknowledge of what a problem these things would be, why didn't he take a moment to say, "Hey everyone! I just want to make it clear that all humans should have rights, and I don't endorse slavery, misogyny, child abuse or harm towards humans in general"?

"If there's no god, there's no justice for evil."

I would *love* to believe that Hitler and Stalin are drowning in a lake of fire, that Bundy and Dahmer are experiencing non-stop torment, that every person who commits an injustice would receive some sort of fair accountability for it. My desires do not amount to truth though. There are people who do horrible, awful things and get away with it. This is yet another reason why secular morality is superior to religion. It understands that this present life is the time for justice and is motivated to achieve it. Secular morality isn't content to let some god handle it in an afterlife.

"Christian values founded Western culture."

When evangelicals invoke these "Christian values", they have to do a lot of cherry picking. *Which* Christian values? The ones that say queer people shouldn't have the same rights as heterosexuals? The values that demand conversion, crusades and genocides? The values that justify enslaving fellow humans and withholding basic rights on the basis of skin color? Conveniently, evangelicals ignore those parts of Christian history when claiming their values are superior. That claim also comes with the suggestion that "Western culture" is somehow superior to anything else, which is a form of eurocentrism common within Christian nationalism. In reality, many of the progressive aspects of what is attributed to "Western" values come from other cultures. Indigenous societies were practicing democracy and federalism long before the U.S. constitution was even an idea, and the Islamic world was a major contributor to mathematics. These are just two examples. This claim also dismisses the immense amount of harm caused by "Western culture" in the form of colonialism and the subjugation and slaughter of Indigenous peoples.

Those things which are deemed "good" or "progressive" about Western culture, such as free speech, democracy and human rights actually come from the Enlightenment period which was largely fueled by secular skepticism and criticism of religious dogma. It was the fight *against* religious rule that brought about advances in medicine, economics, political structures and morality.

CHOOSE TO LOVE

For most of my life I outsourced my standard for goodness to Christian "morals." On the one hand, goodness had been defined for me as a rigid, unchanging law to which I must submit. On the other hand, the morals were cherry-picked from the Bible and evangelical culture, most often by men, and were human concepts purported to be objective truth. There was no examination of what it actually meant to treat others well, or why that could be a beneficial thing to society as a whole. Morality was treated more as a test for whether you were adhering to authority or not. When I finally began to question my faith, I was also forced to question my own values. The contradictions and inconsistencies of Christian values, which others had used to justify colonialism, misogyny, abuse and other acts of dehumanization, became harder to swallow. I realized that "Christian values" is really just code for authoritarianism. Don't ask questions, don't try to learn and grow as a society, don't improve upon your values as you learn more about the world around you: Just obey. Goodness was compliance, not the love and kindness that were so meaningful to me. My religion couldn't contain my values.

Truthfully, goodness doesn't exist–not in the concrete, achievable way religion would have you believe. There would have to be some objective source assigning a definition to it and sitting in judgement to approve or disapprove. Reality shows us that simply isn't true. Don't be afraid of that truth. It exists whether we embrace it or not, but it sure is easier to function when you do. By accepting that the meaning of your life is for you to determine, rather than some external force or law, you free yourself from the constraints and demands of dogma. Humanism (a prioritization of well-being) doesn't advertise goodness as a title you achieve in order to avoid punishment, but as something we can create together. It calls for living in the present, facing consequences in this lifetime and doing better as we learn more. Our path in life, whether grounded in religion or not, has always been subjective. I choose not the one that satiates me with reward, but one that challenges me to love more, take less and enjoy adventures along the way that demand I engage with reality. And what is living, if not that?

Afterword

"The universe is not created with you in mind, and it is not a place where our needs are guaranteed or even cared for. It is entirely indifferent to our existence, and that should make us realize the preciousness of our brief lives and the importance of making the most of them."
— CHRISTOPHER HITCHENS

ONE AUGUST NIGHT IN FINLAND, my husband and I were up late, sitting inside by the fireplace, sharing a glass of wine. We were chatting about what a beautiful summer it had been, living on his family's countryside property, surrounded by lakes, birch trees, flowers and forests that resembled something out of a Tolkien book. My husband stepped outside to grab something he had forgotten, and in his pragmatic, Finnish way calmly said, "Hey, you might want to come outside for a second." Curious as to why, I joined him and was instantly met with the most unreal sight I had ever seen. The sky was ablaze with purple and green colors dancing across a clear sky full of stars. I was lucky enough to be witnessing the Northern Lights. It was the closest to magic I've ever seen. Stunning, breathtaking, wonderful and completely explainable. To be so caught up in that moment, to know exactly what was causing such wonderment, and to be free of anything requiring me to attribute such glory to a creator was deeply grounding and enlightening. The universe is spectacular in and of itself. I don't have to feign self-importance, believing it was all created just for me. The universe just is. The beautiful parts, the sinister parts, and everything in between. Existing in such a world can be scary, uncertain and difficult—yet we persist. And looking up at that sky full of changing colors I found myself thinking, "How lucky I am to be a human."

I lost a lot when I lost my faith. I've gained back so much more. Autonomy, freedom of thought, authenticity, self-acceptance, chosen family, curiosity, courage and a peace of mind that religion promised me but never delivered. One of the most beautiful things I've gained? Moments. Moments for which I choose to be fully present, that I don't have to put in my peripheral while I pause to thank a distant god. Moments that I don't have to step out of to determine what I should or shouldn't be doing differently. Moments of acceptance of what is, and the full embrace of the grief that can come with it, without needing to put a "someday in heaven" band-aid on it to dull the pain. Moments of peace and calm where I can lean on my own understanding, get to know myself and not feel shame or fear. Moments of joy, of bellyaching laughter. Moments of celebrating people without wanting to change them, of not changing myself for them. Giving the extra hug, the extra kind word, the extra time, knowing the moment I am in is it. There is so much heartache to losing your faith, your community, an entire god. But I would do it all a million times over for the weight that was lifted and the space it made for joy, peace, love and freedom like I've never known before. Maybe you're in the stage of losing your faith *right now*, and the pain is unbearable. I see you, I've been you and you're going to be okay. You already have so much to be proud of. Maybe you're just past that, and you feel numb and a bit empty. Sit with it, embrace the discomfort and know that you will feel again and this time the opportunities for happiness will be on your own terms. And getting to live life on your own terms is where the magic happens. You can be good *and* godless. You can have peace and adventure, joy and happiness. You can create meaning and purpose. You can practice loving your neighbor, feeding the poor *and* thinking critically. You can be good and do good without having to cherry pick your ethics from a text that tries to convince you that only it has the answers. You can even define "good" without crediting it to a higher power. The best parts about being human pre-date religion. We're capable of growth, creative and curious. We thrive in community and are often caught offering empathy and kindness to others. We're goofy and fun. We are resilient and brave. We are not the product of an authoritative creator, but a culmination of billions of years of matter and change. We are the result of ancient oceans and earthquakes, plants and animals, tools and languages, wars and ambitions. We are past lovers and survivors, myths and lessons. We're complex creatures that did not become this way in one instance. Who you were yesterday is not who you are today, and this version of you won't stay the same either. Enjoy it while you're in it.

Resource Directory

The following are all invaluable resources for anyone questioning their faith, working to remove themself from an abusive religious culture or struggling to adapt after leaving an evangelical community. There are many others, but these are the ones I believe are the most helpful and effective. I hope you find them of value should you need them.

Recovering from Religion

recoveringfromreligion.org

WHAT IT IS A nonprofit for anyone experiencing fear and/or doubts surrounding their religious beliefs. They offer a 24/7 helpline via phone or chat, in-person and virtual support groups and much more.

CONTACT INFORMATION

app.admin@recoveringfromreligion.org
(844) 368-2848

Secular Therapy Project

seculartherapy.org

WHAT IT IS A network for helping you find non-religious, evidence-based mental health professionals in your area.

CONTACT INFORMATION

seculartherapy.org/contact-us (online form)

The Clergy Project

clergyproject.org

WHAT IT IS A nonprofit offering support and resources for religious leaders who are no longer believers and need help navigating out of their clergy positions.

CONTACT INFORMATION

clergy@clergyproject.org

Secular Student Alliance

secularstudents.org

WHAT IT IS A nonprofit for non-religious students offering community, events and scholarships.

CONTACT INFORMATION

ssa@secularstudents.org
(614) 441-9588

Black Nonbelievers

blacknonbelievers.org

WHAT IT IS A nonprofit offering events, community and support for Black nonbelievers.

CONTACT INFORMATION

blacknonbelievers.org/contact-2/ (online form)

Survivors Network of those Abused by Priests (SNAP)

snapnetwork.org

WHAT IT IS A nonprofit community offering support and resources for victims of clergy and institutional sexual abuse.

CONTACT INFORMATION

snapnetwork.org/contact-snap/ (online form)
(877) 762-7432

Street Epistemology

streetepistemology.com

WHAT IT IS A website offering courses and information on navigating conversations about difficult and sensitive topics.

CONTACT INFORMATION

streetepistemologyinternational.org/contact (online form)
contact@streetepistemologyinternational.org
(210) 384-1987

Index

Index

I

J

K

L

Index

Acknowledgments

To Phil, Noreen, Madeline, Tara, Susan, Amy and the rest of team at Media Lab Books—your practical efforts and personal care for this book have made me feel supported and seen in ways I have not experienced before in life and have given me a new level of healing and confidence in my ongoing journey. Thank you for creating this with me. I couldn't have asked for a better partnership!

To the Järvenpää family—you not only gave me a safe and cozy place to write this book in the beautiful countryside of Finland, but you, as individuals, have been your own safe and cozy places for me. I'm so grateful for a life that led me to all of you. Your home, forests of birch and pine, food, jokes, sauna, deep talks under the midnight sun and love all carried my heart as I wrote about heavy things. Kiitos, olette minulle rakkaita.

To the ones who sparked these conversations for me before I knew I could use my own voice—Matt and Arden, Jimmy, Alyssa, Seth and Dave. My gratitude for your role in challenging the beliefs I held is lifelong, and the encouragement and friendship I have received since speaking up have enriched my world. I'm honored to do this work with you all.

To my parents and siblings—thank you for choosing connection and all of the grief and work and joy that comes with it. All of us have grown and changed in our own ways, and I'm grateful that our love for each other has not.

To my human, my husband—my safest, kindest, most exciting adventure. If only everyone knew how your love in action is the constant kindness nurturing the best parts of me. I love you, Cadus.

About the Author

Promise Backlund is a former evangelical Christian who now identifies as an agnostic atheist after leaving her faith in 2017. She is best known for her popular online platform under the name eve_wasframed, where she engages more than half a million followers in bold conversations about non-belief and life after religion. She's also a frequent contributor to *The Line* podcast and YouTube channel (@TheLinePodcast). Drawing upon her experience of leaving a prominent evangelical family ministry, she speaks with candor, personal insight and a sharpness for exposing contradictions in faith culture.

Through her social media influence, Promise has become a leading voice in the counter-apologetics movement and is known for blending intellect with concise points and accessibility. She collaborates with many high-profile secular thinkers, contributes to the discourse on meaning without religion and has built a reputation for challenging dogma while encouraging curiosity and critical thinking.

When she's not writing, speaking or sparking conversations online, she enjoys her home life in Finland with her husband, Jukka, and their music and songwriting projects.

Media Lab Books
For inquiries, contact customerservice@topixmedia.com

Published by Topix Media Lab
47 Ronald Reagan Blvd
Warwick, NY 10990

Printed in Canada

ISBN-13: 978-1-964487-55-7
ISBN-10: 1-964487-55-2

MCA-B26-1